MASSENET

By the same author

SAINT-SAËNS AND HIS CIRCLE
SAINT-SAËNS ET L'OPÉRA
SACHA GUITRY, THE LAST BOULEVARDIER
THE DUKE OF WELLINGTON
ROSSINI

Translation

FRANCIS POULENC: MY FRIENDS AND MYSELF

MASSENET

by

James Harding

'I would give the whole of Bach's Brandenburg Concertos for Massenet's *Manon* and would think I had vastly profited by the exchange.'

Sir Thomas Beecham, Bart., C.H.

ST. MARTIN'S PRESS
NEW YORK

 For information, write:
St. Martin's Press, Inc., 175 Fifth Ave.,
New York, N.Y. 10010

Printed in Great Britain

Library of Congress Catalog Card Number: 70–132189

First published in the United States of America in 1970

AFFILIATED PUBLISHERS: Macmillan & Company, Limited, London—also at Bombay, Calcutta, Madras and Melbourne—The Macmillan Company of Canada, Limited, Toronto.

For

Phyllis and Bertie van Thal

CONTENTS

ACKNOWLEDGMENTS

In assembling the materials for this book much valuable assistance was received from M. Pierre Bessand-Massenet, the composer's grandson; from M. Yves Leroux, a relative of the family; and from Mlle Éliane Bouilhol, author of a penetrating thesis on Massenet written with the encouragement of her teacher, the late Alfred Cortot. Thanks are due also to M. André Ménétrat, curator of the Bibliothèque de l'Opéra, where the bulk of Massenet's autograph scores is preserved, and to Mlle Henriette Boschot. Information is gratefully acknowledged from the following: Mrs Pauline Green, the daughter of Marie Nordlinger, and Mrs Patricia Prestwich; M. Albert Lisimachio, curator of the Archives du Palais de Monaco; and the omnipresent Herbert van Thal, without whom few books would get written. The quotations from Massenet's work appear by permission of his publishers, Messrs Heugel & Co., 2 bis, rue Vivienne, Paris 2, who are owners of the copyright.

PLATES

INTRODUCTION

It would be difficult to conceive of a more absurd art-form than that of opera. We are asked to accept that in moments of emotion it is natural for men and women to express their deepest feelings in trills and *roulades*. We are exposed to the spectacle of ladies in the rudest of health who tenaciously postpone their dying gasp in a cascade of endless *portamenti*. We see staid and sober gentlemen suddenly break into song when we are convinced they would be more properly employed in some respectable merchant bank or counting house. Empires are destroyed in the space of an intermezzo. Villains are overthrown in the time it takes to gargle an aria. A five-minute duet is all that is needed to pledge a lifelong troth. It is, therefore, strange that some can talk of 'realism' within a convention so obviously, so irrevocably grotesque. One would have thought that the more fantastic an opera was, the more successful it would be on its own terms.

One of the most eminent practitioners in the medium during the second half of the nineteenth century and the first unhappy decade of the twentieth was Jules Massenet. He wrote, besides much else, nearly thirty full-scale works for the stage. His industry was terrifying. The public does not always realize the immense toil involved in writing an opera. The composer must not only provide many hundreds of pages of full orchestral score; he must also cater for half a dozen different sorts of voice and a chorus as well. At every point he must remember so to arrange his work that the demands peculiar to the stage are met. But he still has not finished. At rehearsals he must be patient with the vagaries of stupid *prime donne* whose only virtue is a pretty voice, and he must tolerate the eccentricities of 'producers' who, in their vanity, imagine they are breathing creative life into the work. (We hear so much these days of Signor X's *Traviata* and Herr Y's *Rosenkavalier* that we could be forgiven for overlooking the modest contribution which Verdi and Strauss may be assumed to have made to the evening's traffic of the stage.) After which the long-suffering composer must be ready to see the labour of months, perhaps of years, dismissed in a few hurried sentences thrown together by critics anxious to catch the early edition of their newspaper.

All of this Massenet bore stoically in a career lasting close on fifty years. His dedication to the calling he had chosen was such that he cheerfully condemned himself to the life of a galley-slave. He was up at four every morning and composing steadily, often as much as sixteen hours a day. When his opera was finished there was not an aspect of its production which he did not control. Every detail, from the timing of an entry to the placing of a feather in the leading lady's headdress, was the object of his eager scrutiny. Then he would bury himself in the country to escape the terrors of the first night. And there, before the curtain had fallen on his latest work, he would already be composing his next opera, or deciding which of the half-dozen he kept permanently on the stocks was ripe for the finishing touch. He was the complete man of the theatre and a professional in everything he did.

The reward he earned was great. In his time he dominated the French theatre and was among the few composers to have made very large sums of money from their work. He was the richest musician of his kind in the nineteenth century. From an impoverished start he rose to become an admired and envied European figure, with a handsome flat in Paris and a beautiful country domain at Égreville. He was never cynical about the good things a lifetime of hard work brought him. Just as the only successful general is the one who wins battles, so Massenet reckoned his own triumphs by the number of audiences conquered.

This is not to say that he was a careerist. For all his apparent worldliness his natural simplicity remained unspoilt by the cruelties and vendettas of theatrical life. The price he paid in nervous tension was an almost unbearable one. Yet he would not have had it otherwise. In spite of a sensitiveness that was acute, he was driven by an urge that overcame all the promptings of a desperately shy personality. His wounds he concealed with a bland veneer of fulsomeness.

As a musician he created a style that was unique. It was suave, ingratiating and wholly personal. What is sometimes forgotten is his mastery of orchestration. His music is always the work of an accomplished craftsman. It is never less than adroit. The most superficial glance at his scores will reveal a clever technician who knew how to cultivate his gift and to waste nothing. To all this must be added an instinctive sense of the theatre that was rare indeed.

When his epoch was ended and the audiences for whom he wrote had passed away, it was inevitable that new fashions should take over. What preserves him from the fate of so many of his contemporaries and imitators is the quality of his musicianship. The composer whose influence extended to Puccini, Ravel, Debussy and Poulenc, to name but a handful, is not to be ignored. There are signs that he is at last beginning to receive some of the recognition he has so unjustly been denied since his death. Over the past three years alone, revivals outside France of *Werther, Don Quichotte, Cendrillon* and *Sapho* have testified to his worth. In France, only *Werther* remains in the repertory of the Opéra-Comique.

In a neglected field the explorer is free to follow his own path. The author makes no apology for having his favourites among Massenet's prolific output. The amount of space he has devoted to them will make clear which these are. If the reader objects, he is invited to pursue his own researches in a body of music which proposes many delights and many pleasures. No one will be more gratified than the author if he has stimulated enquiry into Massenet. You are free to dislike his music, but you cannot deny that he was a master on his own ground. Sir Thomas Beecham's sally which forms the epigraph of this book will, it is hoped, be taken in the spirit in which it was offered. The greatest musical executant England has ever known should not be grudged his witticisms, for his genius served the operas of Massenet on occasions that were exquisite and unforgettable.

J.H.

I

PARIS AND THE CONSERVATOIRE—OPERA-PITS AND THE PAWNSHOP

ONE chilly day in the spring of 1814 the Duke of Wellington's staff officers were a trifle alarmed to see their commander suddenly break into a jig and snap his fingers for joy in the streets of Toulouse. A short time before, he had ended the Peninsular campaign by invading France and marching his army from the Pyrenees. The beach at Saint-Jean-de-Luz, which today is so delectably strewn at the height of the season with chic bronzed thighs, offered the less seductive spectacle of weatherbeaten Guardsmen attending church parade and doggedly jabbing their boots into rain-soaked sand. The British Army had pressed on to Tarbes and scuffled briefly with the French under Marshal Soult. The subsequent battle at Toulouse was a confused affair. The Duke was there when news came from distant Fontainebleau that Napoleon had abdicated. And he, capering with delight, exclaimed: 'You don't say so, upon my honour! Hurrah!'

Jubilation on the other side was distinctly subdued. One of Marshal Soult's officers, an engineer captain whose papers identified him as Captain Alexis Pierre Michel Nicolas Massenet, handed in his sword to his leader. He was not yet twenty years old, and the collapse of the Napoleonic adventure had shattered his ambitions. Soult heard him sympathetically while he explained his disappointment. The Marshal was a shrewd man, and cautious like his lawyer father. His sonorous baptismal names, Nicolas Jean de Dieu, seem to have ensured that some benevolent Providence watched over his extraordinarily lucky career. Unlike his colleague Marshal Ney, who was foolish enough to get himself shot in the process, Marshal Soult cheerfully gave his allegiance to violently different regimes and, like Talleyrand, got away with it.

The advice of the prudent Soult was therefore worth having. Alexis Massenet listened carefully. 'You're a graduate of the École Polytechnique', Soult told him. 'Industry will need men of your background and ability.'

So Captain Massenet went back to civilian life and a career in engineering. His family tradition was not, in any case, a military one. His father, who came from Moselle, was professor of history at Strasbourg University. His mother, Françoise Hélène Mathieu de Faviers, was the daughter of a leading Strasbourg politician. This latter was Jean François Mathieu de Faviers, a member of the Chambre des Quinze responsible for the internal government of Strasbourg, which at that time was something of a miniature republic. Alexis' maternal uncle the Baron Mathieu de Faviers, was the only soldier in the family. Napoleon had appointed him *ordonnateur en chef* of the army that fought the Spanish campaign. Uncle and nephew had set off together on the ill-starred journey which was to be punctuated by the melancholy names of Burgos and Vittoria, San Sebastian and Pamplona. It ended miserably at Toulouse.

The young engineer made inquiries and weighed up his chances. With financial help from Soult, he was able to start a scythe factory at Toulouse. The business flourished and soon he was opening new branches in other parts of the region. Anxious to utilize the new steam engine which was revolutionizing industry, he transported his equipment and labour force from Toulouse to Saint-Étienne. The place was, and still is, a bustling industrial complex with a businesslike devotion to steel and textiles. Its prosperity was based on the rich coal seams in the area. Only a few years earlier it had inaugurated the first railway line to be built in France. At Montaud, an outlying suburb, Alexis Massenet founded in 1838 another scythe factory. He married, raised a family, and set up home at 4 place Marengo. His house, built in the familiar anonymous style of French provincial architecture, stared out on to a square which was bleak as its name was glorious.

Subsequent biographers have credited Alexis Massenet with an exuberant paternity of up to twenty-three children. This must be seen as an attempt to inject some dash of colour into an otherwise shadowy figure. He was, to use a suitably vague term, a businessman. The commodity he dealt in was not one calculated to stir the passions. His preoccupations do not seem to have gone beyond those relating to supplies of pig-iron and the maintenance of ledger books. No picture of him has survived, and it has so far proved impossible to discover his exact age. A sober and probably more correct estimate of his paternal achievement gives a figure of eight children by his first marriage. His wife died, and in his early fifties he undertook what has been described as the triumph of hope over experience by marrying again.

The second Madame Massenet was a lady called Eléonore Adélaïde Royer de Marancourt, the daughter of a *commissaire des guerres* under the First Empire. As a child, she had attracted the attention of Marie-Antoinette's daughter, the Duchesse d'Angoulême. For three years the Duchess had been imprisoned with her royal parents, thus earning the sobriquet 'the orphan of the Temple', one of those nicknames which historians in their heartless fashion love to bestow. After her release from the Revolutionaries, the Duchess married the son of the nobleman who succeeded to the throne as Charles X. Although she was never herself to be a queen, her force of character brought her a dominating position in society. She was, said Napoleon in a Corsican tribute to her powerful qualities, 'the only man in the family'.

The Duchess was impressed by little Mademoiselle de Marancourt's intelligence and her personality. She arranged for the girl's education and engaged teachers to give her lessons in drawing, literature and music. In those days, instead of teaching their daughters the art of inscribing arcane symbols in notebooks, parents thought that gentle-folk of the female sort should be able to embroider a little, draw a little, chat of good books a little, tinkle prettily on the piano and sing a little. Mademoiselle de Marancourt was a better pupil than most, and when she completed the studies laid down for her by her royal patron she had become an able painter and an even more accomplished pianist.

By her marriage to Alexis Massenet she had four children, a daughter and three boys, making a total family of twelve. One of the boys, probably the last-born, arrived at one o'clock in the early hours of 12th May 1842. The birth was registered next day at the *mairie* in the names of Jules Émile Frédéric. All unknowingly, the parents had created a source of future discontent for their son. In every other way a model of filial devotion, he was never to forgive them the names they had foisted on him. As he grew up, he came to detest, with a blind and hopeless rage, those inoffensive appendages. They were, at least, an improvement on the nickname which the rest of the family gave to him. On account of his frail appearance, they dubbed him 'Rickets'.

Jules Massenet's earliest recollections were of playing among the trees and flowers of an extensive garden which ran beside the sheds and workshops of his father's business. 'I was born to the noise of heavy hammers of brass, as the poet once said', he later recalled. 'My first steps on the path of music had no more melodious accompaniment.' Before long the brass hammers fell silent. Political events cast a lengthening shadow over the business world. Unable to find the extra capital that had suddenly become necessary, Massenet's father was obliged to take in new partners. The style of his firm was changed to that of Jackson, Génin and Massenet. Although his word still carried weight in the direction of affairs, his position was reduced and his standard of living cut down.

The reign of Louis-Philippe was drawing to its close. The placid monarch had watched benignly over eighteen years of commercial well-being. Restless politicians and bored demagogues clamoured for more exciting prospects. Louis-Philippe's reluctance to strike dramatic attitudes was looked upon as a grave political fault. The deficiency was partly remedied by poets such as Lamartine, who was constitutionally unable to resist the lure of a balcony whence to bewitch an audience with grandiose oratory. In the dying days of Louis-Philippe's rule, while revolutionaries muttered and malcontents plotted, the blast-furnaces of Saint-Étienne sent up fewer and fewer clouds of smoke to hover above the surrounding hills. Alexis Massenet recognized the portents and began to wind up his share in the business. In 1847 he sent his family to Paris, where it would be easier to arrange the children's schooling. Two years later he joined them there.

The Massenets settled in the rue de Beaune. It runs into the quai Voltaire on the Seine, not far from the Pont Royal. In this little street once lived the marquise du Deffand, that imposing queen of the eighteenth-century salons. (As an elderly lady she suffered the double misfortunes of going blind and of falling in love with the spinsterish Horace Walpole.) A few doors away, early in the nineteenth century, lived François René Chateaubriand. A poet infected with Lamartine's weakness for the dramatic gesture, he had stage-managed in the rue de Beaune, for the benefit of a politely uninterested posterity, his resignation from an obscure ambassadorship to an obscure principality. The historical associations of the place counted less for Madame Massenet than the good schools for her children which she found nearby. She was, herself, an excellent teacher. One is, though, a little taken aback at her methods. She taught the infant Jules to read with the aid of Thomas à Kempis' *The Imitation of Christ*. By dint of studying with close attention this account of the soul's journey towards perfection, Jules attained an ease of reading unusual at his tender age.

To help out with the family finances, Madame Massenet also gave piano lessons. It was inevitable that one day Jules should become her pupil. That day, in fact, was a memorable one. It was 24th February 1848, a few months before his sixth birthday. The dawn promised fine weather, but as time went on it became colder. The family had gathered for lunch when the servant erupted into the dining-room bawling, 'Aux armes, citoyens!' and, in her republican enthusiasm, threw the plates helter-skelter across the table. Barricades were going up outside and revolutionaries were marching in the streets. Louis-Philippe sensibly left his throne and slipped away to England, there to die a few years later in the less strenuous surroundings of Claremont in Surrey.

All that day the noise of riots and of breaking glass drifted in from the rue de Beaune. Madame Massenet did not follow her husband in his sympathies with Napoleon, but supported the Bourbons instead. Her childhood memories of the Duchesse d'Angoulême strengthened her dislike of the new regime. Despite her anxiety she went on with the day's routine and gave her son his first piano lesson. By the light of flickering candles she placed his little fingers on the keys, and while the rest of Paris manned barricades and made excited speeches to whoever would listen, the household in the rue de Beaune devoted itself to more adult pursuits.

'To initiate me the better into a knowledge of the instrument,' wrote Massenet, 'my mother . . . had laid along the keyboard a sheet of paper on which she had written the notes corresponding to the white keys and the black keys, together with their positions on the five lines of the stave. It was a clever idea and there was no possibility of making a mistake.'

Within a few years he had made such progress under this maternal tuition that his parents decided to send him to the Conservatoire. On 9th October 1851 he arrived at the ancient building in the rue du Faubourg-Poissonière to take his entrance examination.

> 'The walls of the big room which we entered', Massenet recalled, 'were, like most of the others in that establishment, painted in a grey-blue colour thickly stippled with black. The only furniture in this waiting-room consisted of old benches. A senior official of rough and severe aspect came and summoned the candidates, shouting out their names in the middle of the crowd of parents and apprehensive friends who accompanied them. It was rather like a roll call of the condemned. To each candidate he allotted the number which had to be given on appearing before the examining board. The latter was already assembled in the room next door.'

That 'room next door' where Massenet soon found himself was a place of bitter-sweet memories for all who studied music in France during the first half of the nineteenth century. It was there that the examinations in music and acting were held, and there that preliminary judgments of the Prix de Rome Committee were delivered. From time to time, organ lessons were given in the room. When the venerable instrument used for this purpose was not being played, it was clothed in a dust-sheet, its asthmatic tones thankfully stilled. Few candidates ever forgot the sight of the dim bulk that lurked beside the fatal door through which they made their entrance onto the platform beyond.

Facing the platform sat the judging committee made up of members of the teaching staff. Among them on this occasion was Fromenthal Halévy, composer of *la Juive* and many other successful operas. He never refused a libretto and was seldom guilty of revising a single bar in the whole of his prolific output. Good-natured and industrious, he was apt to forget his classes in the heat of composing an overdue last act. Next to him sat Michele Carafa, who is recorded in history not as the composer of *Elisabetta in Derbyshire* or of *la Prison d'Edimbourg*, which a later age has hastened to forget, but as the sardonic friend of Rossini in his last days. Carafa had begun life as a professional soldier, and at one time or another he had fought, with amiable impartiality, on both the opposing sides during the Italian campaigns. Then he set up as composer in Paris, and dozens of operas flowed remorselessly from his pen. When he was appointed to teach at the Conservatoire his compatriot, the peppery Cherubini, had thoughtfully advised him to study fugue and counterpoint before passing on his erudition to others. A more sympathetic member of the committee was Ambroise Thomas, later to become a good friend of Massenet. He embellished the repertory of the Opéra-Comique with a number of works remarkable for their grace and lightness. Though he may not have been the equal of Goethe or of Shakespeare, his operas *Mignon* and *Hamlet* contain music that is as pleasing as it is unpretentious. One feels that he has been damned for his frivolity by the grave race of musicologists on account of such light-hearted confections as *Mina, ou le Ménage à trois*.[1]

Presiding over the judges was the elegant figure of Daniel François Esprit Auber, then director of the Conservatoire. There can be few brass bands throughout Europe which have not over the years attacked, and defeated, with much carnage, the overtures to *Masaniello* and *les Diamants de la couronne*. He deserves better than that. He wrote nearly fifty operas, which include *Leicester, ou le Château de Kenilworth*, a ritual obeisance to Scott which most musicians of the day felt obliged to make,

[1] 'There are', said the irrepressible Chabrier, 'three sorts of music: good music, bad music, and the music Ambroise Thomas writes.'

and a *Manon Lescaut* which preceded Massenet by a generation. Auber was a shy and disabused man. He was only fully at ease in the company of women, whom he pursued with untiring vivacity into old age. At his grand house in a fashionable district of Paris he entertained his feminine guests to lavish dinner parties, and it was with reluctance that he sometimes agreed to include men among them. As he sat feasting his eyes on the pretty actresses and singers at his table, the conversation revolved around theatrical gossip, slander of society beauties, and Mr Worth's latest fashion show. Music, at the host's unwritten command, was banned as a theme for discussion. He became almost as annoyed with anyone who dared to raise the subject as he once had been with a cabinet minister who toasted him at a banquet as 'this venerable old gentleman'. Auber loved horses almost as much as he did women. However late he may have been the night before, he was up at six every morning to choose his mount from the stable of twelve which he kept. On summer evenings he dined with his guests on a balcony overlooking the courtyard. Then, the *Maître* having chosen a *Maîtresse* to sit beside him, several carriages bore the company off for a trot through the Bois de Boulogne. The winter evenings found him at the theatre accompanied by a retinue of ladies. Auber was much given to long private rehearsals of the feminine star of his current opera. He once demonstrated his musicianship by playing the piano accompaniment with his left hand, and, with his right hand, exploring at the same time the charms of the *prima donna* whom he was rehearsing. So skilled a musician was she, we are told, that her *roulades* continued to soar forth without a tremor.

For his test piece Massenet was to play the last movement of a Beethoven sonata.

> As is usual, I was told to stop after playing two or three pages, and, nonplussed, I heard Monsieur Auber's voice telling me to come down in front of the committee. There were four or five steps leading down from the platform. Overcome by some sort of dizziness, I hadn't at first noticed this and I was about to stumble when Monsieur Auber said, kindly: 'Watch out, *mon petit*, you'll fall.' Then he straightway asked me where I had been able to find such excellent training. After telling him, not without pride, that my only teacher had been my mother, I went out in a flurry, almost running and feeling so happy. HE had spoken to me! Next morning my mother received the official letter. I was a pupil at the Conservatoire!

Soon after entering the piano class at the Conservatoire, Massenet showed that he had a very real gift for the instrument. He enrolled for theory classes and was only just beginning to get to grips with the mysteries of harmony when his father's health made it necessary for the family to move out to the country. It was thought that the air of Chambéry, in Savoy, would help to restore the invalid. Early in 1854 the Massenet family went to the town and stayed with relatives there. Jules found little to delight him in the rustic beauties which had enchanted Rousseau. He felt he had been cut off in the middle of a promising career, and he wandered with unappreciative eyes among the hills and their romantic cascades, their tiny hamlets and their translucent streams. Even the sight of Les Charmettes, where Rousseau had lived with the flighty Madame de Warens, failed to compensate for the loss of Paris and the Conservatoire. So he worked all the harder at his studies, practising '... scales and arpeggios, sixths and thirds, just as if I was destined to become a spirited pianist. I wore my hair ridiculously long, as was the fashion with virtuosi, and this outward resemblance suited my ambitious dreams. It seemed that unkempt hair was the complement of talent!' During his enforced stay in the country he somehow discovered the music of Schumann. The composer was then little known in France. The handful of people who had heard his work declared it for the most part to be absurd stuff. 'Come and amuse us with some of your Schumann and its awful wrong notes!' they would say to young Jules' exasperation.

The frustrations of Chambéry at length became unbearable. One morning, when the first light of dawn had barely touched the mountain peaks, Massenet escaped from the house 'without a ha'penny in my pocket' and made off for Paris. Once in the capital he never returned. His parents, realizing the strength of his vocation, did not attempt to argue with him.

In Paris Massenet lodged with his favourite sister, Julie. She was now the wife of an artist, Pierre Cavaillé, who catered with brisk efficiency for a public taste in historical pictures designed to tell a story and implant a moral. A portrait he painted of the twelve-year-old Massenet shows a fair-haired and attractive little boy with generous, slightly compressed lips. He looks at once mischievous and withdrawn, forthcoming and shy. Sometimes he would join a band of high-spirited young friends and scamper down the rue Rochechouart emitting loud shrieks that brought everyone to the door and struck fear into the bosoms of old ladies. At other times he would sit reflectively on his own and meditate dreamily for hours.

At the Conservatoire Massenet quickly made up for the time he had spent in Chambéry. By October of 1855 he was back in his old piano class, and the following year he won an honourable mention at the end-of-session examinations for his playing of Hummel's B minor concerto. As early as 1858, at the age of sixteen, he gave his first public recital. The engagement took him to Belgium, where in Tournai, on 16th September, he impressed the local music critics with his performance. 'The young pianist Monsieur Massenet,' wrote one of them, 'is shy in front of the audience but full of power and command before the keyboard. He has an admirable touch and the sounds reach his hearers with purity and strength. One could almost liken them to pearls falling into a crystal glass.'

There were, at this period, few pearls or even crystal glasses in the existence Massenet was leading. His father was unable to make him an allowance. At the same time, the boy felt uneasy at living permanently on his sister's charity. During the day, when he was not attending lessons, he went to practise in a studio which had been lent to his elder brother, probably by Pierre Cavaillé. This elder brother had ambitions to be a playwright and lived in the studio with his collaborator, a young socialist called Jules Vallès who later became a well-known novelist. Years later Vallès recalled the scene:

> There were two camp beds we used to stow away every morning when the young brother arrived at nine o'clock to practise at his piano. Our strummer was then fourteen or fifteen years old perhaps, with long fair hair and deep-set eyes. Though only a child, he intimidated and almost inspired us with respect, for he worked so very hard. He was as punctual as the clock itself, coming and seating his bottom on his textbook and attacking the instrument at the given time, brushing aside with the gesture of one obsessed everything likely to hinder his overwhelming compulsion for music.

Even at this early stage Massenet had developed the facility for hard work and the driving concentration which were to be among his most notable characteristics as a man. He had his reward in the July of 1859, when he gained a first prize at the Conservatoire for his playing of Hiller's F minor piano concerto.

At about this time the rising young pianist, anxious to impose no longer upon his sister, took an attic room at No. 5 rue de Ménilmontant. It was not long since herds of cows had grazed on the slopes there. Sheep had cropped peacefully between the country houses and 'follies' that dotted the landscape. Little villages had flourished where traffic now thunders incessantly. Maurice Chevalier's famous song celebrates the working-class quarter it was to become. In Massenet's day the place still kept a few shreds of its picturesque history. Next door to his cramped eyrie lived the clowns and acrobats who worked at the nearby Cirque Napoléon. On Sundays that vast building was taken over by Jules Pasdeloup, the conductor whose popular concerts did so much to mould French musical taste in the nineteenth century. On hot days the audiences who packed into the Cirque Napoléon would clamour for the skylights to be thrown back. Massenet silently blessed their need for fresh air, since up through the open skylights drifted the strains of the concert which he could not afford to attend, even at Pasdeloup's modest prices. In this way he gained his early knowledge of Berlioz and Wagner, the two composers whom he then admired above all others.

In later years Massenet did not speak with nostalgia of his life as a penniless student. He thought the adventures of Rodolphe and Mimi to be romantic nonsense, and all he admired about *la Bohème* was Puccini's music. He could see nothing sentimental in poverty. The friends who chuckled at his carefulness over money and his respect for material success when he was an established figure in the theatre cannot have realized the impression his painful early days left upon him. He never forgot the humiliation of being chronically hard up, and it was only his youthful hope that kept him going. He scraped together a few francs by giving piano lessons at a wretched little school in the area. There was a café in the rue de Belleville that paid him thirty francs a month for playing each night. He made his way there past shady taverns and greasy cookshops. On Ash Wednesday he may have seen the once-famous Carnival setting off as described by Alfred de Musset:

> Bumping and grazing each other, the carriages bearing the masked revellers trundled along in disarray between two rows of hideous men and women standing on the pavements. This wall of sinister spectators had eyes red with wine and tigerish hatred . . . I was standing on the seat in an open carriage: from time to time a man in rags stepped out of the row and spewed up a torrent of insults in our faces, then threw a cloud of flour over us . . .

Less distasteful, though equally exhausting, was his regular engagement as drummer at the Opéra. Every Saturday, when the Opéra ball was held, Massenet laboured from midnight to six in the morning at kettledrum, cymbal, gong and triangle. On three evenings a week he played in the pit for the normal repertory. His other evenings found him in the same humble occupation wherever opera was being given, or doubling up for amateur groups where a friend remembered him jotting down musical ideas on a drumskin between his cues. His perpetual round of nights at the opera taught him the craft of theatre music in the most practical way of all. It was tiring and ill-paid, but nowhere else could he have served such a useful apprenticeship. He came to know by heart all the scores that were played. Night after night he heard the greatest singers of the time and studied how composers had enabled them to show their technique to effect. He learned how music could be shaped to introduce and develop a scene, and how orchestration helped to create atmosphere. And there was that Homeric evening when, from his corner in the pit, he saw the riots at the first performance of Wagner's *Tannhaüser*.

His memories of the time were essentially theatrical. To reach the Théâtre Lyrique, where he was a regular player, he had to pass through the boulevard du Temple. The left-hand side of this thoroughfare was then an almost uninterrupted line of theatres specializing in the bloody melodramas and sensational spectacles which had earned it the nick-name of the *boulevard du Crime*. Among them were the Funambules, where Deburau, the whey-faced Pierrot, acted out his pathetic mimes. Behind the boulevard du Temple ran the old rue des Fossés du Temple, into which opened the stage-doors of all the theatres. On the ill-lit pavement actors and actresses congregated to snatch a breath of air between acts. In their bizarre costumes and fantastic make-up they gave the place the aspect of a *cour des miracles*, a beggars' meet of the type so vividly described in Hugo's *Notre-Dame*. The atmosphere soon lost its romance when one looked closer and saw the fleas which were the faith-ful companions of those tattered entertainers. Even at the Théâtre Lyrique, Massenet remembered, the artists' accommodation was nothing more than an old stable where horses were kept when the management put on a spectacular show. Like the rest of a community whose bread depends on the caprice of the public and the whims of impresarios, Massenet was familiar with the interiors of pawnshops. There were certain places he could never see afterwards without a pang of sorrow at the memory of the precious belongings he had had to barter in the struggle to keep alive.

II

ROME-LISZT-FIRST LOVE

SWEET are the revenges brought by the whirligig of time. In 1860 Massenet presented himself as a student at the harmony classes taught by François Bazin. Bazin was the perpetrator of two comic operas, *le Voyage en Chine* and *l'Ours at le Pacha*, which had gained a certain vogue. His bottom drawer crammed with other unpublished and unplayed operas, Bazin had a successful official career at the Conservatoire and eventually, like a piece of flotsam washed up on some exotic shore, found himself basking on the hallowed benches of the Académie des Beaux Arts. He inspected, with a dogmatic eye, the compositions which Massenet laid before him. The individuality which already showed in these prentice works deeply offended the old pedant. Exclaiming that he had no room for a 'black sheep' in his class, the outraged teacher showed his would-be pupil the door. Eighteen years later, Massenet was not only to take over Bazin's harmony class at the Conservatoire but also to succeed him in his chair at the Académie des Beaux Arts.

In the end Massenet studied harmony under Reber, a much gentler spirit who rejoiced, without much conviction, in the Christian names of Napoléon Henri. Next followed organ lessons with François Benoist who for half a century and more was a part of the furniture at the Conservatoire. (He had written, in collaboration with Ambroise Thomas, an improbable opera entitled *la Gypsy*.) Massenet's youthful excesses which had so scandalized Bazin were greeted with amused tolerance by his new masters. Among them was Ambroise Thomas himself, for whom Massenet quickly became a favourite pupil. 'Let him be', he would say, benevolently stroking his beard; 'when the first excitement of youth is over, he'll soon find his balance and achieve success.'

Two years afterwards Massenet entered the competition for the Prix de Rome. This prize, which is sponsored by the Académie des Beaux Arts, offers the successful candidate a stay of four years in the

Villa Medici at Rome, during which time he is encouraged to develop his art. With it goes a handsome gold medal, although the real advantage of being able to style oneself 'Grand Prix de Rome' lies in the opportunity to begin one's artistic career among the unique influences which Italian civilization can provide. For days on end Massenet was locked into a mildewed little room, as was the forbidding procedure with competitors, and left to grapple with a poem which he had to set to music. It was, on this occasion, a mediocre piece of verse entitled *Louise de Mézières*. The candidate's opinion of its worth was summed up in an epithet he scribbled on the wall: 'Louise la Mercière' [Louisa the Haberdasher]. He did not win the prize.

Next spring he was subjected to the same depressing experience. Having completed his cantata *David Rizzio,* he loitered in an agony of expectation near the Institut where the judges were deliberating. At five o'clock in the afternoon he could stand it no longer. Walking towards the building he saw a group of three people deep in conversation. They were Berlioz, Ambroise Thomas and Auber. Thomas came to meet him.

'Embrassez Berlioz!' he cried. 'You owe him your prize!'

'The prize', replied Massenet unbelievingly. 'I've got it.'

And in his excitement he threw himself on Berlioz and hugged the composer's gaunt frame to him. Then it was Auber's turn, after which the joyful youth buried himself in Thomas' ample beard.

Mary Queen of Scots' unfortunate lover had brought Massenet luck. *David Rizzio* was duly performed. One of its numbers, mysteriously described as a 'Scotch Ballad', was admired and was later published separately. There followed more embracing at the presentation ceremony. As was the custom, Massenet was handed the prize by his own teacher, Ambroise Thomas. His passage towards the rostrum evoked from the unruly student audience punning shouts of: 'Embrasse Thomas!'

Freed for the moment from the drudgery of the orchestra pit, Massenet was now the possessor of a bursary worth over three thousand francs a year. On Boxing Day 1863, he and his fellow prizewinners—sculptors, architects and painters—toured Paris in three hired landaus, to pay the traditional courtesy visits to members of the Académie des Beaux Arts before setting off for Italy. New Year's Day found him at Bordighera where his mother had settled. It was the anniversary of his father's death the previous year, and a visit to the grave was enough to sober Massenet's high spirits. In his mother's little palm-girt villa overlooking the sea, a mood of sadness replaced his earlier exaltation and he was reluctant to leave her. But his friends were waiting nearby in a vast carriage drawn by three horses, and soon the wheels were spinning along roads that led through myrtle and mimosa to Genoa.

Dr Johnson, as usual, has had the last word.

> A man who has not been in Italy, is always conscious of an inferiority, from his not having seen what it is expected a man should see. The grand object of travelling is to see the shores of the Mediterranean. On those shores were the four great Empires of the world; the Assyrian, the Persian, the Grecian, and the Roman. All our religion, almost all our law, almost all our arts, almost all that sets us above savages, has come to us from the shores of the Mediterranean.

It was this admirable sentiment, or something very close to it, which the Académie des Beaux Arts had in mind when it bought from the Grand Duke of Tuscany the estate on Monte Pincio which was to house young French artists and musicians. Before reaching the Villa Medici, Massenet and his friends sampled a foretaste of Italian beauty on the way. In Genoa they paused to wonder at the marble splendours of the Campo Santo burial ground. At Milan they were engrossed by the fading colours of Leonardo's *The Last Supper* (the room had recently been used by Austrian soldiers as a stable, and a door had been pierced in the fresco's centre panel). Then they arrived in Verona, where the romantic Massenet could not resist making the traditional pilgrimage to Juliet's tomb. Unable to afford even Baedeker's modest aid, they spent hours patrolling the waterways of Venice in search of a picture glimpsed momentarily in one of its ninety churches.

And so they came to Rome. 'It was in Rome that I began to live', declared Massenet with a Gallic flamboyance that Johnson for once might have approved.

> It was there, in the course of happy jaunts made with my musician, painter or sculptor friends, and during our conversations under the oaks of the Villa Borghese or the pines of the Villa Pamphili, that I felt the first stirrings of admiration for nature and art. What delightful hours we spent wandering through the museums of Naples and Florence! What delicious and melancholy feelings those strangely dark churches of Siena and Assisi aroused in us! How quickly one forgot Paris and its theatres, its noisy crowds and its feverish bustle!

At Rome the prizewinners were greeted by Victor Schnetz, the director of the Villa Medici. He was a tall man who toured his domain wearing a voluminous dressing gown and a Grecian cap which, like his ample robes, was embellished with plump and splendid tassels of gold. During the years he held his attractive and not very onerous post, he painted many views of the Roman campagna. The landscapes he portrayed, which have a frail old-fashioned charm, often include Sabine brigands who would co-operate with him only after a careful appraisal of his burly frame. In Massenet's day no one had yet thought to excavate the tombs and temples which lay under the rubbish of centuries. The Forum itself was a heap of stones and jagged shafts of columns overgrown with herbs and weeds. On shattered paving where once the city fathers met to govern their city and to declare war or vote a triumph, there grazed flocks of goats watched over by impassive shepherds in broad-brimmed hats and black cloaks with green linings.

There were twenty or so young artists and musicians in residence at the Villa Medici, and Massenet was soon to discover the surprises which they reserved for new arrivals. After dinner on his first evening there they all went out into the dark January night for a stroll in the city. As they stumbled through a ruined basilica Massenet had a confused impression of lurching arcades and coffered vaults poised crazily against the murky sky. He went a little way forward and was confronted with a huge cross lowering from a pedestal. He looked up and saw himself hemmed in by colossal walls. His mischievous comrades had suddenly vanished. The immense and terrifying silence was broken by his footsteps hurrying over the uneven ground and tripping against fallen statuary. But whichever way he took, he always found himself back where he had started. In despair he settled on the steps that led up to the stone cross and fell asleep. At dawn the sharp winter light slanted down over the tiered seats that rose to majestic heights around the Colosseum, and there, in the middle of the amphitheatre, was an exhausted but relieved Massenet. Like a squirrel in a cage, he now realized, he had simply been walking round and round the arena.

Back in his room at the Villa Medici he soon recovered from the misadventure. It was impossible to be depressed for long when he had only to look up from his work table to see from his window '... the city of Popes and Caesars, dominated here by the sovereign cupola of St Peter and there by the pagan Colosseum. Further away there stretched the Roman countryside, already bathed in the vague shadows of twilight as far as the Janiculum, gilded yet by the rays of the setting sun ...' By the spring of 1864 Massenet and his friends were travelling far afield on their exploration of Italy. They put up for the night at primitive taverns where, on one occasion, Massenet feared that the guest overhead was about to set fire to the place, only to realize that what he had taken for sparks was the scintillation of stars glimpsed through a dilapidated ceiling. To celebrate their trip in style, the travellers ordered suits made of white flannel with blue stripes. A little puzzled by the suspicious looks with which the *carabiniere* favoured them as they walked through the streets of Naples, they were enlightened by the explanation that their garb closely resembled the uniform of Neapolitan convicts. For the rest of their stay they limped ostentatiously, as if they had but recently cast off ball and chain.

From Naples they went on to the orange groves of Sorrento and visited the birthplace of Tasso, whose terra-cotta bust mournfully surveyed the half-ruined hovel where he had first seen the light of day. Their hair close-cropped as the result of a tart skirmish with fleas at an Amalfi hotel, they sailed over to Capri. This was the unforgettable climax of their tour. 'To set up house on Capri', Massenet wrote, 'to live and work there, would be the ideal existence, the sort of life one dreams about!' But it was time for Rome again, and autumn mists were rising when they installed themselves once more at the Villa Medici. The notebooks Massenet brought back with him were filled with folk tunes he had heard on his wanderings. Among these rustic melodies was one played by a shepherd on his *zampogna,* or bagpipe, in the woods of Subiaco. It was to serve as the plaintive opening theme of the oratorio *Marie-Magdeleine*. The notebooks in which Massenet had jotted it down were carefully preserved, and as time went on they proved a source of ideas for later works. His musician's ear was constantly on the alert, his subconscious was ever awake to fresh stimuli, and even when he seemed to be farthest away from all thought of music, haggling in a street market or looking at pictures, his mind was storing up new patterns of sound.

Carnival time in Rome, pictured by Berlioz with a frenetic *saltarello* and a blaze of glittering orchestration, brought a host of vivid impressions. The students of architecture at the Villa Medici built a processional car which, decorated by the sculptors, bore them through riotous streets. Massenet remembered throwing flowers and confetti at dark-eyed *signorine* who smiled down on them mysteriously as the ornamental vehicle trundled past the balconies of ancient palaces. Other excitements were provided by the social life at the Villa Medici. Monsieur Schnetz held soirées which were eminently popular with Roman society. He was, we are told by Stendhal, 'regarded by the local aristocracy as one of themselves, with the same way of life as the princes and the same opinions as the cardinals'. His entertainments were lavish and hospitable. Guests drove up to the Villa Medici through an oak-lined avenue. All around lay gardens planned with immaculate care. Lawns neatly enclosed by hedges rolled smoothly down from the Villa, while among the foliage lurked statues of Hermes and marble busts. Schnetz entertained on the first floor in spacious reception rooms hung with Gobelins tapestries. There, with a somewhat disabused urbanity, he received the princes, the cardinals and the nuncios who flocked beneath his celebrated roof, together with numbers of visiting compatriots. Had it not been said that when a Frenchman came to Rome, his first request was to see the Pope, and his second to see Monsieur Schnetz?

No host of that time could afford to ignore Rome's most famous resident musician. Franz Liszt was then living in the city after a career in which he had dazzled Europe with displays of pianism as bewildering as his magnetic personality. Schnetz cared very little for music and was, indeed, prevented by deafness from even attempting to understand it. For some reason he thought Verdi was the only composer whose music was acceptable to him. Bizet, who was at the Villa Medici several years before Massenet, said that so long as you told Schnetz that you were going to play Verdi, you could then go ahead and play Beethoven, Bach or Chopin with complete assurance. So long as Schnetz thought you were playing Verdi he was content. Despite all this Liszt was a frequent guest at the Villa Medici. He had broken with the comtesse d'Agoult, the mother of his two daughters, and had begun his long liaison with that formidable chronicler of the Christian church, the Princess Carolyne zu Sayn Wittgenstein. A black cigar stuck purposefully between her lips, she spent years compiling a many-volumed work of ecclesiastical history, while Liszt, seated at the other end of the room and also puffing at a strong cigar, got on with his composing. The spectacle—and the atmosphere—must have struck awe into the most frivolous visitor. When they settled in Rome Liszt took a separate apartment and began to study for the priesthood. A powerful sense of religiosity had always existed in the posturing showman who courted the applause of crowds, and it was this side of his strange character which now emerged most plainly. Accepted into the minor degrees of priesthood, he had the right to call himself Abbé and to wear the black habit of his calling. It is pleasant to note that among the functions he was authorized to perform—reader, acolyte, doorkeeper and so forth—the musician whose virtuosity struck his hearers as satanic was also qualified as an exorcist. 'Mephistopheles disguised as an Abbé', commented an observer. Yet he was entirely without hypocrisy. No one guilty of that vice could possibly have remarked naïvely, as he did on one occasion, that he had divided his day between studying the Catechism and arranging for the piano a flashy fantasia on Meyerbeer's *l'Africaine*.

Massenet heard him play at the Villa Medici and, like everyone else, capitulated to the magic of the old enchanter. It was just before Christmas. The young student had gone to midnight mass on Christmas Eve and was touched by the sight of the shepherds and their flocks who gathered in the public square to receive the priests' blessing. Next day, walking up the three hundred steps that lead to the Church of Ara Coeli, he passed two women. The face of the younger one immediately caught his eye. She remained a pleasant memory until, a few days later, he visited Liszt at his home. Although he had retired from the concert platform, Liszt still took pupils. Wishing, however, to give more time to religious contemplation, he was seeking other teachers for the attractive girls and fashionable ladies whose delicate white hands he would have been only too pleased to guide over the keyboard in less austere days. His eye fell on Massenet as a suitable repository for one of his charges. The young man, reluctant at first on account of his own studies, quickly changed his mind when Liszt presented him to a girl who was none other than the unknown beauty glimpsed on the church steps.

Her name was Constance de Sainte-Marie, familiarly known as 'Ninon'. Within a short space of time Massenet was hastening to finish a piano trio in order that he might dedicate it to her. She was the cousin of Jules Armingaud, the founder, with Lalo, of a famous chamber-music group. Her brother was an artist who lived at Barbizon and who, as was only natural, specialized in vaporous wooded landscapes in the manner of Corot. At first Massenet was welcomed into the cultured Sainte-Marie family. With his pupil Ninon, who soon became a close friend, he went on carriage rides into the countryside, always, of course, in the watchful presence of her mother and father. 'For the past two and a half months,' he wrote home, 'I've been playing a lot of duets with her. Together we've worked through all the symphonies of Mozart, Haydn, Beethoven, Mendelssohn, and even Schumann.'

It was not long before he realized that he was falling in love with her. He later rhapsodized over the girl 'who was to become my beloved wife, the watchful and often anxious companion of my days'. Apart from this typically florid declaration, there is little which will help us to see more clearly the nature of the girl who so overwhelmed him. We must take his word for it and go on to the next scene, in which he asks Monsieur and Madame de Sainte-Marie for the hand of their daughter. Their answer was foreseeable. As Ninon's teacher he was ideal.As her husband he left much to be desired. While yet a student whose income was soon to end at the expiry of his scholarship, he must wait a little longer before thinking of marriage.

His idyll temporarily suspended, he threw himself with still greater determination into his studies. 'I am working more at the piano,' he wrote to his sister. 'I'm studying Chopin's *Études*, but especially Beethoven, and Bach as the true musician-pianist. I'm also training my memory, which will be useful.' Among the compositions which, according to the rules, he sent back to the Institut for inspection, were a *Requiem*, a concert overture, and a quantity of music which he wrote to please himself. This included the preliminary sketches for his oratorios *Ève*, *la Vierge,* and the *Marie-Magdeleine* already noted. The heroines of these works began to take on a more sensuous quality, and the languorous phrases Massenet composed for them were written with the image of Ninon in his mind.

By the time spring had come round again, Massenet was off once more on his journeys. The Prix de Rome regulations prescribed at least a year to be spent visiting Germany and Austro-Hungary, and the involuntary exile travelled through the main German towns before settling at Pesth. The city which inspired Liszt's *Carnaval de Pesth* also gave Massenet the idea for his orchestral suite entitled *Scènes hongroises*. His notebooks were filling up rapidly. The Czech melodies which captured his imagination were soon joined by a fanfare overheard in Venice on the way back to Rome. Twenty-five years later this fanfare was to appear in the fourth act of *le Cid*.

He returned to take his leave of Rome. The carefree student days were over. He would no longer see from his window the dome of St Peter's mellowed by the setting sun, or hear the distant evening notes of the shepherd guiding his flock through the campagna. Sadly he packed his souvenirs of the Roman years: a mandoline, a few twigs culled from the gardens of the Villa Medici, a wooden Madonna. They nestled among the few worn clothes and piles of flimsy manuscript paper that made up his slender luggage. Envying the other students who came to see him off at the railway station and who, that night, would be sleeping at the Villa Medici while he was jolting in his cheap carriage, he watched nostalgically as the ruins of Diocletian's grandeur moved slowly past the window.

He could not leave Italy without a last visit to Florence, and there he spent a day in the company of Tintoretto, Raphael and Michelangelo. At Pisa he was struck by the solidity of the leaning tower. It must, he reflected, be exceptionally strong to withstand the reverberations of the seven bells which, two or three times a day, rang out in all their force. But these scientific reflections were quite forgotten in the enchantment of his journey by coach along the moonlit Roman road to Genoa. Closely following the edge of the sea, the route plunged deep into olive woods only to emerge, a little later, on mountain peaks before dipping again into a ghostly landscape lit by the moon and the occasional twinkle in the window of a far-off homestead. All too soon Massenet was at Genoa and in the train bound for Paris. He woke from a shivery doze to see the carriage windows laced with arabesques of ice. The train had long since crossed the border into France. The blue skies of Italy were succeeded by the frowning snowclouds of Paris. After settling his travel expenses Massenet found that he had two francs left in his pocket. With them he made a purchase which had suddenly, for the first time in two years, become essential—an umbrella.

III

DELIBES – MARRIAGE – LA GRAND'TANTE

THERE still remained some funds owing to Massenet from his Prix de Rome, and these he hastened to collect. A little room he took on the fifth floor of Number 14 rue Taitbout, in the heart of Montmartre's familiar din, became his headquarters for the next few years. Through streets dripping in wintry rain he went on the rounds of music publishers. Few of them even took the trouble to look at his manuscripts. He was not, at first, too disheartened. 'What was I, after all?' he remarked. 'A complete unknown.' Moreover, he had just secured the first public performance of one of his works, the suite *Pompéia*. This was introduced at a concert given by Joseph Arban, a former cornet player who had set up his own orchestra. In moments of excitement Arban was apt to sing at the top of his voice the most striking portions of the work he was ostensibly conducting. At other times, in order to add a little variety to his programmes, he would entertain the audience with fantasias upon his raucous instrument.

Despite the eccentric behaviour of its sponsor, *Pompéia* was well received. Although it has not been published, we know that it won praise from the critics. One of them went so far as to say that he was reminded of Berlioz' vigorous touch and that the brilliance of orchestration was astonishing in such a young man. Other small pieces were played in the months that followed, but publishers were unimpressed. Then one day, inspired by a new friendship with Armand Sylvestre, a versifier who dwelt obscurely in the shadow of the Parnassian group of poets, Massenet set his *Poème d'avril* to music. The manuscript travelled hopefully from publisher to publisher. It always came back. After four unsuccessful attempts Massenet contrived to penetrate into the office of Antoine Choudens, the man who had waxed exceedingly fat on the huge sums that came his way when he published *Faust*. He showed Massenet the door. So, too, did the publisher of the then sensationally successful Meyerbeer.

Plodding back to the rue Taitbout after one of these fruitless expeditions, Massenet found his way barred by a tall, fair-haired giant of a man.

'I opened a music shop yesterday, here in the boulevard de la Madeleine,' said the stranger. 'I know who you are and I offer to publish anything you want me to.'

The blunt young man was Georges Hartmann, one of the most enterprising publishers French music has ever known. He took under his wing a band of young composers whom he nurtured with fond attention. At a time when Bizet, Charpentier and Franck were finding it difficult to make themselves heard, Hartmann backed his faith in their work by publishing it. He went further and organized, with the help of the conductor Édouard Colonne, an association which created an audience for his protégés by actually performing their works. Wherever new musical developments were taking place in Paris during the second half of the nineteenth century, there Hartmann was nearly always to be found. His most famous protégé was Debussy, whom he subsidized with his own money for five or six years. Hartmann, said the grateful Debussy with truth, had seen sent by Providence 'and played his part with a grace and an amiability which are rare enough among philanthropists'.

Massenet took Hartmann at his word and gave him *Poème d'avril.* The little song made its way into the drawing-rooms, and amateur singers in polite society everywhere were trilling it soon in a variety of well-meaning keys. There were, of course, no royalties, but at least Massenet had the reward of seeing himself in print and of enjoying a kind of celebrity, however modest. To earn a living he had to look elsewhere, and he returned to the hack work that had been his lot before the days of the Prix de Rome scholarship. One of his tasks was to transcribe melodies for a rich American lady, a Mrs Charles Moulton, who interested herself in music. Mrs Moulton was a noted Parisian hostess. In his novel, *le Nabab*, Alphonse Daudet presents her as Madame Jenkins and depicts her in a Renoir setting. The drawing-room blinds are down to keep out the hot sun, and, wearing a summer dress, she sings at the keyboard 'a new song by a fashionable young musician'. Massenet had been introduced to her by Auber. Overhearing one day the strains of *Poème d'avril,* she realized that the young man had other talents than those of a simple amanuensis. The dedication of his next song, *Poème du souvenir,* shows that from then on she used her considerable influence on his behalf. He now had not only a publisher but also an Egeria.

Another helpful supporter was Ambroise Thomas. When Massenet fell victim to an outbreak of cholera which raged in Paris, Thomas hurried with his doctor, the Emperor's own medical consultant, to the little room in the rue Taitbout. The old composer, fussing anxiously over his favourite pupil, and the medical man, a trifle amused by the contrast between the grand surroundings where he usually saw his patients and the humble place in which he now found himself, soon had Massenet on his feet again. The result of a brief convalescence was the *Dix pièces de genre* for piano, ten little salon titbits which included a Nocturne, a Rigaudon, a Fughetta, a Carillon and so forth. The most popular item won even greater fame under the new title of *Élégie* as part of the incidental music Massenet wrote a few years afterwards for Leconte de Lisle's play *les Érinnyes*. Its sobbing swoops in the bass rang out still more plangently on the cello, and there were few instruments to which it was not adapted in the course of its successful career. The *Dix pièces de genre* were a triumph from all points of view, since Massenet was also paid two hundred francs for them—the first money he ever earned with his music.

Once he had recovered from his illness he began to get about again. Ambroise Thomas took him out to receptions given by rich friends, and at one of these he introduced him to Delibes. *La Source,* to which Delibes contributed so brilliantly that he quite outshone his collaborator Minkus, had just made him into a celebrity and revealed him as a born writer of ballet music. Few people have a good word for Delibes these days. The over-familiarity of his work tends to obscure the adroit craftsmanship and subtle handling of melody and rhythm which place him among the select number of composers who have mastered the very difficult art of writing original ballet music. He had perfected his dramatic technique the hard way. While still in his teens he was offered his first chance by Hervé, proprietor of the Folies-Nouvelles. Hervé was the author of more than a hundred and twenty operettas and ballets. In one year alone he wrote over twenty one-act pieces for his theatre. He often sang the leading role himself or conducted the orchestra, though whether the phenomenal worker did all this at one and the same time the chroniclers do not tell us. Hervé's later years were spent in London, where his busy talents provided a stream of box-office attractions at the old Empire music hall. Lacking the gifts of an Offenbach or a Lecocq, he nevertheless deserves his place in the history of French operetta. Delibes accepted the overworked Hervé's commission and within a few days had written the music for a curtain-raiser entitled *Deux sous de charbon*. Its sub-title, '*asphyxie lyrique*', may doubtless be traced to the inspired hand of the librettist, Jules Moinaux, who was the father of Georges Courteline.

For the next fourteen years Delibes turned out operettas and vaudevilles at the rate of one a year. Then, with *la Source* in 1866, he established himself in his true genre. Yet the greater his success the more diffident he seemed to become. His plump, jovial figure and his vast silky beard accorded ill with the modest manner he adopted in society. He was, perhaps, too good-humoured, too honest, for the rough and tumble of the theatre. His frankness cost him his job as chorus master at the Opéra. At enormous expense the director of that establishment had secured the rights of Meyerbeer's latest opera, *l'Africaine,* and asked Delibes to play it to him. Delibes' lack of assurance did not extend to his technique, and he sight-read brilliantly at the piano Meyerbeer's untidy and often indecipherable orchestral score. This *tour de force* took him four and a half hours, at the end of which the director exclaimed 'What a masterpiece, isn't it?' Quavering at his own audacity but determined to tell the truth, Delibes replied: 'Monsieur le directeur, it's—it's *awful*!' To friends who condoned with him on the loss of his job, he said contentedly: 'Look at it this way: if I'd kept it I'd have had to direct the rehearsals of *l'Africaine*!' He was luckier with Ambroise Thomas, who offered him the post of teacher of composition at the Conservatoire. Only too aware of his failings as a student, Delibes protested: 'I know neither fugue nor counterpoint.' 'Very well then,' declared Thomas, 'you can learn them!' And, like Rimsky-Korsakov in a similar plight, Delibes soon taught himself as much as his pupils by the excellent device of always ensuring that he was several pages ahead of them in the textbook.

Massenet looked on enviously as he watched Delibes conducting a choir of lady amateurs at one of the soirées he attended with Thomas. The acquaintance of his new friend quickened the ambitions he already cherished. In the nineteenth century French musicians put their hopes in the theatre as the surest way of making their name and reaching a large audience. The German-born Meyerbeer had shown that theatrical flair, allied with industry and relentless supervision of stage-management and publicity, was the best method of achieving these aims. Mere genius such as Berlioz possessed was not enough. (It is, of course, beside the point that Berlioz is now played everywhere and that Meyerbeer, perhaps a little too unjustly, is left to slumber more or less undisturbed.) In the presence of Delibes Massenet felt he was breathing something of the atmosphere of the real theatre, that world at once terrifying yet alluring which he so much wanted to enter himself. One day, he promised himself, he too would conquer the stage, and one day he too would be invited by hostesses to conduct at their soirées.

Towards the end of 1866 Massenet seems to have at last persuaded Ninon's parents to agree to her marriage. They may have been impressed by the influential friends he was gathering around him in his profession and by the fact that he still had a few thousand-franc notes left from his Prix de Rome scholarship. They were married on 8th October in the little church of Avon, a village near Fontainebleau which was Massenet's favourite retreat. Inside the church is the tombstone of the marquis de Monaldeschi, an early favourite of Queen Christina of Sweden. (The latter was, however, kinder to Descartes, whom she patronized, than to Monaldeschi, who was assassinated on her order at Fontainebleau, so providing Alexandre Dumas with the excuse for one of his bloodier melodramas.) Nearby is the grave of Katherine Mansfield, whose career, in its own way, was little less melancholy. She died there while staying with the philosopher Gurdjeff, and a cross-road in the forest has been named after her. When Massenet stood at the altar it was a soft autumn day, hazy with the changing light that fascinated the artists' community at Fontainebleau. His best man was Jules Armingaud, the bride's cousin. While the priest orated on the Christian duties of marriage, a flock of sparrows glided saucily to and fro chirruping at the holy man and drowning his talk with their cries. Then the bridal party stepped out of church and walked through the forest beneath towering trees. They strolled against a background described by Stevenson: '. . . castles of white rock lie tumbled one upon another, the foot slips, the crooked viper slumbers, the moss clings in the crevice; and above it all the great beech goes spiring and casting forth her arms, and, with a grace beyond church architecture, canopies this rugged chaos'. The newly married couple felt then, and continued to feel for the rest of their life, that, as Stevenson had said, there was no other place 'where the young are more gladly conscious of their youth, or the old better contented with their age'.

After a week's honeymoon at the seaside they were back in Paris again. The old life of genteel poverty was resumed, and Massenet appeared in the orchestra pit once more, gave lessons to unwilling youth, and played for dance bands in obscure suburbs. The future began to look a little brighter in the spring of 1867, when he learned that he would be able to take advantage of the clause in the Prix de Rome regulations which entitled prize-winners to have a one-act opera performed at the Opéra-Comique. This institution, which always seems a little rakish beside its dignified sister the Opéra, traditionally offers entertainment which avoids the spectacular and is satisfied with lighter, more intimate effects. In the old days the distinction between *opéra* and *opéra-comique* was easy to make, since the latter was not above using spoken dialogue. Over the years, however, accidents of history have tended to blur the difference between the two theatres nominally devoted to the genres, so that, while one is not surprised to find *Wozzeck* in the repertory of the Opéra, one searches in vain for anything remotely humorous in the score which will justify the inclusion of *Carmen* or *Pelléas et Mélisande* among the works regularly performed at the Opéra-Comique. Despite these and other equally incongruous operas which, one feels, belong elsewhere, the place has its origins rooted amongst the tumblers and tightrope walkers of the seventeenth-century fairs. Since then, in its various homes, the stage of the Opéra-Comique has been peopled with a bizarre but not unpleasing procession of Richard Lionhearts, Caliphs of Baghdad, Napoleons in the Elysian Fields, Musketeers of the Queen, Postillions of Longjumeau, Thieving Magpies, Daughters of the Regiment, and even a disquieting figure called The Brewer of Preston who, we are assured, sprang from the same fevered imagination that musicked the ballet *Giselle.*

The libretto with which Massenet was presented came to him through the benevolent intercession of Ambroise Thomas. A young man returns from military service in Africa on the death of his rich great-uncle to find that his ancient relative has died intestate, leaving a relict who turns out to be a lovely young woman whom he had married in old age. There is a contest of generosity between the great-nephew and his beautiful great-aunt. It ends, of course, in marriage and riches for them both. *La Grand'tante* was put on in a double bill with a piece by Massenet's old enemy François Bazin. This tactless juxtaposition failed to subdue Massenet's excitement as he sat in the darkened theatre to follow rehearsals. For the first time he could go backstage with an air of belonging and could loiter in the wings among the dust and the smell of paint and stale make-up which, to the nostrils of the theatre lover, bring a whiff of paradise. 'One's first work is like a first decoration! A first love!' he exclaimed.

At half-past seven one Friday evening in April the curtain rose on a set depicting the Breton country house of the great-uncle. The hero was sung by Victor Capoul, a dashing tenor who had given his name to a hair-style which he affected. All the young boulevard dandies now parted their hair down the middle and wore their locks in rings on the forehead à la Capoul. The heroine was the seventeen-year-old Marie Heilbronn who had made her début the year before. Much later she was to be the first Manon.

The composer hung about nervously backstage. Soon after curtain-rise he heard a loud burst of laughter.

'Listen, *mon ami*,' said his librettist complacently, 'it's going well. The audience is amused.'

So they were, but not in the way Massenet hoped. After Heilbronn concluded an aria facing the audience, Capoul made his entry and began to warble: 'What a country! . . . Not a person to be seen!' But Heilbronn had missed her cue, and her partner found himself staring desperately at her back. The laughter died down and the rest of the piece was heard sympathetically—until, when the stage-manager called on the authors to take their bow, a cat sedately prowled across the stage. Despite these mishaps *la Grand'tante* was favoured with good notices. Théophile Gautier, or one of his hard-working ghost writers, spoke kindly of it, and Massenet could feel pleased that his first venture had a run of seventeen performances. On each of these seventeen evenings he experienced again the same thrill of being a composer whose name was on the posters, and the same happiness that his music was actually being performed to an audience, as he had on the first night.

He was gratified, too, by the praise of his contemporaries. His début at the Opéra-Comique marked the beginning of a friendship with Bizet, who had already shown signs of coming greatness in the mingled qualities of *les Pêcheurs de perles*. On another occasion the two young men were rivals in a contest sponsored by a committee of the 1867 Exposition. There were substantial prizes for the winner, and the promise of performance. In spite of Ambroise Thomas's energetic canvassing of the judges, Massenet was only a runner-up and Bizet was not even placed. The prize went to Saint-Saëns for his cantata *les Noces de Prométhée*. In those days Saint-Saëns was a gay and amusing companion, untouched as yet by the professional disappointments and the cruel misfortunes of a personal life which were to turn him into a sharp-tongued and irascible nomad who preferred the company of animals to human beings.

Saint-Saëns promised to use his influence with Liszt on Massenet's behalf. 'There are such good and lovely things in your score that I've just written to Weimar asking for it to be played there,' he said.

Massenet remembered this many years later and wrote in his usual exaggerated terms: 'Only great men can make such gestures!' By then it was too late. Soured by frustration and boiling with rancour at Massenet's success in a sphere which he himself had stormed with great effort and little reward, Saint-Saëns battened on the comment and added a stinging rider: '. . . what he *didn't* mention was the icy coldness with which he received the news that I, expecting a quite different welcome, had brought him'. Saint-Saëns, of course, had the inestimable advantage of outliving his rival and the rare delight of writing Massenet's obituary. Even so, the competition atmosphere of high hopes and youthful nerves could well make it uncertain which of the two contestants' versions was right.

Between *la Grand'tante* in 1867 and the outbreak of the Franco-Prussian War in 1870, Massenet's name began to appear in the programmes of orchestral concerts as the author of various cantatas, suites and symphonic poems. One of these, the *Ière Suite d'orchestre,* was taken up by the valiant Pasdeloup and introduced as part of his efforts to obtain a hearing for young French composers. The audience was not overwhelmed with enthusiasm, and next day, in *le Figaro,* the well-known critic Albert Wolff wrote an amusing but malicious notice. He reported that Massenet's contribution fell victim to its temerity in appearing at the same concert as Mozart and Mendelssohn. After ten minutes, Wolff continued, the weakly score had to be taken to a nearby chemist 'who gave it first-aid, so that at a quarter to four the youthful composer, Monsieur Massenet, was able to take the unfortunate invalid home'. This rather cruel jocularity annoyed one of Massenet's colleagues, Théodore Dubois, who wrote a sharp but dignified letter to *le Figaro* protesting at such heartless behaviour. (Dubois himself was a brilliant musician who later became head of the Conservatoire, though few of his works are played nowadays.) His generous defence inspired Massenet, for the first and last time in his career, to argue with a critic, and he replied to Wolff in great good humour. He had, he said, admired and laughed at the wit of the article. However, intelligent people and fools had this in common, that they were both liable to make mistakes. There Massenet wisely left the matter. He never again, though often tempted, replied to unfavourable criticism of his work. Despite his sensitiveness to unfriendly comment from any source, he concealed his wounds jealously and met opposition with a smile. He would have agreed with Sibelius' remark that no one has ever put up a statue to a critic. He knew that, while today's journalist is quickly forgotten, the artist survives in his work. Most people would prefer to be liked, and in Massenet this characteristic grew into something of an obsession. He went out of his way to be nice to everyone, and if he was rebuffed he only shrugged his shoulders and tried all the harder to charm. From the time of his clash with Albert Wolff it was almost impossible to penetrate the genial discretion into which Massenet retreated, or to draw from him anything but the most effusive flattery of a colleague or an acquaintance.

The birth of a daughter in 1868 brought a new responsibility which emphasized the need for Massenet to establish himself in his profession. While his flat in the rue Taitbout was filled with the cries of the new-born Juliette, he struggled, unsuccessfully, to set Byron's *Manfred.* Then Ambroise Thomas, playing again his part in Massenet's life as a bearded Good Fairy, introduced him to the librettist Michel Carré. There were few composers of the time to whom Carré had not, on his own or in collaboration, furnished libretti. Thomas had had his assistance on *Mignon* and *Hamlet*, and Carré was librettist almost by appointment to Gounod, as well as supplier of quantities of word-fodder to Bizet, Saint-Saëns and practically everyone else who set pen to music paper. Throughout the winter of 1869 Massenet was occupied with him on a three-act opera to be called *Méduse.*

The war of 1870 caused *Méduse* to be still-born. Reluctant to accept the civilizing benefits of occupation by the Germans, France became involved in an ill-fated struggle. Massenet joined up and was posted to an infantry regiment where one of his comrades at arms was the dramatist Victorien Sardou. It is no surprise to learn that Sardou, the instigator of many a stirring melodrama and the barnstorming genius who created what Bernard Shaw nicely described as Sardoodledom, often made the barrack-room walls ring with his ardent declarations of patriotism. Massenet was less demonstrative, and in between guard duties he tried to carry on with *Méduse.* Somehow the repellent features of that unattractive Gorgon persisted in taking on the appearance of Bismarck, and, instead of composing grave measures in keeping with the ancient legend, Massenet could not prevent his unruly pen from scribbling in reminiscences of the *Marseillaise* and scraps of patriotic songs. His thoughts veered anxiously between the Prussian shells that boomed around the ramparts of Paris and the fate of his wife and daughter whom he had evacuated to the safety of the South. The heap of manuscript represented by *Méduse* was left in the end to moulder forgotten.

IV

DON CÉSAR – THE FURIES – MARY MAGDALEN – ÈVE

In the eighteen-seventies a broad and handsome avenue planted with trees used to lead from the railway station into the little Fontainebleau village of Avon. After the war and the blood-boltered days of the Commune which followed, Massenet came back to the spot where he had been married and bought a house there. It is a small, one-storied villa painted white. The forest lies not more than a hundred yards away, with shaded paths and unexpected clearings. On the other side there is a spacious view ending on the horizon at wooded hills that rise gently up from the valley of the Seine. During the next eleven years Massenet composed many of his major works to the rustle of foliage stirred by the breeze and the susurrus of dead leaves underfoot. In these peaceful surroundings he found that music came more readily than among the harassments of Paris. Today a petrol-scented main road bustles noisily in front of the Villa du Plateau de la Gare, and the avenue de Fontainebleau has been re-christened, with scant melody, the avenue Roosevelt.

By the time Massenet settled at Fontainebleau, the gaslit rococo of the Second Empire had crumbled in the humiliation of Sedan. The unofficial laureate of the period, Jacques Offenbach, lived on for another decade, though he had reached his peak a few years before with *la Grande Duchesse de Gérolstein,* an operetta which might serve as a monument to the brassy frivolity that characterized one aspect of Louis-Napoléon's rule. Berlioz had died the year before the war, a disappointed man longing for the end. Gounod was already established as the composer of *Faust* and *Roméo et Juliette,* achievements which he was never to surpass, despite a steady flow of tastefully perfumed oratorios and settings of *There is a green hill far away* and *For ever with the Lord.* The war had thrown his private life into disastrous confusion, and no man who had to grapple, as he did, with the crazed and untameable Mrs Georgina Weldon, could be rightly expected to have much opportunity for serious composition.

Among the younger men Saint-Saëns was emerging as a leader, and his Société Nationale de Musique provided a rallying point for his comrades. Items performed at concerts given by the Société Nationale included several small works by Édouard Lalo, still a little-known viola player in the Armingaud Quartet. César Franck had not yet thrown off the obscurity of the organ loft. Chabrier's exuberance was largely confined to the dusty offices of the Civil Service. Somewhere in the distance it was possible to catch the muffled thunder of Wagnerian storm clouds, but the full force of the deluge had several years to wait. Only a few advanced spirits had succumbed to the allurements of Wagner, and among them were the Conservatoire students who so distressed their teacher, the inoffensive Delibes, with their dangerous enthusiasm. In the meantime Bizet was hard at work on an *opéra-comique* taken from the eighteenth-century novel *Clarissa Harlowe*. One regrets that it was never completed, for the collision between Bizet's vivacity and the slippered unctuousness of Samuel Richardson must surely have produced something unique in French music.

Most of the younger generation were to be met on social evenings at Saint-Saëns' house, where Massenet was a frequent guest. There he cultivated a friendship with the twenty-year-old Vincent d'Indy, an ardent and high-principled musician who retained his youthful flow of moral indignation well into old age. At first he discerned in Massenet a 'sacred fire' and complained warmly at the blindness of impresarios who ignored his new friend's great talent. Massenet, in turn, admired d'Indy's early symphony, though the hearty ruggedness of the composer's style was a sharp contrast with his own softer manner. D'Indy commiserated with him over his recent unfortunate encounter with the uncouth Pasdeloup. Massenet had taken the score of his oratorio, *Marie-Magdeleine,* to the conductor, in the hope of persuading him to perform it. The day was grey and rainy, and the fire in Pasdeloup's drawing room began to smoke. Soon the air was filled with stifling fumes, and Massenet played on at the piano while Pasdeloup crashed about opening and shutting windows. After Massenet had played for two hours, Pasdeloup asked eagerly: 'Is that all?' He was assured that it was. On the doorstep Massenet turned and ventured to ask if he would play it at one of his concerts.

'Play it? Not on your life!' Pasdeloup spluttered asthmatically through his great beard. 'Why, there's one point where you have the singers refer to Christ with the words: "I hear His steps" . . . the steps of Christ!' And Massenet, with tears of disappointment in his eyes, was sent packing to a disgusted accompaniment of: 'I hear His steps! I hear His steps!'

Massenet's wretchedness at this rough treatment was dissipated soon afterwards by a commission to write a four-act work for the Opéra-Comique. True, he had only been asked because the original composer dropped out at the last minute, but the opportunity remained an excellent one. The libretto was *Don César de Bazan* and had been taken from a popular play which continued the adventures of the dashing Don César who figures so colourfully in Victor Hugo's drama *Ruy Blas.*[1] Like the score of *la Grand'tante,* the original music of *Don César de Bazan* was destroyed. It vanished in a fire and Massenet re-orchestrated it over twenty years later with the benefit of experience long gained, so it cannot be taken on trust as representing a wholly genuine work of his youth. The dance numbers, for example, include a piece of music, the *Air de ballet,* a favourite in the days of tea-shop trios, which turned up several years afterwards in the popular *Scènes pittoresques.* Whether it was written at the time, or whether Massenet decided to put it in as an afterthought while rewriting, we do not know. On the other hand, the *Entr'acte Sevillana,* which quickly became a permanent feature in the repertory of casino orchestras and brass bands, is an obvious fore-runner of the *Castillane* from the ballet in *le Cid,* though endowed with less harmonic subtlety.

The score was written in six weeks. Evidence of the haste at which Massenet had to work is shown in the clumsy *mélodrame* of Act IV. Here, against a musical background, the hero recounts certain incidents which are necessary to the development of the plot, but which, obviously, there was not enough time either to dramatize or to set to music. Yet throughout the score there are indications of the later Massenet. The Spanish local colour is neatly touched in—just enough to add a palatable spice—and rhythms are handled with a full measure of theatrical effect. It is, however, the stageworthy quality of *Don César de Bazan* that strikes one most. Massenet here shows evidence of a remarkable gift for the theatre, despite the intrinsic nature of music which today sounds conventional and often faded. The purpose of the stage being to create emotion by means of illusion, Massenet knew instinctively how to achieve it. His natural talent, formed and instructed by years of humble work in the orchestra pit, now began to flower rewardingly.

Though generally well received, except by certain nervous critics

[1] A musician early in the field was the prolific Irishman Vincent Wallace, composer of *Maritana.* His *Don César de Bazan,* based on the same play, was given at Drury Lane in 1845.

who detected a Wagnerian flavour in its harmless double fortes, *Don César de Bazan* ran for only thirteen nights. The fate of his second opera may have inspired Massenet with his dread of the figure thirteen. From then on, the page of his manuscripts between twelve and fourteen was numbered 12 *bis*. He never worked on the thirteenth of the month; neither did he dare start a journey then. It goes without saying that in future no new work of his was allowed to have its first night on that fatal day of the month. The run of *Don César de Bazan* had proved a disappointment, but it marked the beginning of Massenet's stage career. He had shown not only that he could sustain the flow of invention needed for a full-length opera, but also that he had the invaluable sense of theatre without which no writer for the stage can hope to succeed.

When Georges Hartmann was asked to suggest someone to write incidental music for Leconte de Lisle's *les Érinnyes,* he instantly thought of his protégé, the composer of *Don César de Bazan.* Leconte de Lisle was the most prominent figure in the group of poets known as *le Parnasse.* His preoccupation with the doctrine of art for art's sake, his absorption in Greek art and literature, led him to write poems which, at their best, are exquisitely formal in their static beauty. He had, characteristically, found the inspiration for his play in Aeschylus, and he retold the tragedy of Orestes in cold, marmoreal verse. Massenet was allowed the unusual luxury of a forty-piece orchestra. He decided to score his music for thirty-six strings, a tympanist, and three trombones representing the Furies of the title.

The Olympian poet had little interest in the music that was to accompany his play. When he had finally been convinced that music would not actually harm it, his only concern, as a self-respecting literary man, was that the sounds should not drown any of his lovingly quarried words. The rehearsals were not, therefore, occasions of sweetness and light. Despite the author's misgivings, the music was not to blame for the short run of his tenebrous drama. It opens with a grave and Gluckian prelude in slow march rhythm. The choral passages underline the stage action with sombre firmness, and there is a melancholy about the depiction of Clytemnestra and Orestes which, though far removed from the stark passion of Greek drama, is not unattractive. Amateur pianists in the audience could have been forgiven their surprise at the point when Electra offered a libation at the tomb of Agamemnon, for on to the air drifted the familiar melody of the *Élégie* from the *Dix pièces de genre* (Massenet was an economical writer). The weakest part of the score lies in the three Greek dances which provide the ballet.

Their relation to ancient Greece is as authentic as the 'production numbers' which delight patrons of the Folies-Bergère.

Two operas and a suite of incidental music which was to figure often at concerts had now won for Massenet a degree of fame. Hartmann was anxious to build on this foundation and looked around for other means to advance the young man. The oratorio *Marie-Magdeleine* still slumbered unheard after Pasdeloup's brutal rejection. The disheartened composer had put away his manuscript and was only reminded of it some time later at Pauline Viardot's house. The singer's public career was then nearly over, but her interest in new music remained as lively as ever. After dinner Massenet was asked to sing something. Taken by surprise, he sat at the piano and played extracts from his oratorio. Pauline Viardot leaned over the keyboard and said excitedly: 'What's that?'

'Oh, something I wrote when I was young, *Marie-Magdeleine,* which hasn't a hope of being performed', Massenet said with a shrug.

'What?' said Madame Viardot. 'It *will* be performed and *I* shall be your Marie-Magdeleine!'

Madame Viardot's sponsorship was welcomed delightedly by Hartmann. His friend, the conductor Édouard Colonne with whom he worked on so many projects, was approached and agreed to perform the oratorio. In her eagerness to hear the complete work, Madame Viardot always arrived early for rehearsals and supervised the proceedings. On Good Friday 1873, *Marie-Magdeleine* was given at the Odéon before a large and fashionable audience. It was highly successful. The work had a theme—the courtesan who mends her ways—which never failed to thrill a public that adored the hothouse romanticism of *la Dame aux camélias.* Presumably the audience was able to enjoy the titillation of vice with a clear conscience in the awareness that redemption was just around the corner. Then there was the music. Much of it dated from Massenet's time in Rome and had been heavily influenced by Gounod. Yet although sweet Gounodian reminiscences abounded, they were inflected with a quality that was Massenet's own. This was a languorous, short-breathed type of phrase which exuded feminine charm and gently cajoled the hearer. At one stroke Massenet had found both a distinctive style and a public which was ready for it. The young composer was hailed for having transformed the boring medium of oratorio into something fresh and appealingly graceful. *Marie-Magdeleine* brought him a first taste of the enormous popularity that was soon to be his.

'Our school has never produced anything to compare with it,'

Bizet declared. 'You'll drive me mad, you dog! . . . By Jove! you're becoming oddly disturbing . . . upon which, believe me, *cher*, no one is more sincere in his admiration and affection than your Bizet.' Even the watchful Saint-Saëns was impressed, and, while pointing out the debt to Gounod, he praised the deftness with which Massenet handled his material. Vincent d'Indy greatly admired some of the choral writing and asked Massenet: 'How did you manage to hit on such music? Sometimes it seems quite heavenly.' To which Massenet, rendered somewhat light-headed by his triumph, joked in reply: 'Oh, I don't believe in all that creeping Jesus stuff . . . But the public likes it—and we must always agree with the public.' It was a remark which left the earnest d'Indy speechless. Thenceforth he considered his frivolous colleague fit only for the outer darkness, to which he despatched him with a suitable meed of weeping and gnashing of teeth.

The first performance of *Marie-Magdeleine* found Massenet in a state quite different from the facetiousness that prompted his remark to d'Indy. The presentation of a new work always reduced him to a mood of collapse, and while Pauline Viardot enraptured the audience with her singing of the title role, the unhappy composer wandered distractedly through the corridors of the Odéon. He left before the evening was ended and joined his wife in packing for the trip to Italy which they had planned to start on the following day. When they arrived at Naples they had still not heard of the sensational triumph of *Marie-Magdeleine*. An enthusiastic letter from Ambroise Thomas broke the news.

'You were able to move people's emotions because you yourself were moved', wrote Thomas. 'I was captivated like everyone else, even more so . . Rest assured. Your work will be played again and will have a permanent place . . . '

Heartened by the congratulations of his old teacher and friend, Massenet was about to take the boat for Capri when a large packet of letters and press reviews was handed to him. Friends had written accounts of the oratorio's warm reception, and the critics' notices were all highly favourable. The one that gave Massenet most pleasure was by Ernest Reyer, the formidable critic of the *Journal des Débats*. Reyer had succeeded his friend Berlioz in the post and was himself a composer of some talent. His own operas represent a novel fusion of Wagnerian techniques with those of Berlioz, and although they never remained long on the stage he was too robust a character to be easily depressed. His journalism, combined with a sinecure as curator of the library at the Opéra, where he lost his way when he tried to visit the scene of his notional duties, kept him in reasonable comfort. He looked and spoke like an old soldier, and his sarcasms were enough to quell even the most independent-minded conductor who shouldered the task of performing one of his operas. Massenet, though, seems to have found a chink in Reyer's abrasive exterior, for the critic wrote admiringly that *Marie-Magdeleine* contained passages of such tenderness, delicacy and purity as could not be surpassed by any other music. It was, assuredly, one of the best notices Massenet ever received, and he preserved it for many years to come.

Massenet continued with his sentimental journey. He had first seen Italy as a young man and unknown student. Now he was revisiting all the familiar places, Naples, Capri and Sorrento, as a composer who enjoyed Parisian acclaim. Scarcely had he and his wife arrived in Rome than they were invited to the Villa Medici. There, in the director's study hung with rich tapestries, he looked out once again on the stately lawns and brooding oaks that had formed the background of his early days. Then he dined with the students beneath a series of portraits of Prix de Rome winners which, he noted with a pleasurable shock, included his own. The amiable Victor Schnetz, who was director of the place in Massenet's time, had been succeeded by the mild figure of Ernest Hébert. Although a painter, Hébert was more of a musician than Schnetz and went so far as to play in a string quartet. One of his predecessors at the Villa Medici had been Ingres, whose passion for music had given rise to the expression *le violon d'Ingres* as a synonym for a hobby. Like everyone else, Massenet was curious to know just how well Ingres played his famous violin. The only evidence he was able to find was provided by the amusing comment Delacroix made when asked the question. 'He played it,' said Delacroix, 'like Raphael.'

In company with his wife Massenet re-lived the time of their courtship at Rome. They took a carriage to Ostia and picnicked at Castel Turano, the place that had witnessed their joyous excursions eight years ago. When they returned to Paris in a cloud of memories, they found awaiting them the new and spacious flat which was to be their Paris home for the next three decades. It was on the fourth floor of No. 46 rue du Général-Foy. On the walls Massenet hung pictures of his two favourite authors, Jean-Jacques Rousseau and Beaumarchais. They were significant preferences. Jean-Jacques corresponded to Massenet's ready emotionalism and to the transports of feeling which rural prospects or a sentimental tale could so easily arouse in him. On the other hand, the author of *le Barbier de Séville* appealed to his taste for elegant wit, for cunningly dovetailed intrigues in eighteenth-century drawing-rooms, and for clever stage technique. It was only natural that beside them should also hang pictures of his favourite composers, Mozart and Gluck. The rooms were furnished with large, plush arm-chairs, fringed and bobbled door curtains, and massive low-hanging lamps. Vacant surfaces were filled with the bibelots and porcelain Massenet loved to collect around him, including the Tanagra statuette which had been the focal point of his meditations while composing *les Érinnyes*. Soon he was to add a desk reputed to have once belonged to Diderot. It was all very snug and cosy and cheerful.

In the autumn of that year Massenet scored another success with his orchestral suite, the *Scènes pittoresques*. Its four items include the *Air de ballet* which appears so mysteriously in *Don César de Bazan*, a little march, a Courbet-inspired *Angélus*, and a riotous *Fête bohème*. He was encouraged to follow these up with the *Scènes dramatiques* which look to Shakespeare, by way of Gounod's *Roméo et Juliette*, for their provenance. Desdemona, like Juliette, is given a dulcet *Sommeil*, while Ariel triumphantly crests an allegro scherzando, and Macbeth grapples with banquets and witches, only to resolve into a Gounodian close. German scholars, of course, have a word for this sort of thing. According to them, works like *The Maiden's Prayer*, or *In a Monastery Garden* by Alfred Ketèlbey (once described by a lyrical advertisement manager as 'Britain's Greatest Living Composer') may be classified as *kitsch*, that is to say light productions of a decidedly trivial nature. One may argue, though, that Massenet's suites escape this category by virtue of their handling. His orchestration has neatness and superior craftsmanship. He himself had no illusions about the product he was offering, and he labelled it accordingly with 'pretty' words such as *pittoresque*. Like Elgar, he had a genius for the polished salon trifle.

On a rather different plane was the overture to *Phèdre*, which Massenet wrote in the autumn of 1873. It sprang from a commission by Pasdeloup, who, rather late in the day, had decided to encourage French music by asking Massenet, Bizet and Ernest Guiraud each to write an overture for him to play at his concerts. Bizet's contribution was *Patrie*, a clamorous and bombastic piece in which his gifts for once deserted him. A pathetic irony ruled that this unimportant work should be the only occasion when Bizet could claim a wholehearted triumph in his lifetime. It was dedicated to Massenet, who told him exultantly of the 'salvoes of applause' that greeted *Patrie* at its first performance. Their other colleague, Ernest Guiraud, never managed to produce his overture. He had written an opera at the age of fifteen, and it may be that this precocious achievement left him with only enough energy to compose agreeable little ballets like *Gretna Green* and harmless comic operas such as *Piccolino*. He lingers on in reference books because he orchestrated Offenbach's *Contes d'Hoffmann* and added the recitatives to *Carmen*. (His academic career, in the course of which, somewhat to his surprise, Debussy and Erik Satie figured as his pupils, was a long and respectable one.) Massenet's overture was as popular as Bizet's when introduced by Pasdeloup in 1874. Its impassioned allegro recalls a similar theme in Liszt's *Tasso* of some twenty years before, though whether Massenet already knew that symphonic poem is dubious. This feverish attempt to compress 'C'est Vénus tout entière à sa proie attachée' into musical terms is followed by a ripe melody of great appeal but with small reference to the acrid longings of Racine's heroine. Even so, it is not uncreditable, and Debussy, who preferred it to Massenet's other music, described it as '. . . the work of a true musician'.

Next year Massenet followed up *Marie-Magdeleine* with the oratorio *Ève*. Anxious to strike while the iron was hot, the diligent Hartmann had interested the conductor Charles Lamoureux in playing *Ève* at his newly founded Concerts de l'Harmonie Sacrée, which, for lack of better accommodation, were held in the profane surroundings of the Cirque des Champs-Élysées. Lamoureux had married the heiress daughter of a toothpaste tycoon and was able to subsidize his efforts to give French audiences the music he felt they ought to hear. Wagner and Chabrier were among the causes he championed, and at his concerts of religious music he had already, with much success, introduced unfamiliar Handel oratorios. There was little love lost between him and his ageing rival Pasdeloup, and he hoped to go one better than the founder of the Concerts populaires by sponsoring a full-length work from Massenet.

Ève exploits the vein Massenet had discovered with his previous oratorio. It luxuriates in what d'Indy appropriately termed a 'discreet and semi-religious eroticism', although the amorous exchanges between Adam and Eve might be thought more congruous than those between Jesus and Mary Magdalen. *Ève* set a style which was to influence French composers for a long time ahead, and Mr Martin Cooper, with his usual perceptiveness, points out a connecting link with Debussy in its occasional hints of the whole tone scale and its triplet thirds foreshadowing *Pelléas et Mélisande*. *Ève* confirmed Massenet's popularity with oratorio audiences. It also impressed his colleagues, and Gounod issued one of those ex-cathedra pronouncements of which he was so fond: 'The triumph of one of the elect should be a time for rejoicing by the Church,' he announced.

> You are one of the elect, dear friend; Heaven has marked you with the sign of her children: I can feel it in all that your beautiful work has stirred in my heart. Prepare yourself for the role of martyr: such is the lot of all that comes from on high and troubles that which is base. Remember that when God said: 'This one is the vessel of my choice,' he added: 'and I shall show him how much he must suffer in my name . . .'

On the night of the first performance Massenet sat alone and anxious in a café across the street from the Cirque des Champs-Élysées. During the intervals a friend rushed over to report the progress of *Ève*. At the end Massenet was dragged unwillingly on to the platform to acknowledge the loud cheers of the audience. In the midst of the applause came an eerie fulfilment of Gounod's muddled prediction about suffering. A servant arrived to tell Massenet that his mother was very ill. On arriving at her house Massenet was greeted by his sister with the news that she was already dead. His devotion to her had been one of the mainsprings of his life. That she had died at the very moment of his latest triumph made the bereavement doubly poignant. At about the same time occurred the death of his wife's mother, and the summer at Fontainebleau that year was a time of mourning. As if to emphasize the Chekovian mixture of joy and sorrow that comprised this period of his life, Massenet heard that *Ève* had gained him his first official recognition in the shape of the Légion d'honneur. At any other time the red ribbon would have given him unreserved delight, for he prized the outward signs of achievement. He accepted it now with listlessness.

Very soon another event arrived to cast its pall of gloom. In March he had gone to the first night of *Carmen* and had admired this perfect revelation of his friend Bizet's genius. 'It's a great success . . .' he had written at two in the morning after coming home from the theatre, '. . . bravo with all my heart.' A bare three months later Bizet died in his thirty-seventh year. Massenet went to his funeral in tears. At Fontainebleau the June weather was unusually oppressive and hot. He started writing a *Lamento* in memory of Bizet. His hand stuck sweatily to the paper as he struggled with lassitude brought on by the sultry heat. A summer storm broke out, and while blinding sheets of rain dashed against the window Massenet fell asleep over his score, worn out by emotion and fatigue.

V

THE KING OF LAHORE – PROFESSOR AT THE CONSERVATOIRE – THE TASTE OF GLORY

IN the early eighteen-sixties Parisians watched with curiosity as an area just off the boulevard des Capucines was fenced round and large holes were dug. On the land now enclosed by streets miscellaneously named after Scribe, Gluck, Halévy, Meyerbeer and Auber, a vast building rose majestically over the next few years out of a cocoon of scaffolding. The new opera house was to be the permanent home of an institution which, in the two centuries of its existence, had occupied at one time or another twelve different theatres. The architect was Charles Garnier, a ubiquitous figure in felt hat and sombre clothes who continually promenaded the site bearing a long stick with which he drew sketches on the ground or tested a joint.

Before construction work began it was necessary to drain off a lake beneath the soil, since Garnier planned underground scene docks at least twenty-four yards deep to accommodate back-drops. Night and day for a period of eight months, steam engines pumped out huge quantities of water, and, by the time they finished, had dried up all the wells for a quarter of a mile around. In 1862, when a formidable basement lined with cement, concrete and bitumen had once and for all kept the water at bay, the foundation stone was laid. By the following year the first floor was already built, and so quickly did the work proceed under the direction of Garnier that, in 1870, all the main sections were completed. The Franco-Prussian War interrupted this last and perhaps most unnerving example of Louis-Napoléon's *folie du bâtiment,* and throughout the duration of the struggle the biggest theatre in Europe was used as a store for tons of rations by the hundred thousand, while from its roof busy semaphores winked out government messages. After the war the Communard insurgents took over, and the roof became a launching pad for the balloons they despatched carrying proclamations to other French towns as yet unenlightened about the benefits of the Paris Commune. Then a less strenuous form of government established itself and Garnier once more was to be seen scurrying everywhere with his long stick and tape measure.

Soon afterwards the destruction by fire of the Salle Ventadour, where the opera was currently housed, made it imperative for the new building to be prepared as quickly as possible. Garnier bestirred himself to such effect that the Opéra was ready for occupation by the end of 1874. His achievement, known ever since as the 'palais Garnier', was an endearing riot of Victorian exuberance and a perfect compendium of the artistic ideals of the time. The topmost cupola, glinting with gold, is crowned by Millet's statue of Apollo, who, besides holding his lyre on high, also carries a lightning conductor which in stormy weather channels the electricity down his marble flanks. If Garnier had been undaunted by the technical problems of the earlier stages, he was to meet even tougher dilemmas when choosing the nine composers to be immortalized in medallions on the façade. No one could agree on who should appear. At last Garnier went ahead with Mozart, Beethoven, Spontini, Auber, Rossini, Meyerbeer and Halévy, defiantly arranging them in chronological order of birth to avoid charges of favouritism. For good measure, the two most famous librettists, Quinault and Scribe, were each placed at one end. Four medallions on the lower portion presented to the world the astonished gaze of Bach, Haydn, Pergolesi and Cimarosa.

Carpeaux's famous group, *la Danse*, which once disported itself at the top of the steps, caused much argument and even fist-fights when it was unveiled. One morning a furious art lover threw a bottle of ink at it, and though the stain quickly faded from the voluminous stony thigh of his female target, controversy went on. Countless tons of statuary and ornament embellish the Opéra both inside and out, and the unwary visitor is constantly delighted at the imagination of sculptors who have depicted corybantic figures handling bizarre musical instruments which are known neither to God nor to Saint Cecilia. More realistically, there is, in the grand foyer, a panel representing national instruments, though English pride will be hurt to see that Great Britain has to depend on the Scottish bagpipe and the harp of Erin for her presence there. Elsewhere, a group of eight Muses looks glassily down—eight only, because there was no room for *la Philosophie*, who doubtless took her dismissal philosophically, since she already has a statue nearby. As if this were not enough, twenty gilded statues are there to remind us of the qualities needed by an artist and to point out that *l'Imagination* still has need of *la Tradition,* and that *la Prudence* is no less necessary than *la Modestie.* Acres of mirror, platoons of chandelier and a colourful mileage of panelled allegory make the Opéra one of the richest confections of nineteenth-century art. Enclosed within its sturdy structure of Aberdeen granite, Spanish brocatello, Finnish porphyry, Italian marble and Mont-Blanc jasper, it stands four-square with a confidence modern architects would be fearful of emulating. It has, magnificently, the courage of its convictions.

From its ceremonial opening in 1875 onwards, the Opéra was as much a social as a musical centre. A perfect setting for State occasions, when the massy lustres twinkled down on casqued ranks of the Garde républicaine lining the grand stairway, it also played an important part in the life of the prosperous middle classes. Comfortable families who otherwise had little interest in music were regular attenders at the Opéra, and it was distinctly fashionable to be an *abonné*, or subscriber. Until 1914 every employee behind the scenes, including the electricians and the foreman of the stage crew, wore evening dress and a top hat. A chorus master who dared to appear in a day suit would be instantly sent off to put on the proper clothes. The orchestra included many fathers who on retirement handed over to their sons. They spoke respectfully of the place as 'la grande maison', and proudly of themselves as 'nous autres, de l'Opéra . . .'

Together with patrons of the smaller Opéra-Comique, the audiences at the Opéra formed a sizable and well-defined public for musical spectacle. They included newly married couples with social ambitions, fathers of families who used their subscriber's ticket as a means of celebrating births and engagements, bankers who looked in with their mistresses, and elderly senators who came to ogle the *corps de ballet,* many of whose members owed their luxurious apartments and expensive jewellery to the solicitude of their ancient admirers. But in spite of Degas' pictures of top-hatted satyrs thoughtfully eyeing pretty ballerinas in a spray of *tutus*, the Opéra was essentially a bourgeois institution. Great was the reward for any composer who knew how to cater for a house which seated well over two thousand spectators at each performance. If he could please everyone, from the occupants of the expensive *parterre* to those perched on high in the modest *loges* beside the giant chandelier which dominated the auditorium, then his fortune was made. The existence of this public explains why opera in the nineteenth century was about the surest way for an ambitious composer to achieve riches. It paid dividends which in our day might be compared to the return which film rights can yield for a lucky novelist.

If this situation had not existed, then Massenet's career would have been very different. He lived, however, at a time when there was an opera public to be wooed, and when audiences were to be won over. His earliest attempt had been a Meyerbeerian opera entitled *les Templiers,* which he started when he moved into his flat in the rue du Général-Foy. After completing some two hundred pages he showed the result to Hartmann. His publisher shrewdly advised him to try a different theme and told him to see Louis Gallet, the librettist with whom he worked on *Marie-Magdeleine* and *Ève.* Massenet came away from the hôpital Beaujon, where Gallet worked as almoner in between bouts of feverish industry as a versifier, with the plan of *le Roi de Lahore.* The action takes place in ancient India and features kings, queens, wars of religion, fanatical priests, revolutions, and a love affair between a royal minister and a priestess of the temple. Here were all the ingredients necessary to the sort of grandiose entertainment in which the Opéra specialized. There was even a third act set in the Hindu paradise giving excellent opportunities for the ballet which no Opéra production could do without. The formula was impeccable.

In February 1877, Massenet put the finishing touches to his five-act opera. The dates he inscribed on the last page, ranging from 1872 to 1877, show that, economical as always, he had not wasted the music already composed for *les Templiers.* His eleven hundred pages of score are written for the usual size of orchestra, to which he adds a saxophone and, in the *divertissement,* four saxhorns. Apart from these, he relied for the exotic effects he wanted on pseudo-oriental harmonies and discreet use of the triangle. *Le Roi de Lahore* is neither very original nor substantial. Massenet's obvious model was Bizet's *Pêcheurs de perles* of a decade or so earlier, and although it had not retained the public's favour, Massenet was too expert a musician not to appreciate the technical lessons to be learned from his friend's work. Bizet's influence is flagrant, for example, in 'C'est un Dieu qui l'inspire!' of the fourth act, where the noble duet 'Au fond du temple saint' from *les Pêcheurs de perles* is imitated even down to the shimmering harp accompaniment.

Halanzier, then director of the Opéra, had no misgivings when Massenet played the work to him in his flat overlooking the place Vendôme. *Le Roi de Lahore* went immediately into rehearsal. Conscious that he had a ready-made success to hand, Halanzier spared no expense on the production and laid out two hundred thousand francs for costumes alone. As it was Massenet's first venture at the Opéra, Halanzier took charge of all rehearsals while the composer sat beside him, listening, learning, and noting changes on the score in blue and red pencil. On the morning of the first performance a note from Gustave Flaubert was delivered at Massenet's home. 'I pity you this morning. I shall envy you tonight!' the novelist had written.

This 27th April was the vital point of Massenet's career. That evening *le Roi de Lahore* was played to a full house at the Opéra, with the President of the Republic in one box and the Emperor of Brazil in another. On the steps outside ticket touts were selling *strapontins* for a louis apiece. Joséphine de Reszke, sister of Jean and Édouard, sang the part of the heroine and was rapturously applauded. The audience marvelled at the sumptuous procession of houris and dancing girls, and was dazzled by the kaleidoscopic lighting effects. As the hero, Jean Lassalle made his reputation and subsequently became leading baritone at the Opéra. Massenet himself realized as if in a dream that his ambition was fulfilled. The patriarchal Gounod arrived from on high to clasp him in a wet embrace and to rave: 'Dans mes bras, mon fils. Embrasse papa!' Charles Garnier, the architect of the scene of his triumph, wrote to congratulate Massenet on his 'admirable' work; and next morning he awoke to read ecstatic press notices which compared him with the composers of *Fidelio*, of *Freyschütz*, of *Tannhaüser* and of *Guillaume Tell*.

In the year of its creation *le Roi de Lahore* had thirty performances. At none of them did receipts drop below the figure of eighteen thousand francs which only the most successful operas of the time were able to draw. By 1879 it had reached its fiftieth performance and was being played everywhere in Europe. In Italy, above all, it was especially popular. This was to some extent due to the enthusiasm of Tito Ricordi, who was just then consolidating the fortunes of the publishing concern which his father had started. With Ricordi Massenet travelled around the principal Italian opera houses directing rehearsals of his work and settling publication rights. This connection with Italy, the land he loved best next to France, was delightful to him, and his affection for Ricordi lasted until his death. To tell the truth, Massenet confessed, he was not over-fond of travelling and the discomforts it involved. As he pointed out to the students who later gathered round him, no conscientious composer should fail to have a hand in productions of his operas. A perfectionist in every detail, however small,

Massenet attended wherever a foreign performance of his work was to be given for the first time. To the conductor, the orchestral players, the producer, the singers and the costumiers he gave explicit instructions. With *le Roi de Lahore,* as with all his other operas, he took great pains to make sure that everyone, from *prima donna* to stagehand, knew the exact reason for the directions they were given. There were special consolations for the exile in Italy, where he could talk with aged singers who remembered the first night of *il Barbiere di Siviglia* and the young Rossini, and where, after a sentimental pilgrimage to the Villa Medici, he spent a month near Lake Como with his wife and his daughter Juliette. It can only have been the stern call of duty which brought him to London to conduct concert selections from *le Roi de Lahore* on the windy heights of Crystal Palace.[1]

Whether he was travelling or staying at home, Massenet sedulously followed the daily routine which he had evolved before reaching his thirties and to which he adhered for the rest of his life. It was a routine planned so that every hour of the day could be thriftily used to ensure the maximum amount of work and the closest attention to the project in hand. In winter and summer alike he rose every morning at four o'clock. Those early hours, when the rest of the world slept and only an occasional bird-song disturbed the silence, were, he found, his best time for composition. He was solitary but not alone, since the companions of his imagination were Salome, Manon, Thaïs, Sapho, Charlotte, Cinderella, and all his other heroines whose music flowed more freely in the still air of dawn than at any other time. He wrote very quickly, so quickly, indeed, that he could never remember for long what he had written several days previously, and when he accompanied his own work he always had to rely on the score. The opera he was currently writing occupied his mind to the exclusion of everything else. His first step was to memorize the libretto. Then he would let it rest in the deeps of his imagination until it had germinated and taken musical shape. The process might last for a few weeks or several years. When intuition told him that the music was ready to be written, he fell to work at speed. The clarity and neatness of his manuscripts always surprised people who did not know that most of the real work had already been done in his mind.

At this stage he never touched a piano to try out his ideas. He liked,

[1] *Le Roi de Lahore,* the first of his operas to be staged in London, was given in Italian at Covent Garden on 28 June 1879. It was well sung, well received, and later revived.

in fact, to mystify people by claiming that there was no such instrument in the house. (Only close friends knew that the rather oddly shaped bureau that stood in his room had a false top which could be slid down to reveal a keyboard.) When he knew he was ready to start writing, out would come the notebooks on which he had scribbled stray themes and ideas. Smoothly, he would cover page upon page of the hand-made music paper for which he had a regular special order at his stationer's. It was thick, luxurious to the touch, richly watermarked, and was known in the trade as 'papier Massenet'. The dates and times at which he began or interrupted work were scrupulously noted on the manuscript. He also recorded the state of the weather, a factor which had great influence on him. A dull and rainy day lowered his spirits, while sunshine lifted him up. Other details he listed usually included the mood he was in—'toujours triste de tout!' or 'transports de joie!'—dinner dates, family events, and, as time went on, the number of performances reached by other operas of his which were running at the time. The words and music were first written out in pencil and then neatly inked over. The rare mistakes or revisions were either cleanly erased with ink-remover or symmetrically blacked out. There were very detailed and careful instructions for the conductor to follow, and special effects were described at length. Nowhere are his instructions so deeply pondered and so precise as at the point where he wished the curtain to fall on a dramatic climax. In *la Navarraise,* for example, much concentrated thought was necessary before he moved the time of the curtain-fall from the beginning of a given bar to the end of it; and in *Werther* he emphasized that the curtain must descend on the exact note which he specified.

When the manuscript was finished—except, of course, for the page thirteen which Massenet superstitiously replaced with 12 *bis*—it went off to the printer for engraving. By having the score printed before it went into rehearsal he guarded against interference from producers and singers. On its return the manuscript was bound, very beautifully, in half-leather or marbled boards, and joined others of his works that the composer had had dressed just as handsomely for his shelves. This unique collection was destined eventually for the library of the Opéra, where today the ranks of deep red bindings form a solid witness to his industry.

By twelve o'clock Massenet had usually finished with composition for the day, though sometimes, if the need were urgent or he particularly wanted to finish a scene, he would write for twelve or fifteen hours at a stretch. Even illness, which prevented him from going out, was not allowed to stop him composing, and friends reported with awe how he would sit up on his sick-bed, pale and exhausted, turning out pages of orchestration without a halt. After lunch he would give lessons or go to rehearsals. Pupils and singers alike found him a benevolent and sympathetic taskmaster. He hated to upset anyone and wrapped his judgments in the cottonwool of ambiguity. A tenor who once, unknowingly, set Massenet's teeth on edge with his singing in *Manon*, approached him afterwards eager for compliments. He was not disappointed. 'You sang,' he was told with an innocent smile, 'like a composer'. On the other hand, there were times when even Massenet lost patience. An ill-tempered *prima donna* rebuked him for inadvertently trampling on the train of her ermine cloak. 'Madame,' he replied coldly, 'you are trampling on my music.'

Between five and seven in the evening he would hold court in a room which Hartmann furnished for him at his music shop. There he auditioned singers for his operas. Journalists came to interview him, composers arrived to ask his opinion of their work, and the room was soon filled with all sorts of people hungry for favours and influence. They met with unfailing amiability. Massenet's exquisite courtesy was partly the result of a natural wish to be nice to his fellow human beings. It was also due to his own sensitiveness. He suffered agonies himself from criticism and he did not enjoy seeing others going through like tortures. The slightest adverse remark, even from a friend, was enough to plunge him into melancholy. He was not thick-skinned enough to bear with equanimity the barbed attacks of newspaper critics, and an unkind review haunted him for weeks. That was why he always stayed away from his own first nights and fled to the country, where, in quaking dread, he waited for reports from friends rather as a convict awaits his sentence. His pathetic anxiety to like and to be liked won him the reputation of a *bénisseur*. It would be truer to say that his outwardly bland temper was both a kindness to others and an insurance policy to protect his own highly strung nerves.

While in Hartmann's office he took the opportunity of keeping abreast of the mounting wave of correspondence that fame brought him. Here again his compulsive neuroses expressed themselves in quaint little habits. His writing style was of a floridness that defies translation into sober Anglo-Saxon terms. Remote acquaintances were saluted '. . . with deep emotion, but! . . . but you'll be at the Opéra on Sunday evening, won't you? I'd be so happy! To know you were there, to see you!' Librettists were encouraged with flattery of their work: '... I've the greatest desire to have the text—and to live with it—I'm sure you've written a little miracle . . .' Ladies who invited him to their soirées were hailed: 'il me tarde de vous embrasser . . . à vous, de coeur', by 'Votre très fervent et respectueux admirateur.' The singer, Martial Teneo, who sometimes read proofs for him, received '... chères et admiratives félicitations à notre cher Teneo'. Words and whole sentences were heavily underlined, in the manner of Queen Victoria, often as much as four times, and the allowance of exclamation marks was liberal. For all the flamboyance with which he wrote, his correspondents were able to tell how they really stood in relation to him by studying the form his signature took. His abhorrence of the name Jules has already been mentioned, and it became so obsessive that his visiting cards often bore the unusual style 'Monsieur Massenet'.[1] If, therefore, your letter was signed M. (for Monsieur) Massenet, you knew that on this occasion he regarded himself as a public figure and was keeping you at arm's length as one of his distant admirers. When you became a little more intimate he signed himself J. Massenet, though even here there was hesitation, and letters during the intermediate stages bore an initial that hovered uncertainly between M and J. At last, when he signed himself Massenet *tout court*, you learned that you were accepted as a close friend. Variations were still possible, though, and disagreements or long absences were apt to bring back the more formal signatures.

On leaving Hartmann's office it was Massenet's custom to visit the theatre where his current opera was playing and to check the takings. This, for some reason, has always amused the high-minded, who hold the amateur's opinion that artists worthy of the name are unconcerned with money. (Picasso, asked by some well-meaning prig to discuss art, said that he left such matters to the critics but was quite ready to talk royalties and contracts, on which he was an expert.) Having experienced the horror of poverty when young, Massenet had no wish to repeat the experience. He knew that, far from ennobling, it brought about a crippling of the spirit. Like any sensible man who lives by the favour of the public, he was careful with his money. Although, at the height of his fame, he was said to earn the equivalent of something like twenty-five thousand pounds a year in royalties, he realized that at any time,

[1] The treasurer of a committee formed to put up a monument to Sully-Prudhomme was incautious enough to use the forbidden name in his appeal for funds. 'I am sending you twenty francs because you called me Jules,' wrote Massenet. 'But for that you'd have had a hundred.'

overnight, the flood of prosperity might just as easily dwindle into a trickle. He could not repress a certain feeling of guilt over his good fortune. In later years, when he looked in at the offices of the Société des auteurs et compositeurs dramatiques, he was embarrassed at the size of his earnings. While other composers less fortunate were collecting slim little envelopes, the cashier was counting out great bundles of banknotes for Massenet.

'It's too much, it's really too much!' Massenet would cry. 'Don't think it'll always be like this, *mes bons amis*! But I've worked so hard, and then I've been lucky. And I'm old, very old.' His voice would falter. 'You'll collect big money like this . . . even bigger . . . you'll see!' Stuffing the wads of notes into bulging pockets, he would emphasize his elderly stoop, make himself look as decrepit as possible, and would quaver in a Methuselah voice: 'You'll see, my friends . . . When you're old . . . you'll see . . . ' There was, of course, a dash of malice in this well-known performance, and it did nothing to placate those who spoke of his meanness and complained that he rarely invited them to dinner.

When, in 1878, his old friend Ambroise Thomas offered him the professorship of composition at the Conservatoire, he accepted for a number of reasons. It gave him academic standing as well as recognition of his place in the profession. There was the wry satisfaction of filling a post in which his predecessor was the late François Bazin, the man who had refused to accept him as a student in his class. Neither was the salary of two thousand eight hundred francs to be disdained. Even so, Massenet's enjoyment of teaching and the pleasure he took in the company of young people were his chief motives. Twice a week, on Tuesdays and Fridays, he arrived at the Conservatoire to give his lessons. He began on the dot of half-past one, for punctuality was yet another of his manias. The dusty old room where he taught was reached by way of a dark, narrow passage which concealed, inevitably, two treacherous steps. The only furniture was a venerable piano, a chair for the teacher, and two stools reserved for senior students. The others stood and crowded round the piano. The grimy windows, unopened, it was believed, since the time of Cherubini, shook incessantly at the noise of the traffic that passed through the rue du Faubourg Poissonnière outside. The light was so poor that teaching often took place by the dim gleam of guttering candles.

The meanness of the surroundings did not curb the enthusiasm Massenet's students felt for him. With their scores laid out on the ground before him, he would indicate with the ferrule of his umbrella the passages that needed revision. 'The orchestration's too heavy there. Take out the brass,' he would say. And then, pointing again with his umbrella: 'Here it lacks body. Put in a couple of horns.' The atmosphere was pleasant and informal. Massenet's charm put his students at ease, and his obvious wish to help them gained their confidence from the very beginning. Among his more notable pupils was Gustave Charpentier, who said: 'I owe an enormous amount to Massenet because he made me understand music and, above all, love it.' Another was Alfred Bruneau, a humble proof-reader whom Massenet encouraged to persevere with composition. Henri Rabaud, Charles Koechlin, Florent Schmitt and Gabriel Pierné were names that also appeared on his class lists, together with others less famous but equally well grounded in their art by Massenet. Each year it was a member of his class who carried off the Prix de Rome, and he totted up the score with proud satisfaction. He shared whole-heartedly in his pupils' successes, and was as downcast as they were at any setbacks they experienced.

Massenet has often been accused of producing mere imitators of his style. If this is so it must surely be due to a lack of originality in his pupils, for in his teaching method he deliberately went out of his way to avoid forcing his style on them. One of his most exotic disciples was the young Venezuelan Reynaldo Hahn, himself an impeccable craftsman, later to be the most Parisian of figures and the close friend of Proust. To the charge that his teacher taught them to 'faire du Massenet', Hahn replied emphatically:

> Never, never did Massenet impose his own ideas, preferences or style on any of his pupils. On the contrary, he identified himself with each of them, and one of the most remarkable features of his teaching was the faculty of assimilation he showed when correcting their work. Whether it was only a detail to be changed or a sweeping alteration of the general plan, construction, colour or feeling of the work he had under his gaze, whatever he pointed out or advised did not seem to come from *him*. He drew it, so to speak, from the pupil himself, from his own temperament, character and style. Massenet revised the piece of work just as the pupil would have done spontaneously had he had the necessary experience . . .'

Other students have confirmed that Massenet would only speak about his own music with extreme reluctance. He much preferred to go through their work with them, silver pencil in hand, divining what they

Massenet as a boy

Massenet at the
Villa Medici

Massenet aged
twenty

Massenet in his thirties

Massenet working at his desk during the time of *Manon* and *Werther*

Massenet trying out an arpeggio on his dummy keyboard

Massenet (*seated*) rehearsing a scene from *Thérèse*

Right: Sybil Sanderson as Manon

Far right: Lucy Arbell as Persephone

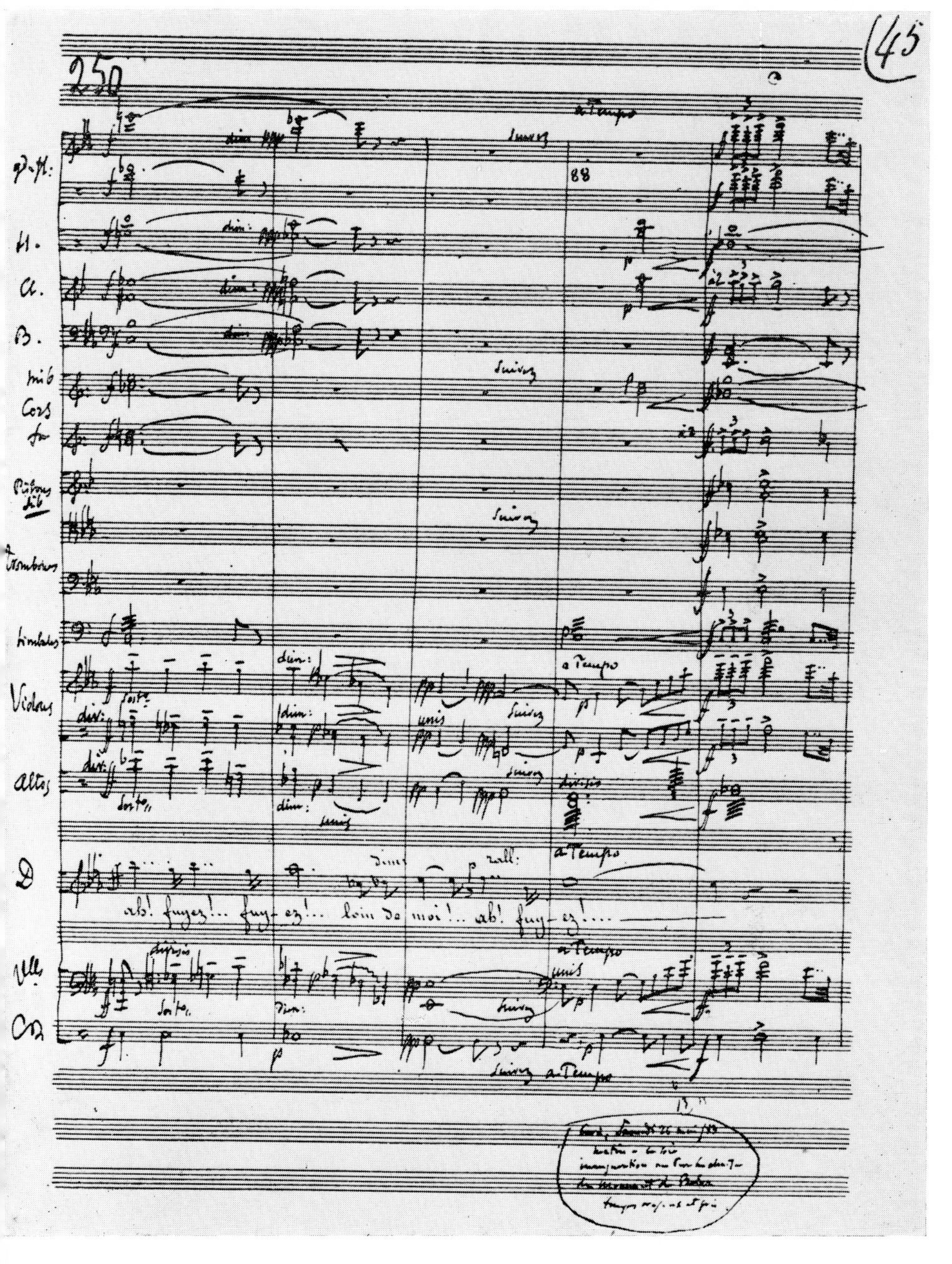

A page from the manuscript full score of *Manon*, Act 3: 'Ah! fuyez!' (Des Grieux). As usual with Massenet, a note at the bottom comments on the events of the day (Friday, 26th May 1883) and the state of the weather

Two posters for Massenet operas—*Esclarmonde* and *Sapho*. The composer always took a direct hand in the publicity for his works

Massenet's country house at Égreville

Massenet talking with a reporter in the garden at Égreville

Massenet in conversation with Prince Albert I of Monaco

One of the last photographs of Massenet, aged seventy, sitting in his flat in the rue de Vaugirard—to the left are some of the ornately bound autograph scores of his operas

were trying to achieve and helping them to do so by leading them on to develop their own resources.

At his classes he did not limit himself to music. He spoke about painting, literature and poetry. His meetings with students were not confined to working hours at the Conservatoire alone. On Sunday afternoons they came to see him at home in the rue du Général-Foy. Alfred Bruneau remembered visits there and how his memories centred upon two items of furniture: the chair in which Massenet worked and the famous 'bureau-piano' noted earlier. 'The chair, which swivelled round and could also be tipped up, was decked out with a colourless and indeterminate piece of American cloth on the seat and back, while the arms, innocent of any covering, were utterly shabby', wrote Bruneau.

> It was the sort of chair that might belong to a punctual and conscientious clerk. Permanently bent forward at his endless, feverish labour of writing, Massenet, of course, did not lie back in it for a moment to reflect, to meditate, or to relax his over-excited nerves. He was riveted to this chair by a ceaseless, demanding and pitiless task. The bureau-piano looks like an ordinary table of polished black wood. Its top is covered with very worn green leather bordered with a slim gold thread. A board can be lowered to reveal a cleverly concealed Pleyel keyboard . . . I used to walk right into his bedroom—he never had a study. He slept little, and, the moment he woke up, before dawn, he got out of bed and went and sat in the chair of which I have spoken. I would find him in front of the bureau-piano I have tried to describe. He did not as yet wear the red robe and purple skullcap which he adopted for comfort in his determined seclusion and which made him look like a youthful cardinal. Over his night dress he put on some loose-fitting garment or other in which he could be comfortable, and hastened to begin his daily task. He was then getting on for forty, although he retained his boyish manner and did not try to over-awe us, either in his own home or in class, with the weight of his authority. I was, however, far from feeling proud as I placed my scattered music sheets on the table top. He read them, approved or criticized them in the same good temper, and, when he was in doubt, sought with a pair of tentative hands to clear up the point on the hidden keyboard . . .

Massenet was soon established as a teacher whose classes were popular and whose students invariably won the highest academic prizes.

Passing one day an organ-grinder who performed at the entrance to the Jardin du Luxembourg, he was flattered to hear some of his own music clanking forth. He took over and himself gave the handle of the instrument a few turns. Ever afterward the organ-grinder displayed a card which read: 'Pupil of Massenet'.

In the year of his appointment to the Conservatoire Massenet also won election to the Institut. He had thus, in the course of a twelvemonth, made his position doubly secure. As a member of the Académie des Beaux Arts he could congratulate himself at having put the seal on his career. Like all postulants to that exalted sphere, he had had to make the formal round of visits to other members in the task of garnering support for his candidature. It was a duty, we may be sure, to which he brought the full force of his charm. The winning candidate has to receive an absolute majority over his rivals. In Massenet's case two ballots were necessary. After the first had been taken and other contestants had dropped out, he found himself opposed to Saint-Saëns and Ernest Boulanger. (The latter, an accomplished musician, was also the father of Lili, a gifted composer who died at the age of twenty-four, and of Nadia, the distinguished teacher.) The second ballot gave Massenet the number of votes he needed and he duly became the youngest member of the Académie.

Saint-Saëns never forgave him. Although he was to join Massenet at the Académie on his second attempt three years later, the memory rankled fiercely and strengthened dislike of his rival.[1] Massenet countered his tart comments with unruffled politeness. He had, though, a fund of malice on which to draw from time to time. Towards the end of the year, in company with Saint-Saëns and Gounod, he was invited to conduct at a festival concert. On the night of the performance, quite unknown to his colleagues, he arranged for massive reinforcements of brass players to augment the orchestra. Confronted with this sly manoeuvre, Saint-Saëns, who was a poor conductor, could only fume helplessly with anger. Gounod, as usual, diplomatically hid whatever reactions he felt in a benign round of embraces, while Massenet, who handled orchestras well, directed a performance of a scene from *le Roi de Lahore* which overwhelmed an audience already stunned by the unexpected blaze of extra brass.

That was not the only time when Massenet unsheathed his claws. A new member of the Institut is expected by tradition to deliver an

[1] A fuller account of this feud is given in the present author's *Saint-Saëns and His Circle*, Chapman & Hall, 1965.

eulogium of his predecessor. The occasion is often a piquant one. Paul Valéry, for example, succeeded Anatole France, a writer whom he loathed, and everyone looked forward with keen enjoyment to seeing how he would resolve the delicate problem. He mentioned France's name but once. Massenet was in a similar situation. The previous occupant of his chair, as at the Conservatoire, had been the unlikeable Bazin. He settled the old score with gentle irony. After mentioning the slender works that Bazin wrote for the stage, he went on: 'A stylish composer, the popularizer of an art which he loved passionately and which brought him the chief happiness of his existence, Bazin was also a teacher of the highest order. Perhaps it was this which made up his originality as an artist and his true personality.' By oversight or intention, Massenet never re-published his speech on Bazin.

VI

HÉRODIADE – SCENES FROM ALSACE – MANON – LE CID

ON Tuesday 27th April 1880, Massenet noted in the margin of the score he was working on: 'Three years ago to the day was the first performance of *le Roi de Lahore* at the Opéra, 27th April 1877.' Two days later, with paternal fondness, he recorded: 'Juliette's First Communion.' Early next month, at the foot of a neatly orchestrated page, the comment was: '10 in the morning to 11 . . . *Vierge* at the Opéra . . . ' With *la Vierge* he had returned to the earlier style of the oratorios *Marie-Magdeleine* and *Ève*. He had hoped for a repetition of his earlier success. Around a libretto which took as its main episodes the Annunciation, the Wedding of Cana, the events of Good Friday and the Assumption, he had woven a musical tissue which aimed at blandishment rather than austerity. It was the mixture as before. It failed.

The vast proportions of the Opéra were, to begin with, unsuitable for a work conceived as straightforward oratorio without the trappings of scenery and costume which habitués expected. Massenet himself conducted and suffered from the ' . . . icy silence of the audience. My work, written with such love and passion, crumbled into thin air. And I was on that cursed rostrum—it was impossible to escape. I trembled with shame and vexation. What a cruel disappointment! The players in the orchestra, usually so reserved, looked at me as if to say: "Poor chap!" ' The press reviews were hostile and Massenet realized that public taste was changing. One item alone raised enthusiasm, and it had to be encored three times. This was the prelude to the fourth section entitled *le Dernier sommeil de la Vierge*. Salved from the wreckage by Colonne, who frequently played it thereafter, it became a popular item at concerts and survived as a favourite 'lollipop' of Sir Thomas Beecham. [See example, page 69.] Massenet had learned the lesson of changing fashions. It was twenty years before he wrote another oratorio.

As always he returned to his main consolation, that of work. In the month that saw the collapse of his hopes for *la Vierge* he had completed the first act of his new opera. The idea came from Hartmann, whose reading of Gustave Flaubert's *Trois contes* suggested to him that the story of *Hérodiade* had the makings of an opera. Both publisher and composer aroused the interest of Ricordi, who had influence at la Scala in Milan, and an Italian *première* was planned simultaneously with

the Parisian first performance. By early August Massenet was in the middle of the second act, breaking off only to note an official honour that helped to soothe his feelings over *la Vierge:* '11.30 in the morning. Stop here. Raining in torrents. Prize ceremony at the Conservatoire yesterday. I receive the *palmes d'académicien!* . . . transports of joy!!!'

Much of the work that remained to be done on *Hérodiade* was completed at Pourville. In this little seaside resort near Dieppe, Madame Massenet and Juliette spent their summer holidays while Papa wrote his score in a shady room. His librettist and Hartmann would sometimes come to pass Sundays with him, though, as he said, ' . . . I scarcely gave those excellent friends the benefit of my company. I was accustomed to working between fifteen and sixteen hours a day. I gave six hours to sleep. My meals and daily chores took up the rest of my time. I must say, it's only in this way, in steady toil kept up tirelessly over several years, that one can produce large-scale works.' A near neighbour was the dramatist Alexandre Dumas *fils*, whose royalties from *la Dame aux camélias* had paid for a luxurious house by the sea. He would send over his carriage at seven in the evening to bring Massenet to dinner. At nine o'clock sharp—for Dumas knew his guest's reluctance to spend long periods away from his work—the carriage would take him back to Pourville and the stacks of music paper waiting to be covered with his neat writing. When the days were sunny he would, to remind himself that he was technically on holiday, hire a cabin on the beach, where, occasionally, he looked up from his score and glimpsed the distant jetty of Le Tréport.

Hérodiade was orchestrated and ready for rehearsal in the June of 1881. Ricordi immediately started preparations for the Italian performance and Massenet called on the director of the Opéra to discuss the French *première*. But Halanzier, who had welcomed *le Roi de Lahore*, had been succeeded by Vaucorbeil, and the new management was unimpressed by Massenet's proposal. The scenery of his earlier opera, Massenet learnt with dismay, had been relegated to the warehouse as a sign that the administration did not wish to keep it in the repertory. Moreover, said Vaucorbeil, the plot of *Hérodiade* was badly in need of rewriting. 'Bring me another opera,' he added, 'and the doors of the Opéra will be open to you.' In other words, the Opéra wasn't interested in him.

Without a doubt, Saints Matthew and Mark would have been as surprised as Vaucorbeil at the changes Massenet's librettist had wrought in their original account. A few brief verses had been all they needed to unfold a stark tale about the lustful Herod Antipas, his implacable wife Herodias and his nubile stepdaughter Salome, which culminated in the beheading of his prisoner John the Baptist. The holy chroniclers would have been just as disconcerted at Gustave Flaubert's story, in which events separated by many years are condensed within a period of twenty-four hours. It would, one feels, be idle to speculate on their reaction to Oscar Wilde's fantasy on the same subject, or to ponder their feelings about the steamy opera that Richard Strauss based upon it. Still, it was not historical truth that Vaucorbeil was after but the refashioning of a plot that seemed to him ineffective in its treatment.

A few days later Massenet was strolling disconsolately along the boulevard des Capucines when he met the director of the Brussels Théâtre de la Monnaie. The latter asked him point-blank for *Hérodiade* and insisted on being given the privilege of presenting it. October found Massenet in the Belgian capital singing and playing his work to the assembled cast. Whenever he rose from the grand piano to make for the generously laden buffet at which he cast longing glances, the singers begged him not to stop. At last, when he had played the final note, he rushed at the goodies displayed and, oblivious of the artists crowded around and cheering him, conquered his nerves and his hunger by scoffing the lot.

If Paris did not want *Hérodiade*, then Brussels was only too glad to make up for the oversight. The opera was given a fine production and an excellent cast. The management was determined to make a success of it, and the first night vindicated their hopes. The Théâtre de la Monnaie was packed that evening with generals, nobility, leaders of fashion, government ministers, and almost every French composer of importance. Special trains from Paris had to be laid on to carry the flock of compatriots who were anxious to see how Massenet acquitted himself. The fervour of the audience increased as the acts went by, and at the end there were innumerable curtain calls. The composer was invited to the Belgian Royal Court and came away a Knight of the Order of Leopold. He opened his newspaper and read reviews that were, almost without exception, unanimous in their praise. *Hérodiade* ran for fifty-five consecutive performances and the receipts each night amounted to more than four thousand francs, in addition to the subscriptions already taken out by regular patrons of the Théâtre de la Monnaie.

Looking at *Hérodiade* nearly a century later, one feels that Vaucorbeil's objection to the plot holds good for the characterization as well. Massenet tells his story in a suave idiom which he uses indiscriminately to express the yearnings of Salome and the savage outbursts of John the Baptist. Although this was doubtless one of the main reasons for the opera's success, it now seems a little odd that Salome, 'mysterious and seductive, a flower of evil blooming in the shadow of the temple,' should express herself in the accents of Marie-Magdeleine, and that Herod should woo her with a honeyed grace more evocative of the salon than of the torrid Eastern setting in which the action occurs. The paradox of *Hérodiade*, and that which makes it of interest in Massenet's development, is the fact that he happened to evolve his mature and most characteristic style in an opera totally unsuited to it. Salome's aria, 'Il est doux, il est bon,' provides the model which his later heroines will follow:

Rather like the Symbolist poets, Massenet breaks up the conventional rhythm of a line, shifts the accent, and introduces *enjambements* which enable him to extend the melodic curve in a novel way. The parallelism of the first three bars quoted above induces a languor which is something new for the time.

In the same way, Herod's 'Vision fugitive' sets the style for the exclamations of des Grieux and Werther:

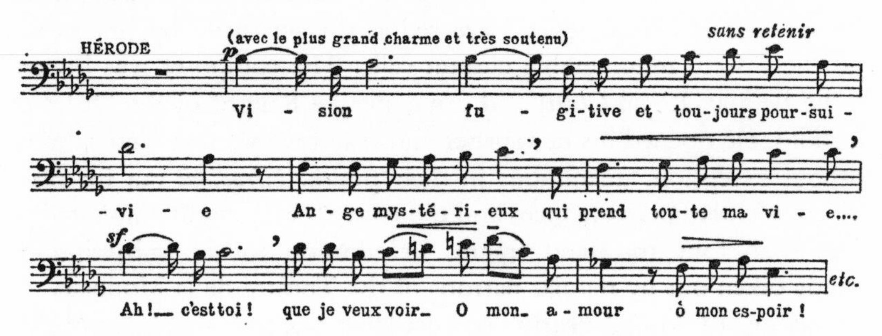

While this form of sung declamation gives a brief nod in retrospect to the musical recitation of the seventeenth century, it also has links with Debussy's *Enfant prodigue* and looks forward to the freedom, the unreality and the 'évanescences rêveuses' of *Pelléas et Mélisande*. If, however, Massenet had discovered the right method for the wrong opera, *Hérodiade* is not to be written off completely in all other respects. His craftsmanship permits him to make good use of traditional Hebrew themes and to indulge in discreet modernism, as, for example, with chords of the ninth in the orchestra during Salome's prayer. As Gabriel Fauré remarked, the whole work contained the imprint '. . . of a personality which, if it does not always succeed in persuading us, is always able to keep us charmed and captivated, even when it relies on the mediocre plot in which the legend is distorted and the characters are so oddly travestied'.

It was a long time before *Hérodiade* made its way to the Opéra in Paris. The first performance in France was at Nantes, and despite a successful presentation at the Théâtre Italien with Victor Maurel and the de Reszke brothers, the Opéra did not acknowledge it officially until 1921. Paris was much quicker to recognize the *Scènes alsaciennes* which came out the year after Massenet's Belgian success. The seventh and the finest of his orchestral suites, it was first played by Colonne, to whom it was dedicated, and has never lost its original popularity. The source of the work is found in Alphonse Daudet, many of whose short stories in the *Contes du lundi* are set in Alsace round about the time when Germany took over the region after the war of 1870. The subjects range from the thoughts of a puzzled little boy receiving his last French lesson (*la Dernière classe*), to episodes illustrating the confusion into which ordinary folk were plunged by the tragic division in their lives.[1] One story in particular, *Alsace! Alsace!*, a chain of nostalgic memories, gave Massenet the quotations with which he prefaced each of the four movements. *Dimanche matin* evokes the empty streets of an Alsatian village when all the inhabitants are at Sunday service. *Au cabaret* is a bustling rustic dance, cut into by vigorous woodland fanfares. In *Sous les tilleuls* a pair of lovers wander along the avenue of limes in the hot afternoon. The final movement, *Dimanche soir,* ends in a skilful working-up of Alsatian peasant tunes.

Massenet wrote in detailed instructions for the players of this suite. For the distant bugle and drum representing the French withdrawal, the off-stage trumpeters were asked to walk up to the stage while playing and then to turn and move into the distance. Throughout the score he was anxious to ensure the success of his patiently prepared effects. The result, an exquisite and subtle piece of orchestral writing, is fully justified. *Sous les tilleuls* is certainly the most affecting of the movements, with its long and pensive adagio dialogue between cello and clarinet against a quivering sheen of violins. Paul Dukas, a composer and critic of stern judgments, preferred *Dimanche matin,* where an old Protestant chorale is woven into the texture to suggest music faintly heard from the church down the street. The movement was, he wrote, '. . . exclusively symphonic, with its cleverly handled chorale, delicate structure and charming instrumental effects.'

But the approval of concert audiences, agreeable though it was, did not stimulate Massenet as much as applause in the theatre, and he was already preparing another opera. The librettist was Henri Meilhac, who, with his collaborator Ludovic Halévy, provided libretti for Offenbach and Bizet. Meilhac wrote, in addition, a number of wittily turned boulevard comedies, including the one that eventually gave birth to *The Merry Widow*. Temporarily separated from Halévy, he had offered Massenet a libretto which the composer found utterly impossible to set. Massenet broke the news to him in the library where the dramatist did his writing. While Meilhac sat beside his Louis XIV table, dumbfounded, Massenet looked embarrassedly elsewhere, his eye roving uncertainly along the handsome bindings on the shelves. His attention was caught by one in particular: it was *Manon Lescaut,* the novel by the abbé Prévost.

[1] Albert Schweitzer was born there. When, as an old man, he reminisced about his early life, his hearers were struck by the way he lapsed unconsciously into French or German according to whether the event he was relating had taken place under either of the two regimes.

'*Manon!*' he cried, pointing out the book to Meilhac.

'What? It's *Manon Lescaut* you want?'

'No! *Manon*, just *Manon*, that's all. It's *Manon!*'

The eighteenth century was rich in original personalities, and few of them were more curious than the licentious abbé Prévost. In his youth he fluctuated between the professions of soldier and of priest. After a disastrous love affair he settled down as a member of the Benedictine order which he suddenly quitted a few years later. This impulsiveness brought about his exile from France. In London, where he lived as tutor to a rich family, he completed an interminable work of fiction called the *Mémoires et aventures d'un homme de qualité*. Other romances from his pen included *Cleveland* and the intriguingly titled *Doyen de Killerine*. The rest of his life was spent on the move between Holland, Britain and France, usually a few steps ahead of his creditors. A vexing imbroglio in London which involved a forged letter of exchange, a rapacious mistress and several months' imprisonment, was cleared up by the forgiveness of his victim, and from then on the buoyant abbé devoted himself to turning out dictionaries, histories, biographies and translations of the works of Richardson. He lived quietly with a succession of ladies of a mature age, among them a complaisant widow known as Loulou, who were unlikely to cause him the perturbations he had experienced with their flighty predecessors. The end of this endearing personage was macabre. He fell unconscious from an attack of apoplexy. The village doctor, taking him for dead, began a post mortem examination to ascertain the cause. Thus brutally revived by the probing knife, the abbé opened his eyes again. This time, thanks to the attentions of the good doctor, he really did die.

It was the seventh volume of the *Mémoires et aventures d'un homme de qualité* which took the public's fancy on its appearance. The book sold even more copies when it was condemned by the authorities. The full title is: *Histoire du Chevalier des Grieux et de Manon Lescaut,* and it contains the story, told by des Grieux himself, of his chequered love affair with Manon Lescaut. A young gentleman hitherto esteemed for his sober conduct, he suddenly falls in love with the beautiful Manon Lescaut. They fly to Paris and set up what des Grieux imagines, with typical masculine fatuity, will be a love nest. But Manon is a girl who loves the luxury and high life which he cannot afford to give her. While the poor fool is burbling bemusedly about love in a cottage, the practical Manon is already laying plans to conquer the town and to find the lovers who will finance her whims. She becomes a fashionable and well-known figure, while in the background to the scenes of which she is the heroine mopes the sad but faithful des Grieux. Misfortune strikes, and she is deported to America as a *fille perdue*. There she dies, and her lover buries her tenderly in the soil of Louisiana.

Prévost's short novel is but a tiny portion of an immense output which otherwise is known only to scholars. This 'passionate and beautiful romance', as Lytton Strachey called it, is an artistic achievement which has retained its superior place in French literature. The precision, the clarity, the restrained pathos remind one of Mérimée's genius for simplicity. Although the hero is nominally des Grieux, readers of the novel overlooked him in their fascination with the character of Manon. On its appearance Montesquieu and Voltaire both referred to it simply as *Manon Lescaut,* despite the author's declaration that he had intended to draw a picture of des Grieux, '. . . a blind young man . . . a mixture of virtues and vices, a perpetual contrast between worthy feelings and bad actions'. Manon it is, perverse and capricious, who has ensured the long life of the novel, and Massenet was right to build his opera around her. His predecessors in the field were Halévy, who wrote a three-act ballet on the subject, and Auber, who with characteristic nonchalance had never got round to reading the novel itself and was content to set Scribe's footling libretto.

The very next day after he had proposed the subject to Meilhac, the composer was astonished to receive the first two acts of the opera. Massenet's enthusiasm was fully shared by his librettist, and with the aid of a new collaborator, Philippe Gille, the words were delivered to him as fast as he could set them. His moods followed the usual course when he was writing an opera. The initial excitement and fulsome compliments showered upon Meilhac and Gille were followed by misgivings about the scenario. There were long strolls through the forest at Saint-Germain, where Meilhac had taken a house for the summer, during which Massenet would cut, change, transpose and revise the libretto to his collaborator's deepening chagrin. 'Good day yesterday,' Massenet wrote on one such occasion.

> Eleven in the morning, excellent conversation with Gille—change *accepted!* Half-past twelve, lunch, good appetite. Two o'clock, session at the Institut, paid 8 francs, 3 centimes (attendance fee). Six o'clock, my pupil Hillemacher carries off the 20,000 francs Grand Prix de la Ville de Paris. Eight o'clock—dinner with the Prefect—my neighbour is Delibes. Eleven o'clock. *Found Gille's letter—am absolutely delighted to see this new proof of my very dear collaborator's hard work . . .*

By the time the broad outlines were established and every ounce of dramatic value had been squeezed out of the subject, Massenet was satisfied. But only for a short while. He relapsed into doubt and uncertainty, and his harassed collaborators were summoned to give him new assurance. He needed consolation and he exaggerated his despair, like a child who attempts to wheedle as much sympathy for himself as possible out of indulgent parents. He was, wrote someone tolerantly, like an Aeolian harp that quivered at every breeze, however light.

Through the good offices of a wealthy Dutch music-lover, Massenet was able to work on his score at The Hague in a room once occupied by Prévost himself. It still contained the large bed, shaped like a gondola, for which the enterprising abbé had found many a use, and in this appropriate ambiance Massenet speedily mapped out the broad sketch of his work. If inspiration began to flag, he would take meditative walks on the dunes of Scheveningen, or contemplate with a sentimental eye the graceful deer which gambolled through the royal woods. Manon's adventures continued to occupy his spare moments during the première of *Hérodiade* in Brussels. After conducting a wildly successful performance in Hamburg and being engulfed in a voluminous laurel wreath, he hurried back to his hotel room and the lamentations of des Grieux. At Nantes he escaped from the orchestra and singers who gathered by the stage door to greet him with an impromptu serenade, and buried himself once more in the fortunes of his elusive heroine.

In the April of 1883, ('6th anniversary to the very day of the 1st performance of the *Roi de Lahore*'), he reached the end of the second act with 'great weariness'. At seven o'clock on the morning of Sunday 15th July 1883, he completed the orchestration of the whole opera. He played his work at the piano to Carvalho, the manager of the Opéra-Comique and a producer notorious for his meddling with the works he staged. Massenet presented him, as was his practice, with the bound and engraved score of *Manon*. 'My friend,' said Carvalho in a tone of ironic frustration, 'your work will be performed as though you were already dead.' His wife, Miolan-Carvalho, who had been the first to sing Gounod's Marguerite, exclaimed: 'If only I were twenty years younger!' Fortunately she was not, and the part of Manon went to Marie Heilbronn, the singer who appeared in Massenet's first work for the stage, *la Grand'tante*. Since then her public career had been neglected for a private life in which a succession of wealthy lovers shrewdly chosen conducted her at last to marriage with a nobleman. After Massenet played the opera to her she burst into tears and said: 'It's the story of my life . . . my own life!' Two years afterwards the creator of Manon on the stage died suddenly in her early forties.

It had not been easy to fill the all-important role of Manon. The difficulties Massenet encountered are amusingly illustrated by the conversation he had with a theatre manager who controlled the services of the singer he wished originally to engage.

'*Illustre maître!*' exclaimed the manager, 'what happy chance brings you to see me?' Massenet explained. '*Mon cher Monsieur*,' was the cool reply, 'what you ask is impossible.'

'For good and all?'

'Completely. But if you write an opera for my theatre, then I will let you have her services—agreed, old chap?'

At last rehearsals began. Massenet watched jealously over everything. He was, said an observer,

> . . . an outstanding producer who had the gift of elucidating a character, of bringing out a nuance in the acting, and of expressing in gesture and attitude a fleeting emotion however difficult it may have been to define . . . How typical of him was the remark he would make to the players in the orchestra: 'My dear colleagues, I shall not be taking any notice of you, but remember, I am present.'

On a cold January night in 1884, the first performance of *Manon* rewarded Massenet's hopes and all the obsessive care he had given to it. The audience at the Opéra-Comique cheered his opera with frenzy and demanded encore after encore. Although next day the reviews were mixed, the public instantly took *Manon* to its heart. During its first ten years in the repertory *Manon* earned close on two million francs at the box-office. It has by now been played well over two thousand times at the Opéra-Comique alone and is in this respect a near rival to *Carmen*. It conquered the imagination of nineteenth-century audiences in a way that is pleasantly shown by Massenet's encounter with a husband who complained of his wife's lack of interest in him.

'Here', said Massenet, 'use these tickets and go with your wife to the Opéra-Comique. Each time she cries, take her hand gently.'

'But we're not on that sort of terms.'

'Never mind,' replied Massenet, 'try all the same. It won't cost you anything.'

A little later he met the husband again, still in the depths of melancholy. 'Didn't my little trick work?' he asked, 'didn't you take your wife's hand at the sentimental moments?'

'Yes,' came the lugubrious answer, 'but when, during the third act, I tried to grab her hand, I found it was already held by the man in the seat next to hers.'

'*Mon ami*,' riposted Massenet, 'it proves that her neighbour was more of a musician than you . . . !'

The mellifluous and caressing style which had been so inapt for the harsh tang of *Hérodiade* was perfectly suited to the eighteenth-century atmosphere of Manon. Here Massenet had a subject which engaged his musical and theatrical talents with the smoothness of a key fitting into a well-oiled lock. A setting of dainty boudoirs and rococo gaming rooms, an atmosphere of flowered waistcoats, silver shoe-buckles and swaying panniers, above all a heroine of ravishing coquetry and charm, were the elements that moved him to write his masterpiece. The scheme he followed was simple.

> The whole work [he said] moves and develops upon some fifteen *motifs* which typify my characters. To each character a *motif*. Manon alone, who is a mixture of sadness and gaiety, has two, the better to emphasize her alternate moods. These *motifs* run the length and breadth of the opera and are reproduced from act to act, shading off or coming into prominence, like the play of light in a picture, according to the situations. In this way my characters keep their personalities distinct until the end.

There was nothing Wagnerian about this. 'Of Wagnerism', wrote Bernard Shaw briskly, 'there is not the faintest suggestion. A phrase which occurs in the first love duet breaks out once or twice in subsequent amorous episodes, and has been seized on by a few unwary critics as a Wagnerian *leitmotiv*. But if Wagner had never existed, *Manon* would have been composed much as it stands now . . . ' The phrase to which Shaw refers is the one where des Grieux falls captive to Manon:

It is a luscious tune which is no less appropriate for the fact that it echoes, involuntarily or otherwise, a similar passage in Franck's oratorio *Ruth*, and others in Massenet's own work—a duet in *la Vierge* and the *Angélus* section of the *Scènes pittoresques*.

When Manon dismounts from her coach and finds herself in the bustling courtyard of the Amiens hostelry, she expresses her shy confusion in a rhythm which is ingeniously displaced:

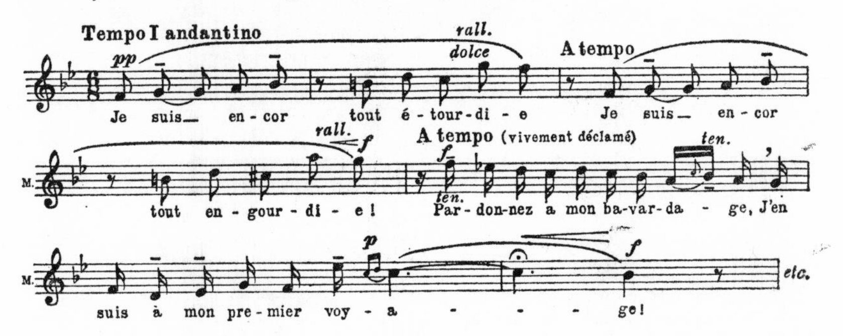

The same technique is just as effective in depicting the sadness with which, at her parting from des Grieux, she bids farewell to the little table where they had taken so many of their meals together. [See example, page 80.]

On her emergence as a notorious and much-courted woman of fashion, the music she has to sing becomes increasingly bejewelled with precipitous *roulades* and dizzy *ports de voix*. Not all of Massenet's interpreters were able to encompass the hair-raising dangers of the *fabliau* he wrote for one outstanding singer to perform instead of the more conventional Gavotte in Act III. Manon's death scene justifies the liberty taken in switching it from Louisiana to Le Havre, since the operatic possibilities of the American episode in Prévost's novel are few. Here the orchestra accompanies, with a murmured rise and fall of the violins, the pathetic last words of the broken butterfly.

Without a doubt the opera belongs to Manon, but the men also have their chances. The father of des Grieux is given a fine bass aria, '*Épouse quelque brave fille*,' in which he admonishes his son to find a companion worthy of himself and of the family name. The object of his reprimand also has many excellent opportunities, and the tenor who cannot make a success of des Grieux's idyllic '*En fermant les yeux*', or of his impassioned '*Ah! fuyez, douce image*', has chosen the wrong profession. On the purely orchestral plane Massenet is unfailingly inventive throughout the opera. Every French composer worth his salt can turn out eighteenth-century pastiche, and Massenet was better than most. The score is embellished with many delicious pages of minuet, gavotte and ballet which add splendour to what are known in the business as 'production numbers'. Still more impressive are the crowd scenes where Massenet conjures up the hustle of a coach arriving at an inn, or the breathless excitement of the gaming table.

Manon is perfection of its kind. With his heroine Massenet added a well-defined 'type' to the gallery of operatic women. She embodies all the characteristics of the flirtatious girl who takes a healthy enjoyment as much in the sentimental as in the physical aspect of an affair. There is nothing degraded about her, and the wholehearted innocence she brings to the game accounts for much of her success with men. She is tender, superficial and quite brainless. What more could a sensible man want? People have sometimes argued that the portrait Massenet has drawn lacks entirely those depths of character which philosophers, in moments of optimism, like to attribute to women. It is a criticism which opera-goers of the Third Republic preferred to ignore.

Less than a fortnight after *Manon* had begun its triumphant career *Hérodiade* arrived at last in Paris. It was played in the Italian version which had been used for the Milan première two years before. The role of Herod Antipas was sung by Victor Maurel, whom Sir Thomas Beecham once reckoned to be the finest baritone he ever heard, and John the Baptist and Phanuel the astrologer were taken by Jean and Édouard de Reszke. To everyone involved in that production *Hérodiade* brought luck. It added considerably to Massenet's reputation with Parisian audiences, who, denied the work by the Opéra, now crowded into the Théâtre Italien to applaud it. For Victor Maurel, who also produced, the opera was one of the landmarks of his season at the Théâtre Italien. As for the de Reszke brothers, they were henceforward to enjoy unequalled admiration and loyalty from their public. Jean de Reszke was thirty-four years old and had not sung a great deal before then. It is thought that this late start preserved the vocal agility which enabled him to sing with unique brilliance in styles as far apart as those of French, Italian and Wagnerian opera. Massenet hastened to sign him up for his latest work, *le Cid.*

The Spanish national hero was already the undeserving subject of no less than twenty-six operas. He seems to have exercised a peculiar attraction for nearly twenty minor Italian composers, among them the luckless Paisiello, who was not only to have his *Barber* overshadowed by Rossini but was also to be eclipsed by Massenet. The composer of that persistent *Scherzo* for piano and orchestra, Henry Litolff, was guilty of a *Rodrigue de Tolède,* and the vague figure of Peter Cornelius completed a brace of stage-works by adding *Il Cid* to his *Barber of Baghdad.* Even Handel gestated a *Rodrigo,* and from time to time both Weber and Bizet had toyed with the idea. The lists were full, and one is reluctant to claim that Massenet, the twenty-seventh composer to try his hand, was the ideal choice for the story.

He had for some time wanted to write an opera about *le Cid.* When handed a five-act libretto, ready made, he asked his collaborators to insert another scene inspired by his reading of the Spanish epic. While working on the music he suddenly remembered the fifth act of another drama lying at the bottom of a drawer somewhere. This, too, was jigsawed into the plot. To make things worse, his librettists, while basing their original work on Corneille's great tragedy, had also interpolated many of the poet's lines into their own dialogue. The result is a plot of clumsy dimensions and clumsier language, where Corneille's stolen gems shine all the more incongruously for being surrounded with paste of the most derisory nature.[1]

Nonetheless, *le Cid* had an excellent reception at the Opéra, where it was first performed in November 1885. Massenet spent the evening over at the Opéra-Comique, trying to forget his anxiety in chit-chat with the cast of *Manon* and in strolling tight-lipped in the wings. As he made his way home past the Opéra he saw the audience pouring out and calling for their carriages. A journalist he knew came up to him and said: 'It's a fantastic success, *mon cher*'. So it was, both for Massenet and for the de Reszke brothers who again served him well. By 1900 *le Cid* had been performed a hundred times at the Opéra, and in the nineteen-twenties it reached its hundred and fiftieth performance. Since then it has been little heard. Despite its contemporary success, the opera was always something of a hybrid. Quite apart from the inadequacies of the libretto, the music is rarely at one with the setting and the characterization. Heroic attitudes and Castillian haughtiness were strangers to Massenet's muse. He lacked ability to convey the turbulent emotion which *le Cid* demanded. The most successful aria, and the least appropriate, is Chimène's *Pleurez, pleurez mes yeux,* for, while it is

[1] One of the three librettists was Adolphe d'Ennery, a jovial journeyman credited with the authorship of over three thousand plays, including *Michael Strogoff* and dramatizations of Jules Verne. He was, in private life, a man of sharp and epigrammatic wit. Asked why he never put any of this into his plays, he answered contentedly that if he did so his wide public would think someone else had written them and would be disconcerted.

neatly written in the style of *Manon*, it strikes a false note in a score which ought to be striving for something else.

The ballet suite from *le Cid* serves as a further indication of Massenet's gift for light music. The tune of the *Castillane*, which opens the ballet, he had heard while on his student travels in Spain. Guitars and flutes had played the theme to accompany a marriage celebration, and he had already used it, though less adroitly, in *Don César de Bazan*. The sparkling layout and attractive flamboyance of this suite have preserved it, though it is a pity that the *Rapsodie Mauresque* is not played as well. Massenet wrote the ballet while in Marseille to supervise a production of *Manon*. His room in the hôtel Beauvau, he learned with delight, had once been occupied by Paganini. Previous distinguished residents there also included George Sand and Alfred de Musset on one of their amorous itineraries. It was spring, and from his historic room decorated with bunches of carnations sent by his admirers, Massenet could look out over the old port. 'Isn't this the place', he wrote with pleasant hyperbole, 'where you can sugar your coffee by leaving it out on the balcony because the sea is made of honey? . . .'

VII

A CHARACTER IN MAUPASSANT–THE CASE OF SYBIL SANDERSON–ESCLARMONDE–LE MAGE–WERTHER–LE CARILLON

For someone who claimed to dislike travelling, Massenet contrived to cover a lot of ground in his time. While *le Cid* was still rehearsing, he set off on an extended trip to Hungary as one of a party of distinguished Frenchmen who had been invited to a gala organized by a students' association. Among the forty or so ornaments of French culture were the poet François Coppée, the painter Georges Clairin, and Massenet's old friend Delibes. The leader of the party was Ferdinand de Lesseps, engineer-impresario of the Suez Canal. He was then in his eightieth year and astonished everyone by his vitality. After arranging the day's programme, checking routes and planning visits, he would rise at four in the morning and go riding. 'One has to spend one's youth somehow,' he would remark jauntily. A few years afterwards his scheme to build the Panama canal was to explode into one of those sensational scandals that make the history of the Third Republic a favourite study for connoisseurs of political corruption. Half the enormous sums raised by public subscription were found to have trickled away into the ample pockets of deputies, officials and journalists. Small investors were to throw themselves under trains, families were to be ruined, and de Lesseps, fallen into a second childhood, was to gape confusedly as the prosecution unwound the tortuous tangle of which he had been more dupe than creator.

But as the Orient Express whistled through the night towards Budapest, de Lesseps was the genial and tireless host of a gay party that had still not broken up when dawn came. Each evening in Hungary there were dinners, receptions and festivals in honour of the visiting Frenchmen. Time passed in a haze of Tokay and practical jokes.

Taking the rostrum at the Royal Theatre in Budapest to conduct the third act of *Hérodiade*, Massenet looked down to see before him the score of the first act of *Coppélia*. He conducted, hopefully, from memory. Needless to say, the unknown joker had similarly arranged for Delibes to be confronted with the *Hérodiade* score. Wiping his brow, puffing and blowing in anguished perplexity, the wretched composer waggled his baton and committed himself to God.

This riotous trip was a unique episode in Massenet's otherwise quiet and hard-working existence. His wife did not accompany him, and she may have thought, with her usual self-effacement, that it would be good for him to get away for once on a bachelor outing. Since their marriage she had organized her life around him and their daughter Juliette. Although she could have had a successful career as a pianist, she gave up her ambitions for the sake of the family. Forswearing the excitement of virtuoso concert tours and the possibility of a reputation in her own right, she contented herself instead with ruling her husband's music paper, copying out libretti and doing all she could to create surroundings in which he was able to dedicate himself entirely to composition. There must have been times when she was nervous about the attractions of the beautiful singers with whom Massenet was obliged to associate professionally. The free-and-easy ways of the theatre are not particularly favourable to the bourgeois institution of marriage. Massenet's men friends envied him the opportunities that were daily put in his path. Gossip inevitably linked his name with that of his current leading lady.

Against rumours of a varied love life it may be argued that Massenet was in the position of a confectioner who, perpetually surrounded by sweetmeats, soon loses his appetite and comes to regard them simply as the items of his trade. In support of this theory we are told that the owner of the Folies-Bergère, who died recently at the age of eighty-seven, was remarkable for the blameless purity of his morals. This happy state of affairs owed much to the ingenuity of a wife who followed the classic advice of women's magazines and revived her husband's interest, jaded with the sight of the world's loveliest chorus girls, by appearing before him every day in a seductive new *toilette*. It may also be said that Massenet's arduous work routine left him few opportunities for amorous conquest—although, as wives are quick to point out, a man can always find time, however busy, for the purpose. The popular belief in the figure of Casanova-Massenet was summed up by the author Paul Léautaud, when he wrote:

> I can't remember where I read that he was very fond of women, even when he was rather elderly. In any case, he had some very beautiful ones who were his singers. Sybil Sanderson, for example, a splendid piece of womanhood to judge by her photographs. The last one, Lucy Arbell, was another of his singers . . . It was obviously from these affairs that he must have drawn afresh the colour, the ardour, the amorous tones of the new work he was writing at the time, a sort of rejuvenation, a new flame of inspiration with each new love. Just like Wagner, for whom each passion generated a new work. Men like that have really lived.

Lucie Arbell only makes her appearance in the closing years of Massenet's life. Sybil Sanderson he was to meet when he was in his mid-forties, that sad, far shore of regret for youth and of unease at the approach of age. Not long after he made her acquaintance he was portrayed under the name of 'Massival' in Guy de Maupassant's novel *Notre coeur*, a story which is set in the fashionable society of the time. Massival, we are told, is a very successful composer and a popular guest in the leading salons of Paris. 'Many women had loved him, and, it was said, still pursued him . . . Massival, in fact, was married. Before the period of success he had contracted one of those *unions d'artistes* that drag on through fame until death . . . ' Massival, like his model in real life, often plays his own music at soirées: ' . . . the musician began with a slow, a very slow succession of notes which seemed like a recitative. There were pauses, light repeats, chains of little phrases, sometimes languishing, sometimes nervous, disturbing perhaps, but unexpectedly original.' He has an affair with the marquise de Bratiane, whom he accompanies when she sings to her guests. One evening, to the delight of malicious friends, the composer's wife bursts in and makes a terrible scene. 'Massival, bewildered, tried to lead his wife away, to drag her off, while she hit him in the face, tore at his beard and hair, bit him and ripped his clothes.'

Although Madame Massenet stopped far short of such dramatic measures, the picture of her husband in society is a true one, and Maupassant catches perfectly the atmosphere of the salons with their lionized composer and admiring hostesses. Despite his reluctance to encroach upon the precious hours he reserved for his work, Massenet found it impossible to refuse all the invitations that his fame increasingly attracted. After all, he had eagerly sought, and worked hard for, the recognition he now enjoyed, and to be guest of honour at some of the greatest houses in Paris was not among the more unwelcome penalties of fame. Massenet was not like his rival Saint-Saëns, whose boredom on such occasions usually found a vent in disobliging ruderies directed at the simpering women around him. The composer of *Manon* accepted the social conventions with grace, flirted smoothly whenever the chance arose, and greeted compliments with a flattery that charmed and reassured even the most diffident.

One invitation that arrived for him in the summer of 1887 he had already once refused. Then the invitation was renewed in such a gracious fashion that he had no alternative but to capitulate. It came from a well-known American family then in Paris. Massenet took his place at table next to a diplomatist and a lady noted for her musical aspirations. The following dialogue assailed his ears:

> *Diplomatist*: You are still a child of the Muses, a new Orphea?
> *Lady*: Isn't music the consolation of souls in distress . . .?
> *Diplomatist*: Don't you find that love is more powerful than mere sounds to ease the pains of the heart?
> *Lady*: Yesterday I felt consoled on setting *le Vase brisé* to music.
> *Diplomatist* (poetically): A *nocturne,* doubtless . . .

The conversation took a hurried turn as other guests chuckled at the ribald double meaning of the innocent diplomatist.

At the end of what had seemed to be a wasted evening, Massenet was about to slip away when he was approached by a mother and her daughter. The former, he noted expertly, was still a handsome woman, but the latter was extraordinarily beautiful. She had chestnut hair flecked with gold and a slight but captivating American accent. Her name was Sybil Sanderson, her birthplace Sacramento, in California. Her father, a Judge of the Supreme Court, had recently died and left her, along with her mother and sisters, a comfortable fortune. She was anxious to take up a career in opera and had studied with the famous teacher Marchesi. Would Massenet, she asked, hear her sing? He politely agreed and accompanied her in the difficult aria sung by the Queen of the Night in *Die Zauberflöte.* Her performance thrilled him. 'What a fantastic voice!' he noted. 'It went from lower to upper G, three octaves both at its loudest and softest. I was astonished, stupefied, overcome! . . . I must say that, together with the rarity of such a voice, I had recognized in the artist she was to become an intelligence, an inspiration, a personality, that were reflected in her wonderful look. These are qualities of the highest importance on the stage.'

Next morning he hurried round to announce the new discovery to Hartmann. His publisher listened patiently, and then, dismissing the subject with a preoccupied air, asked if he would be interested in setting a new libretto that had just come in. 'It's urgent, because the music is wanted in time for the opening of the Universal Exhibition. It's arranged for two years from now in May 1889.'

Massenet took the libretto and glanced at a few scenes. 'I've the very singer for the part!' he exclaimed rapturously. 'The very one! I heard her yesterday. It's Mademoiselle Sybil Sanderson. She will be the first to sing Esclarmonde, the heroine of the new opera you've just offered me!'

So began an intense relationship between the composer and the singer whose art he admired as much as her person. He showed her off proudly to his friends and listened greedily to their tributes. She had, said Alfred Bruneau, who was granted the privilege by Massenet of hearing her in Hartmann's office, a voice that was 'accurate, flexible, wide ranging, agile, ethereal, and notable for its crystalline limpidity and voluptuous tenderness'. She was only twenty-two years old, and her beauty was as fresh and radiant as her voice. Massenet could think of nothing but his new protégée, and under the influence of her charm he began to write an opera lovingly planned to display every facet of her talent.

For the next two years the Massenet household lived in an odd state of resentful excitement. While Massenet himself plotted with feverish enthusiasm to launch Sybil Sanderson in the operatic world and to tailor his new work for her personality, Madame Massenet, discreet as ever, remained loyally in the background. Although she did not speak of her feelings about the much younger woman who now obsessed her husband, the effort it cost her to repress them created smouldering undercurrents which flickered through an atmosphere that sometimes became too charged for comfort. Regardless of all this, Massenet rushed ahead with his plans for Sanderson. An opportunity to test her gifts arose with the Dutch *première* of *Manon* at The Hague in January 1888. Under the name of Ada Palmer, for her protector thought it a wise insurance at this stage to use a pseudonym, she took the leading role in the opera. Massenet discreetly alerted the newspapers, among them *le Figaro*, which, as an influential and widely read journal, he had always cultivated with good results. Correspondents were assiduously briefed, important people were deferentially told of what was afoot, and never had Massenet's charm been employed to more effect. A cold

Sanderson had picked up on travelling to the Dutch city nearly frightened him out of his wits, but she recovered in time to give a performance that confirmed his high opinion of her.

That summer she holidayed in Switzerland with her mother. Massenet came to join them at the Grand Hôtel de Vevey. During the day he worked on the score of *Esclarmonde,* and in the evening he rehearsed with her what he had written. It was a disturbing period overshadowed by her mother's illness with an eye affliction. Anxiety for her mother was followed by doubts about her ability, and one evening, distraught, she resolved to give up her role. Only Massenet's desperate pleas made her change her mind. His manuscripts at this time are more than usually indicative of his moods. The letter S, written large and so thickly inscribed that it sinks deep into the paper, frequently recurs with a meaning that may easily be divined. 'A painful evening last night' alternates with remarks such as, 'Sleepless night, a sad future . . . ' or, 'Sad end to the S evening . . . ' A 'beautiful sunrise over the mountains' cheers him temporarily, but a drive in a carriage alone with S leaves him reflecting, 'a sad day . . . ' The weather, his 'grave preoccupations' with S, the nervous strain of his work, all combined to turn the holiday into five weeks of emotional trial. The strange thing is that despite all this he managed to orchestrate the whole of the first three acts of *Esclarmonde* during his stay in Switzerland. It is hardly needful to add that Madame Massenet spent the summer elsewhere in the company of their daughter.

The opera was completed on his return to Paris. At Massenet's insistence, the woman for whom he had written it added her signature to his on the last page of the manuscript. A graphologist would readily deduce from her handwriting the background to those stormy days in Switzerland. The large initial letters denote ambition, the slope in size from left to right bespeaks an awareness of superiority, and the remarkably long stroke over the t's may be read either as a protective or as a patronizing impulse towards others. Massenet's hand, upright and tending to the angular, suggests the inflexible determination which, as we know, underlay the apparent yielding blandness of his manner. It is clear that Sanderson had all the temperament, if not the experience, of a *prima donna,* and that in Massenet she had encountered a personality worthy of her metal.

Esclarmonde, described as an 'opéra romanesque', was accepted for the Opéra-Comique, whose director, overwhelmed by Massenet's enthusiasm, agreed to pay the large fee asked on behalf of Sybil Sanderson.

What is more, the composer was allowed to take full control of the designers and costumiers so that the production should come closest to realizing his own ideas. Each costume, each piece of jewellery to be worn, each stroke of paint on the scenery, had to be personally inspected and approved by Massenet. He was allowed twenty-two rehearsals with the singers and fifty-seven on stage, of which ten were accompanied by full orchestra. To the fears that always tormented him about the success of any of his operas was added trepidation about the début of his admired Sybil Sanderson. At one point, wearied by the grinding toil of rehearsals, he gave way in the company of friends and wept uncontrollably, shaking like a schoolgirl. People were deliberately turning their backs on him! They were conspiring against him!

'And yet,' he groaned, 'I'm no longer a beginner. Remember the operas I've got behind me! Let people think what they will, they can't take *them* away from me. I *have* achieved something, after all . . . '

It was ironic that the talent of this sensitive man should have led him into the jungle of the theatre, where malice and jealousy are perhaps more active than in any other field. He wanted so urgently to feel that people liked him and to please them with his successes. And then, the encouraging (though not disinterested) smile of a singer, the compliments of a second violin, would lighten his despair, and he was the happiest man in the world, all eagerness to start rehearsals again.

In May *Esclarmonde* attracted large audiences to the Opéra-Comique and Massenet was overjoyed with the double triumph of his work and of Sybil Sanderson. The opera benefited from the holiday atmosphere created by the Exhibition of 1889, and visitors to Paris swelled audiences who cheered the beauty of the heroine and the splendour of the scenic effects. The subject, taken from the ancient French romance of *Partenopeus de Blois*, allowed ample scope for spectacle. The emperor Phorcas, who combines his royal duties with the practice of sorcery, has a daughter called Esclarmonde. She falls in love with the knight Roland. Sworn to secrecy, he departs to fight the Saracens with a magic sword. In the course of the wars he betrays his oath, the penalty for which is death. He meets Esclarmonde and her magician father in the forest of the Ardennes, where he must compete in a tourney if he is to save himself from the consequences of his act. He emerges as the victor and is rewarded with the hand of Esclarmonde. The fantasy in this tale of medieval chivalry was embodied in settings which represented magic palaces and enchanted gardens. Roland was transported to a mysterious island to be welcomed by Dream Spirits, and a series of coloured back-projections depicted the proud knight hunting and then setting off from the shore in a galley of ornate art-nouveau design.

To the end of his days Massenet stubbornly declared that *Esclarmonde* was his favourite work. This preference, most likely, was due to the sentimental associations it had for him. It was Sybil Sanderson's opera, and any criticism of it was resented by him as a slur on his lovely *prima donna*. Musically there is not a great deal of the composer of *Manon* in it. Esclarmonde's invocation, when she hands over the magic sword to Roland, is, however, a reminiscence of Manon's farewell to the little table, invested for the occasion with an air of heroic mysticism:

On the whole the opera is bewilderingly eclectic—which is a polite way of paraphrasing the sharp-eared critic who claimed to have detected in it the traces of Wagner, Gounod, Meyerbeer, Verdi, Reyer (who must have been flattered), and even a suspicion of operetta. The critic Henri Gauthier-Villars, doomed to posthumous fame as Colette's first husband, but known in his day as the sponsor of many ghosted novels and purveyor of highly entertaining music reviews under the name of Willy, had some pertinent things to say about *Esclarmonde*. He had been an early champion of Wagner, then later of Debussy, and he paid a typically back-handed compliment to Massenet by describing him as one of the very few

> . . . to seize on the evolution of the public, to follow it and, if need be, speed it up. His method is wonderfully flexible. He

> constructs his opera in such a way as to include things that will please fools and others that will hold the attention of connoisseurs, if only for a minute. He knows his Wagner; to a certain extent he prepares the crowd for Wagner's music. Never, at least, does he fall into musical obscurity or into those dead-ends where musicians too simple, too narrowly convinced so easily find themselves.

A fair enough sample of the processional pomps, by Wagner out of Meyerbeer, which fatten up the structure of *Esclarmonde*, occurs in the second act:

Two years later Massenet presented to his public a new opera entitled *le Mage*. Its hero is Zoroaster, the legendary Persian warrior and founder of the religion named after him. While the subject undoubtedly contained operatic potential, Massenet was not the composer to exploit it. Confronted with the task of portraying barbaric soldiers and the primitive manners of an oriental community that lived over fifteen centuries ago, he could only produce what Willy mockingly labelled as 'glockenspillages'. 'It's very odd!' went on the merciless critic. 'When I hear Massenet's operas I always long for Saint-Saëns'. I should add that hearing Saint-Saëns' operas makes me long for Massenet's.' Zoroaster, to Massenet's disappointment, vanished after thirty-two performances and returned into the dust of the ages whence he had been momentarily rescued.

Throughout the whole period occupied by *Esclarmonde* and *le Mage*, the composer had also been working on and off at an opera totally different in character from either of these exotic tales. In the August of 1886 he had gone to Bayreuth with Hartmann for a performance of *Parsifal*. At the time Massenet was keen to write an opera based on Henri Murger's *la Vie de bohème*. Murger was a personal friend, and Massenet knew in real life all the people who had served as models for the leading characters of the book. An offer, in fact, was made to him through Hartmann, but his publisher turned it down, having what he thought to be a better subject, and so left the field open to Puccini.

On their trip to Germany Hartmann showed Massenet the sights with a cunning showmanship born of his deep knowledge of German literature and language. In Wetzlar they visited the house where Goethe had written *The Sorrows of Young Werther*. Hartmann knew how to handle the impressionable musician. At the point when Massenet's emotions were at their keenest among those evocative surroundings, he produced a copy of the book and told him to read it. They went into a nearby tavern filled with noisy students, and, over a couple of bocks, Massenet immersed himself in the letters which tell of the unhappy romance between Werther and Charlotte. At first he was but mildly interested. Then, as he read on, his feelings were aroused by the lovers' fugitive happiness, Charlotte's marriage with Albert her betrothed, and Werther's despairing suicide. Forgetful of the reek of beer and pipe smoke, he gave in wholeheartedly to the charm of a love story which had entranced generations of romantically minded readers.

'Such rapturous and ecstatic passion brought tears to my eyes', he exclaimed. 'What moving scenes, what thrilling moments it could all give rise to! *Werther* it was! There was my third act'. Hartmann was a clever psychologist.

Several other operatic versions preceded Massenet's, among them a *Werther et Charlotte* by Rodolphe Kreutzer, the French violinist who, not content, it seems, with the dedication of Beethoven's sonata, was also the composer of some forty operas. All fire and flame for his new project, Massenet orchestrated his score in less than six months. Hartmann gave him a scenario and set him up with a spacious apartment at Versailles, where he could work in quietude overlooking the stately gardens planned by Le Nôtre. The workroom had eighteenth-century panelling and antique furniture. 'The table at which I wrote was itself the purest Louis XV,' said Massenet. 'Everything had been chosen by Hartmann at the most famous antique dealer's.'

So far as English readers are concerned, the pathos of Goethe's novel is for ever spoilt by Thackeray's Anglo-Saxon jokery. It is difficult nowadays to separate from the tribulations of Werther those famous lines in which:

> Charlotte, having seen his body
> Borne before her on a shutter,
> Like a well-conducted person
> Went on cutting bread and butter.

And although Massenet's Latin temperament was proof against such ridicule, his choice of *Werther* is at first sight a curious one. His greatest success had up to then been achieved with *Manon*, where his seductive melodic line wound its way through the world of Crebillon *fils* and of airy feminine perversity. *Werther* offered him, instead, a lovelorn boy, an altruistic heroine, and a bourgeois German setting far different from the milieu of scented intrigue which he knew so well how to reproduce. It is a token of his versatility—and of Hartmann's perceptiveness—that this *gemütlich* production stands among the peaks of his work.

The director of the Opéra-Comique was disappointed when the new piece was played over to him. Understandably, he remarked: 'I'd hoped you were bringing me another *Manon*. This depressing subject lacks interest. It's doomed in advance . . . ' Massenet was soon to have his revenge. The very next day the Opéra-Comique burned to the ground.

Some time after this Massenet was in Vienna, where the success of *Manon* had endeared him to the management of the opera house. He was asked if he could give them a new work. Nettled by the attitude of the Opéra-Comique, Massenet promptly offered them *Werther*. He never had cause to regret his decision. Throughout rehearsals he was treated with deference and luxuriated, for once, in an aura of good intentions. With the tenor van Dyck in the leading role, *Werther* received tremendous acclaim at its first performance in the February of 1892. A year later it made its belated appearance at the rebuilt Opéra-Comique. As usual Massenet stayed away from the theatre. It was very cold, and he marched restlessly up and down the courtyard of the Conservatoire in a flurry of snow. As the January night deepened the snow fell still more thickly and blizzards prevented carriages and buses from moving. Many of the audience had to remain in the Opéra-Comique until morning, and at eight o'clock next day Massenet learned from the lips of friends still in the evening dress they had worn for the performance that *Werther* had conquered. Nearly seven years had passed since he started to think about *Werther*, and it had taken a German opera house to show his French compatriots how wrong they had been in their opinion of the work.

The visit to Bayreuth confirmed Massenet's professional esteem for Wagner, who casts a long shadow both in *Werther* and in *Esclarmonde*. The cut of the melodies in *Werther* has become looser than in his previous work. The acts are conceived as unities rather than as a series of individual 'numbers', and the orchestral texture is rich in Wagnerian sonorities. Massenet knew which way the wind was blowing and shared with Puccini a flair for adapting whatever suited him best in the work of contemporaries and assimilating it into his own formulas. Yet he was very much more than an astute snapper-up of good ideas. Even Saint-Saëns was forced to admit: 'Massenet has been widely imitated. He, on the other hand, imitated no one.'

Werther contains some of his most individual features. The naïf little melody of the brief prelude, which returns in a murmur from the orchestra on Werther's first appearance and at his death, is a sister of the *bondieuseries* which had so annoyed Vincent d'Indy early in Massenet's career. There is, throughout all the passages to do with Charlotte's family and the village life of Wetzlar, a flavour of the innocent lyricism which inspired the *Scènes alsaciennes*. It occurs notably in the children's choruses, which are interpolated with fine dramatic sense. This simplicity runs like a silver thread through the famous moonlight scene of Act I, *bien chanté et soutenu avec un sentiment pénétrant*, as the orchestral direction runs. Here, for the first time, both Werther and Charlotte realize the impossibility of their love. The tune is introduced by an exquisite instrumental filigree of eight crisp measures supported by the harp, and then repeated in warm surging phrases from the violins, when suddenly, delicious in its unexpectedness, Charlotte's opening line, '*Il faut nous séparer*', starts in unison with the final cadence. The idea is simple yet so beautifully placed:

And again, just before Werther's despairing '*un autre! . . . son époux!*', a master's hand transfers this same dying fall to the woodwind. Touches like these abound in the score and are a constant delight.

The example quoted above is worth looking into more closely, since there is nothing more characteristic of Massenet's turn of phrase than this. The first bar traces a curve which is paralleled symmetrically in the second. The third bar takes up the melody in an ascending line and then comes to rest in bar four. Next, the original pattern occurs again, with, in bar seven, a parallel with bar three, and in bar eight a descent into the conclusion. The first half of the eight bars rises, as it were, in happy hope to a culminating point, while the second half slips into a downward curve with an impression of sadness.

Another typical feature is the way Massenet breaks up a line and varies it with displaced accents. This is shown in Sophie's lighthearted aria when she attempts to cheer up her sister Charlotte:

Here the method serves to characterize the skittishness and youthful inconsequence of Sophie—as, indeed, it has done earlier on with her song '*Du gai soleil*'. That the device is a versatile one is shown by Massenet's use of it to express Charlotte's lament for her mother in '*Si vous l'aviez connu*', and in the dying Werther's '*Là-bas, au fond du cimetière*' where the rhythm subtly suggests a funeral march.

The portrait of Charlotte is drawn in rather greater depth than Massenet had attempted before. There are, perhaps, traces of an Hérodias in '*Qui m'aurait dit la place que dans mon coeur il occupe aujourd'hui*', or in '*N'est-il donc pas mon coeur*'. Yet she has a self-denial and nobility that are foreign to his other heroines, with the possible exception of Grisélidis. Werther himself, of course, has some fine moments. His meditative '*O nature*', when he appears for the first time outside Charlotte's home, must be one of the last examples of the old-fashioned cavatina in the style of Faust's salutation of Marguerite's 'pure and chaste dwelling'. His tender '*Lorsque l'enfant revient du voyage*' is a more deeply felt extension of des Grieux' wistful vision of love in a cottage. Where he really comes into his own is with the celebrated aria which had gained an independent fame as *la Désolation de Werther:*

This violent expression of despair is a showpiece for the singer. It was added after the original score was completed, at the urging, so one account goes, of van Dyck who was the first to sing the part. If this is true, then both he and Massenet knew what they were about.

In general Massenet is too concerned with proportion and design to allow the orchestra a dominating role. He uses it more as a way of underlining or commenting on the action. The orchestra he writes for in *Werther* is of normal size, includes four horns and three trombones, and easily produces the thunderous *fortissimi* to which he was on occasion over-partial. In its function as commentator it is cleverly employed—one thinks of the combination of glockenspiel with cellos in the third act, and of the wintry *grisaille* in descending sixths which accompanies Charlotte as she starts to read Werther's letters. Elsewhere the orchestra is given a freer rein. It speaks alone in the scene where Albert hands over the fatal pistols to Werther's messenger, and in the prelude to the suicide it builds up to a climax not far removed from the manner of Tchaikovsky, a composer whose influence was from now on to appear several times in Massenet's operas.

Taken on its own terms *Werther* is an artistic success. The sequences are shaped with perfect balance, climaxes are developed with sureness, and the variety of mood and action is wonderfully maintained. It is one of the most obvious examples of the freshness, the command of the stage, and the grateful writing for voice and orchestra that characterize Massenet at his best. It also shows how he could husband his gifts to the utmost and use them so as to achieve theatrical effect in every bar he wrote. Played in the concert hall or studied in the library, theatrical music tends to sound exaggerated and unsubstantial. It should be heard on the stage, where it was intended to be heard, before it can properly be judged. That is why Massenet needs a theatre to make his full impact.

Apart from a solitary echo of *Don Carlos*—the orchestral bars preceding Charlotte's '*Va! laisse couler mes larmes*' reproduce exactly, by a queer trick of memory, a figure used by Verdi in Act IV of his opera—*Werther* is an authentic and mature expression of Massenet's personality as a composer. Many people consider it to be his best opera. Even Bernard Shaw, who was by no means an admirer of what Arthur Koestler has described as French Polish, had kind words for it. He was lucky enough to hear Jean de Reszke sing it in the Covent Garden production, and after having made legitimate fun of the story, with assistance from Thackeray, he went on to remark:

> Werther is a more congenial subject for Massenet than even Manon was. When he gets away from the artificial and rhetorical into the regions of candid sentiment and the childlike sincerities of love and grief he is charming. Des Grieux, a hero whom we forgive even for cheating at cards, suited him well: Werther suits him still better. The surroundings suit him too. The constant noisiness of the children when they are not rehearsing their carol or munching the bread-and-butter, make the first act quite delightful to a jaded critic sitting in a well-situated and comfortable stall . . . At all events, he [Massenet] has succeeded in keeping up the interest of a libretto consisting of four acts of a lovelorn tenor who has only two active moments, one when he tries to ravish a kiss from the fair as aforesaid, and the other when he shoots himself behind the scenes.

Shaw's approval of the first act was shared by Gabriel Fauré, who wrote:

> It takes place almost entirely in an intimate family atmosphere created by fluent and expansive orchestration which remains pleasantly engaging in its simplicity until the moment when, at nightfall, the drama is emphasized with the delightful appearance of Charlotte and Werther by moonlight. At this point the music, blossoming out in gentleness, raises itself to a pitch of the most concentrated, all-embracing and enveloping charm. Here M. Massenet reveals himself constantly and completely with his finest gifts, his most attractive qualities, and an extraordinary sureness of touch.

It is interesting to have the opinion of another French composer who, like Fauré, wrote music criticism as well. In private Debussy had a very low opinion of *Werther* and compared it with the unfortunate effects wrought on *Faust* and *Hamlet* by Gounod and Thomas respectively. Such people, he said in a private letter written in 1893, were nothing less than forgers. Some years later, in his public capacity as music critic to the *Revue blanche,* he was much more circumspect. Massenet now was to be praised for standing out against the boring imitators of Wagner.

> Massenet was the most genuinely liked of contemporary composers. It was this very affection people had for him which, by the same token, placed him in the special situation which he has not ceased to occupy in the musical world. His colleagues find it hard to forgive him that ability to please which is rightly a gift. To tell the truth, such a gift is not indispensable, particularly in art, and one may assert, among other examples, that Bach never pleased in the meaning of the word when it comes to Massenet. Have you ever heard it said of young milliners that they hummed the *Passion according to Saint Matthew?* I don't think so, yet everyone knows they wake up singing *Manon* or *Werther* in the morning. Let us make no mistake about it, this sort of delightful reputation is secretly envied by more than one of those great purists who have to rely on the somewhat laboured respect of cliques to revive their spirits.

Despite his lack of enthusiasm, Debussy could not help being influenced by Massenet in his own earlier works such as *l'Enfant prodigue, la Damoiselle élue,* the *Suite bergamasque,* the *Arabesques* for piano and the *Petite suite.* His ambiguous attitude towards Massenet is a little puzzling. One wonders why in public he diplomatically chose to sidestep the issue rather than to express the damning judgments he passed in his correspondence. Perhaps he did not relish the prospect of being a voice that cried in the wilderness. He was, in nearly everything, many years ahead of his time, and he may have been content to leave the task of puncturing Massenet's great popularity to the later generations who have done the job so well.

Throughout Europe *Werther* provoked a generally favourable reaction from the critics. It was a slow starter with the public and did not really establish itself in France until the beginning of this century. Since then it has been a regular feature at the Opéra-Comique, where its hero has committed suicide on more than one thousand four hundred occasions. During the rehearsals for the première in Vienna the tenor van Dyck, who was on very friendly terms with Massenet, produced the scenario of a ballet he had written in collaboration with a friend. Massenet liked it, and, as a by-product of the *Werther* period, composed a score in a few weeks while 'holidaying' by Lake Geneva in Switzerland. The scene was Courtrai in the fifteenth-century and the plot involved a watchmaker and his love for the daughter of a wealthy brewer. *Le Carillon,* an exercise in the style of Delibes, was put on at the Vienna Opera a few days after *Werther*. This *pièce d'occasion* left pleasant and comradely feelings behind it—and, one may add, no posterity.

The only event that clouded the success of his new opera for Massenet was the catastrophic and totally unexpected bankruptcy of his publisher. After many years of service to French music and of championing young composers whom other publishers were unwilling to risk their money on, Hartmann was faced with commercial failure. All the works on his list were put up for auction and he was ruined. 'My anxiety, as you can guess, was extreme', wrote Massenet. 'I expected to see my work of so many years dispersed among every publisher there was. Where would *Manon* end up? What would be the fate of *Hérodiade*? Who would get *Marie-Magdeleine*? Who would have my *Suites d'orchestre*?' For months his habitual state of anxiety was heightened by worry about the future.

Then Henri Heugel and his nephew Jacques Léopold Heugel stepped in. Proprietors of a family firm established in the eighteen-fifties and soundly based on the textbooks and manuals which, in music publishing, are the only sure foundation of prosperity, they bought up the whole of Hartmann's copyrights and goodwill. Though the price they paid was large it represented an excellent investment, and the firm has continued to publish Massenet ever since. Like Hartmann before them,

Heugel gave their star composer royal treatment and set him up on their own premises with a rehearsal room and office. Some time afterwards, while reporting a concert for his paper, the acidulous Willy saw Hartmann '... looking very seedy. They tell me he's trying to console himself for Massenet's departure by preparing a most interesting study of German literature. It is to appear shortly under the title *Heugel et Heugelianisme* ...' The punster's virtuosity did not excuse his cruelty.

VIII

THAÏS – LE PORTRAIT DE MANON – LA NAVARRAISE – A CALL ON VERDI – SAPHO

In Chapter 38 of *The Decline and Fall of the Roman Empire,* Gibbon turns the 'flutes and hautboys' of his measured style to a consideration of monastic life in the days of the early Christian church. Egypt, 'the fruitful parent of superstition', was then the home of innumerable hermits who congregated in the region known as the Thebaïd. The extravagant penance which these holy men inflicted upon themselves is described in pleasing detail:

> They sunk under the painful weight of crosses and chains; and their emaciated limbs were confined by collars, bracelets, gauntlets, and greaves, of massy and rigid iron. All superfluous incumbrance of dress they contemptuously cast away; and some savage saints of both sexes have been admired, whose naked bodies were only covered by their long hair. They aspired to reduce themselves to the rude and miserable state in which the human brute is scarcely distinguished above his kindred animals; and a numerous sect of Anachorets derived their name from their humble practice of grazing in the fields of Mesopotamia with the common herd. They often usurped the den of some wild beast whom they affected to resemble; they buried themselves in some gloomy cavern which art or nature had scooped out of the rock; and the marble quarries of Thebais are still inscribed with the monuments of their penance.

As the perfect example of this depressing form of zeal, Gibbon cites the 'aerial penance' invented by Simeon Stylites.

> Within the space of a *mandra,* or circle of stones, to which he had attached himself by a ponderous chain, he ascended a column, which was successively raised from the height of nine, to that of sixty, feet from the ground. In this last and lofty station, the Syrian Anachoret resisted the heat of thirty summers, and the

> cold of as many winters. Habit and exercise instructed him to maintain his dangerous situation without fear or giddiness, and successively to assume the different postures of devotion. He sometimes prayed in an erect attitude with his out-stretched arms in the figure of a cross; but his most familiar practice was that of bending his meagre skeleton from the forehead to the feet; and a curious spectator, after numbering twelve hundred and forty-four repetitions, at length desisted from the endless account. The progress of an ulcer in his thigh might shorten, but it could not disturb, this *celestial* life; and the patient Hermit expired without descending from his column.

Little more than a hundred years after Gibbon another writer was attracted to the subject. He brought the same irony, the same erudition, and the same delight in the absurdity of human nature. As early as 1867 Anatole France had written of how the desert monk Paphnutius converted Thaïs, the beautiful Egyptian harlot, and turned her into a fourth-century saint. In his poem, *la Légende de Sainte Thaïs,* France introduced his heroine with a graceful *enjambement*:

> En ce temps-là vivait une femme au pays
> Des Égyptiens, belle, et qu'on nommait Thaïs . . .

Twenty years later he was still obsessed by the lady, and this time he devoted a full-length novel to her. Those charming and very personal books, *le Crime de Sylvestre Bonnard* and *le Livre de mon ami*, had by then given him a reputation, and his ungainly person now moved, a sardonic smile on his lips, among the best literary salons in Paris. Vigorously taken up by the formidable Madame de Caillavet, the easygoing writer, who much preferred to while away the time reading or browsing in the second-hand book-boxes, found himself becoming a novelist and journalist of remarkable industry. *Thaïs* was the first novel he published under the regime of Madame de Caillavet.

Originally entitled *Paphnuce*, after the monk who transforms the courtesan into a saint, the novel was largely written on notepaper belonging to the Bibliothèque du Sénat where France had a sinecure post. It is doubtful whether Thaïs ever existed, and her story is thought to be a pious invention designed to encourage devoutness in the reader. The only Thaïs known to history is the Egyptian mistress of Alexander the Great. In order to clothe the scanty framework of his tale, the novelist drew on his wide reading of the legends and histories in which he loved to immerse himself. From the writings of the Abbess Roswitha he gleaned useful incidents, from the Egyptologist Maspero came factual information, and from various chroniclers and hagiographers he culled details and episodes which he embodied in prose both elegant and supple. The opening pages of the novel, for example, describe the country of the Thebaïd with great beauty. France's version of the ancient tale is typically mischievous in that Paphnutius, so admired for his piety, falls desperately and carnally in love with Thaïs. While the courtesan goes on to attain sanctity, the holy man slips irretrievably into sin. This is the novelist's revenge on a character whose joyless chastity and drear over-zealousness arouse in him the same distaste as Gibbon experienced at contemplating the excesses of Paphnutius' kind.

Madame de Caillavet persuaded the influential *Revue des Deux Mondes* to publish *Thaïs* as a serial. The author's Voltairean mockery of religion provoked the same annoyance as had Gibbon's, and controversy stimulated the circulation of the magazine in which the serial was appearing. Even the editor himself—he had, incidentally, been shrewd enough to change the title from *Paphnuce* to *Thaïs*—deplored the immorality of it all while at the same time admiring the artistry. When *Thaïs* came out in book-form its success rose to still greater heights. It gave Anatole France an established place among the leading writers of the day and inaugurated a period of literary fame and international celebrity that lasted for some thirty years.

Not long after the novel had made its sensational appearance Massenet's old colleague, the librettist Louis Gallet, came to visit him in his room at Heugel's offices. Supported in his arguments by Heugel himself, Gallet had little difficulty in prevailing on Massenet to choose *Thaïs* as the subject of his next opera. His task was made all the simpler by the composer's vision of Sybil Sanderson in the title role. Now that *Werther* had been successfully launched Massenet was ready to start on a new enterprise. In the autumn of 1892 he began composing *Thaïs* at Pourville, where, with his wife and daughter Juliette, he spent the holiday which preparations for *Werther* earlier in the year had delayed until now. 'I took with me a friend who never left me, day or night', he remembered,

> a huge grey Angora cat with long and silky hair. I worked at a big table placed before a verandah against which the sea waves, building up sometimes with violence, smashed themselves into foam. The cat, lying on my table and almost resting on the sheets

> of my manuscript with a freedom that delighted me, could not allow of such a strange and noisy splashing, and each time it happened she stretched out her paw and showed her claws as if to repel it!

Although both *Hérodiade* and *Thaïs* have an Eastern setting and take place within several hundred years or so of each other, it is the second of the two operas which is by far the more successful. The civilized atmosphere of Alexandria and the last refinements of Greek decadence early in the Christian era were sympathetic to Massenet, and he wrote the music in the space of a few months. The short score was already completed on arrival at Pourville, and the orchestration of the first two acts had been finished on his return to Paris three weeks later. Work on the last act was interrupted by several chores that took up valuable time, and it was not until the October of 1893 that he was able to reach the final page. Still very much preoccupied with Sybil Sanderson, who was to be his Thaïs in the first production, he wrote at the end of Act I: 'This evening in Paris, 152nd performance of Manon. S.' She was now appearing in most of his operas being played at the moment, and next day he recorded happily that she had sung to a big 'house' with receipts of more than six thousand francs.

Another distraction was his visit to Givet, in the Ardennes, where he represented the Académie des Beaux Arts at the inauguration of a statue to Méhul. A prolific composer of opera with an output that rivalled Massenet's own, the musician of *le Jeune Henri* and *Joseph* had a similar taste for colourful subjects which ranged from the Bible to Ossian. Méhul and the composer of *Werther* resembled each other at many points. They both started from obscurity and worked their way up, giving music lessons in the hard early years, toiling to develop their theatrical gifts, and eventually winning the affectionate admiration of society and their pupils. With deep fellow-feeling Massenet remarked in his speech:

> There is many a time of weariness, doubt and discouragement in the life of an artist. Méhul knew this more than any other. He had sometimes to battle against ill fortune, against plots and jealousies, and even private sorrows. During those days of bitterness Méhul would turn aside to his flowers and rediscover among them hopeful vistas and scented balm. He would forget his worries in long happy sessions looking at a flower-bud where all the colours harmonized before his eyes as did sounds in his

musician's mind. Tulips especially enthralled him, and some of them in his garden had such bright and varying colours that they excited him quite as much as the choice melodies that bloomed in his fertile imagination.

Massenet himself disliked chauvinism and always deplored the overblown pomposity that reaches its height on 14th July each year. But he could not avoid mentioning the *Chant du départ*, that patriotic song known to millions for whom the operas of its composer are a dead letter, and he flavoured the grandiloquent oratory expected on the occasion with a gentler tone:

> This statue of the patriotic musician whose inspired songs led the sons of France to defend its sacred soil should therefore be turned towards the frontier. Put beside it lyres and roses, lyres to symbolize his genius and roses because he loved them tenderly, but do not forget to add the trumpet that sounds the note of victory.

A few days afterwards he again paraded in the cocked hat and ceremonial sword of the Académie to attend Renan's funeral. There was little enough time for him, like Méhul, to pass the days looking at flowers, or even, as was reported by an imaginative journalist, to indulge in the fashionable craze for bicycling. It was said in a sporting magazine that he had become a member of the Union vélocipédique de France, and that at the banquet given by his fellow velocipedists he had celebrated by riding a bicycle around the tables. A jaundiced critic remarked that he had probably joined in the hope of recruiting a sizable *claque* among the numerous enthusiasts for the sport.

A more credible event was the act of friendship Massenet performed on behalf of his old friend Delibes. The jovial Léo had died at the early age of fifty-five, and the orations delivered at his funeral had a stronger vein of sincerity than is usual at such gatherings. Everyone liked him. He himself needed friendship so much that he would often call on one of his collaborators in search of some non-existent libretto as an excuse to sit beside a congenial acquaintance while he composed. Like all his friends, Massenet cherished Delibes' simplicity and good-heartedness, and was interested to hear that he had left an unfinished opera behind him. The task of completing it fell to Ernest Guiraud, who, by the decree of an unkind fate, is today remembered for the posthumous odd jobs he performed on behalf of Bizet and Offenbach rather than for his original works.[1] Guiraud died before he could set about it, so Massenet stepped into the breach. The opera was entitled *Kassya* and took its plot from several short stories by, of all people, Sacher-Masoch, whose inventive private life must surely have been unknown to the innocent Delibes. The setting is placed in Galicia, and it reminded Massenet of the trip he had taken with Delibes to Hungary and of the Balkan folk songs they had heard and noted there. The work took him longer than he would have needed for something of his own, as is always the case when another man's creation is taken over by a foreign hand, and for months he fiddled about replacing the spoken dialogue with recitatives and adding extra numbers to bridge the gaps left by Delibes. At last the opera was complete and was put into production at the Opéra-Comique. After reaching its eighth performance *Kassya* had to be withdrawn, leaving Massenet with, if nothing else, at least the feeling of duty well done.

By the end of 1893 *Thaïs* was ready for rehearsal at the Opéra. The whole of the winter was taken up with the usual crises and fluctuations between joy and despair that Massenet always experienced. Another trial he had to bear was his wife's attitude towards his *prima donna*. She had been discreet enough about Sybil Sanderson at the time of *Esclarmonde,* but she could keep up the façade no longer. She had formerly attended all the rehearsals of her husband's operas. Now she ostentatiously absented herself from the preparations for *Thaïs*, and Massenet and Sanderson, doubtless to their relief, were left to work with the rest of their colleagues undaunted by Ninon's disapproving eye. It was all the more important for Massenet that *Thaïs* should succeed, as Sanderson had just finished a short run in the opera *Phryné* by his old rival Saint-Saëns, and he was anxious not to be outdone.

On the eve of the first night Massenet slipped away to be alone with his fears at Dieppe and to escape, if possible, 'the throbbing anxieties which inevitably surround every work on meeting the public for the first time'. It was as well that he did so. At one dramatic point unforeseen by the libretto, a recalcitrant hook in Sybil Sanderson's glamorous costume played traitor and enabled the audience, in Willy's gleeful phrase, '. . . to see Mademoiselle Seinderson naked to the waist. She, much put out by the incident, didn't know which breast to turn to next'. (*Sein* is the word for that part of her anatomy involuntarily

[1] Although, by a neat turning of the tables, he died leaving his own opera *Frédégonde* incomplete, and this time it was Saint-Saëns who effected the ministrations for which Guiraud had become noted.

revealed by Sanderson and explains Willy's pun.) Next morning Massenet came back to Paris and was confronted with glum reports by the directors of the Opéra. The press notices were divided; general opinion declared *Thaïs* to be immoral, as it had the novel, and everyone thought they had a failure on their hands. Massenet refused to give up. He added the oasis scene, one of the best in the opera, and also a completely new ballet. Gradually *Thaïs* recovered from its unfavourable début and Massenet's faith in Sanderson was justified once again. When he came to write his reminiscences he was able to say: '... for close on seventeen years now the opera has been in the regular repertory, has been played in the provinces and abroad, and has long since passed its hundredth performance at the Opéra.' He could afford to ignore Willy's gibe: '*Thaïs* the question, *Thaïs* is money ...'

There is no place for subtlety on the stage, or at least for the subtlety which permeates the sophisticated periods of Anatole France. The author was at first displeased with the libretto Gallet showed him, and in future, whenever composers asked permission to adapt his novels, he would insist: 'Surtout, pas de Louis Gallet!' His reaction to Gallet's version was one of dismay: 'I didn't recognize my own novel', he complained. First there was the question of Paphnuce, the monk who converts Thaïs. Poor Gallet could think of few suitable rhymes for the name and got little further than words such as *puce* and *prépuce*. So he changed it to Athanaël, which rhymed with more acceptable words like *ciel* and *autel*. Then, when France saw his hero on stage, a young man with a fine black beard, he remarked sardonically: 'I see that my Paphnuce has become an elegant cavalry captain.' There were other more serious reasons for his discontent, and in the end he had to resign himself to the sacrifice of shades of meaning to the broader strokes which are necessary in the theatre. France was first and foremost a literary man, and he had little aptitude for the stage. The successful dramatizations of his novels in which Lucien Guitry appeared depended on the skill of the actor, who was also largely responsible for adapting them.

Massenet, then, fixed his attention on dramatic contrast and the evocation of atmosphere. The Thebaïd is brushed in with sober, dark-coloured orchestration and stately perorations by the hermits. There is nothing here of Gibbon's or France's elaborate jeers. Fresh from a visit to Alexandria, the sinful capital, Athanaël is tortured by memories of Thaïs, and the calm of the Thebaïd is shattered with frenzied harps accompanying his vision of the courtesan. Sudden exaltation comes to him in the resolve to save her from the bonds of the flesh, and he declares himself with a Meyerbeerian air:

The manner is virile and straightforward, with little hint of the careful and extended analysis France devoted to his hero's psychology.

The sybaritic life of Alexandria is presented with an exciting glitter heightened by Athanaël's sombre musings as he reproaches the city for its luxury and brilliance. The bustle of rich households and the chatter of gay serving girls is reproduced with the freshness and naïvety of similar episodes in *Werther*. What charming music the composer makes

out of: 'Hermodore! Aristobule! Callicrate! Dorion!' Crobyle and Myrtale try to render the churlish monk presentable in a duet of appealing impudence. [See example, pages 110-11.]

Another irresistible phrase occurs when Thaïs vamps the distrustful Athanaël and cajoles him with a tune in the composer's most alluring style. Even Anatole France came under the spell of this passage and chose it as one of his favourite episodes in the opera:

An example of the compression necessary for the stage is shown in Thaïs' famous Mirror aria. She realizes that, for all the throng of rich admirers who crowd after her, she is a lonely woman. 'We have loved each other for one whole week', she tells her latest protector after he has dissipated the greater part of his wealth on her. He agrees that such a long time proves remarkable constancy and he does not complain that soon she will be free and far away from him. But is she really free? she asks herself. Alone with her mirror she decides that men are brutal, women are wicked. The hours pass so very slowly. Her soul is filled with boredom. She does not know the meaning of true happiness. Her only solace is her beauty—but that too, she knows, will fade. Yet, seeing her lovely image in the mirror, she tries desperately to efface this melancholy thought from her mind and pleads with the goddess Venus to still the uncomfortable voice that whispers: '*Thaïs*, thou wilt grow old! The day will come when *Thaïs* is no longer *Thaïs!*'

Into this aria Massenet concentrates what took France many pages of detailed description. Though he works in much cruder colours, the effect in stage terms is successful.

The same type of problem was solved later in the opera by the much-abused interlude known as the *Méditation.* This was intended to symbolize the courtesan's dilemma as she wavered between thoughts of conversion and of carrying on her old life. Again, Massenet had to depict in a very short space of time an event which France, in the leisurely pages of a novel, could describe with ample and convincing detail. Like Saint-Saëns, who in *Samson et Dalila* had to dispatch the battle of Hebrew and Phillistine in a few minutes of busy orchestration, Massenet hopes the audience will play the game and fall in with his device. The *Méditation* has been offered up so frequently and so ruthlessly to the genteel tinkle of tea-cups among the palms, that it is worth recalling Ernest Newman's words:

Unfortunately the violin solo is almost invariably made far more sickly than it need be or should be, simply because it *is* a violin solo. It is the great chance of the evening for the leader of the orchestra. What concern of his is dramatic psychology? What's this Thaïs to him or he to Thaïs? The one thought in his mind is that here and now is the chance to show the audience what a good violinist he is; and so he sugars the solo with so much 'expression' of the type traditional among violinists that it becomes, on occasion, not merely saccharine but maudlin. Nothing of that sort was in Massenet's intention. The essence of 'Meditation' has already been heard in the orchestra in the scene of Athanaël's vision of the theatre in the first act, where it suggests the immensity of Thaïs' seductive power. The violinist and the orchestra should bear this in mind while playing the interlude: they should try to convey something at least of the contest that goes on within her, in those long night hours of lonely musing, between old passions and present regrets and aspirations.

So far there has been no conventional love duet such as Massenet's public expected of him. It finally occurs in the scene at the oasis which he added after the first production of the opera. Shuddering chords from the orchestra, followed by a slithering woodwind figure superimposed on a murmur of harps, creates a very effective impression of the sun striking ruthlessly down from on high, of heat dancing in the air and distorting the vision, and of dazzle that blinds the eye. Urged on by the triumphant Athanaël—'Break thy body, annihilate thy flesh'—Thaïs makes her way painfully over the burning sand towards the monastery that awaits her. In the midst of Athanaël's jubilation at having rescued her from sin, a spark of pity shows itself. They stop by the oasis and he brings her fruit and water. While she drinks and bathes her exhausted body they sing:

(très soutenu, tendre et intime)
THAÏS
pp
dolce
Bai-gne d'eau mes mains et mes lè - -
ATHANAËL (près de Thaïs, lui offrant la coupe)
pp
dolce
Bai-gne d'eau tes mains et tes lè - -
p
pp
dolce
p
dim.
pp
Th.
- vres, don - ne ces fruits, don - ne ces fruits, Bai-gne d'eau mes
A.
- vres, goûte à ces fruits, goûte à ces fruits, Bai-gne d'eau tes
dim.
dolce
f
pp
mains et mes lè - vres. Ma vie est à toi, Ma vie est à
mains et tes lè - vres. Ta vie est à moi, Ta vie est à
dolce
f
pp
sf
p
f
toi, Dieu te la con - fi - - e. Je t'ap-par-
moi, Dieu me la con - fi - - e. Tu m'ap-par-
sf
p
f
sf

'My life is yours, God has entrusted you with it', sings Thaïs, and Athanaël echoes, with a slightly different meaning, 'Your life is mine, God has entrusted me with it'. For by now he loves her with a carnal passion. As she enters the cell which has been prepared for her he exclaims, to the strains of the *Méditation,* 'I shall never see her again!' In the weeks that follow he is obsessed with longings for her. The holy calm he knew before he met Thaïs has vanished completely and his dreams are haunted by the provocative courtesan she once had been. Her beauty wasted away by the fasting and penitence she has imposed on herself, Thaïs dies in religious ecstasy. While she murmurs of the saints and prophets she sees waiting for her and of the heavens opening up, Athanaël, too late, confesses his love and pleads hopelessly that only life on earth is real. 'Pitié!' he moans as he sees before him a future of endless regret.

Anatole France, who liked Massenet personally, bore him no grudge for the havoc wrought by Gallet, and congratulated him in terms that showed he had nothing to learn from the composer so far as honeyed exchanges were concerned: 'You have raised my poor Thaïs to the front rank of operatic heroines', he wrote. 'It is you who are responsible for my most cherished reputation . . . I am happy and proud to have supplied you with the theme on which you have developed phrases of the highest inspiration.' The opera gave a new lease of life to his novel, and the *Méditation*—in a terrifying variety of transcriptions for every sort of instrument, including ocarina and harmonium, and once, even, reborn as a fox-trot—kept alive the memory of Thaïs long after people had ceased to read France's work. Only in 1956 did *Thaïs* drop from the repertory of the Opéra, where it had been performed nearly seven hundred times and had given opportunities not only to the violet-eyed Sybil Sanderson but also to Lina Cavalieri, Aïno Ackté and Mary

Garden. From the point of view of characterization Thaïs differs little, it must be admitted, from all the other heroines in Massenet's collection. Yet the music that she and the rest of the characters has to sing is so ingratiating, the orchestration so inventive and supple, that the charm of the opera still acts on a receptive ear. A few months after it was performed came the first hearing of *l'Après-midi d'un faune,* where Debussy's fluid melodic line developed still further the direction Massenet had taken with his flexible phrasing and broken rhythms. It is also worth quoting Poulenc's remark: 'I can never hear the second of [Debussy's] *Chansons de Bilitis,* which belongs to 1897, without thinking of "Miroir, dis-moi que je suis belle" in *Thaïs.*'

The opera crossed the Channel some fifteen years later. The English attitude towards Massenet was one of curiosity but not of enthusiasm. Among his operas, *le Roi de Lahore* had been well received, but *Hérodiade,* re-named *Salomé* out of deference to the Lord Chamberlain, achieved only two performances at Covent Garden, despite the prudent conversion of Herod into 'Moriame, king of Ethiopia', and of Hérodias into 'Hésatoade'. *Manon* was luckier, though Sybil Sanderson failed to repeat her foreign triumphs. Aware of the peculiar difficulties involved in presenting opera to the inhabitants of this island, Massenet expressed satisfaction with Joseph Bennett's 'clever and most interesting adaptation' of *Manon.* 'With perfect tact', he went on delicately, 'you have avoided what might have been difficult to make acceptable in England, and that is something it was essential to succeed in doing. You have succeeded!' Though praised by Shaw, *Werther* had never caught on with a large public. *Thaïs* made little stir in London and has rarely been heard here. Things were different, however, with *la Navarraise,* Massenet's next big opera, since not only was it given its first world performance at Covent Garden, but it also aroused more excitement than had any of his other works.

Before coming to London Massenet supervised the production at the Opéra-Comique of *le Portrait de Manon,* a sort of pendant to his earlier opera in which we meet again the chevalier des Grieux. He is now an older and calmer man who lives with the memories of his romance and jealously preserves a miniature portrait of his love. Remembering his own tragedy, he forbids his nephew to marry. But the girl his nephew has chosen slyly appears to him dressed so as to be the image of the Manon shown in the portrait. Overcome by the resemblance, des Grieux consents to the marriage and realizes that, in thinking to protect his nephew from the trap of passion, he was destroying his chance of happiness. The score, as Willy pointed out, is little more than a thematic catalogue of *Manon* and interweaves most of its principal tunes. 'Better late than never!' said Willy. 'Monsieur Massenet has at last found his way. No more huge operas like *le Cid* or *le Mage*, cluttered up with big drums and big pretensions, but a nice little opéra-comique in one act for four characters—two men, two women—including little choruses off-stage, a little peasant song, and a little marriage to end up with, the whole orchestrated with a skill that verges on artfulness. It's perfect.' Apart from enabling admirers of *Manon* to spend a nostalgic hour with an old favourite, this innocent little sketch gave a useful role to the singer Lucien Fugère who was later to triumph on a bigger scale in *le Jongleur de Notre-Dame*.

The first six months of 1894, which was a busy year even by Massenet's standard, saw the productions of *Thaïs, le Portrait de Manon* and *la Navarraise*. Until he came to write *la Navarraise* he had chosen for his operas subjects which were invariably remote from contemporary life, obviously believing that for such an 'exotic and irrational entertainment', as Dr Johnson defined opera, exotic and irrational settings were necessary. The inspiration for his eleven operas to date had come from sources as varied as Indian legend, Biblical literature, French eighteenth-century *galanterie*, Spanish epic, medieval tales, Persian religion, German romanticism, and early Christian hagiology. The reason for his choice of *la Navarraise,* a modern story, can be traced back to the appearance a few years earlier of Mascagni's *Cavalleria rusticana*. Mascagni introduced a novelty into the opera of his time, a suggestion of 'realism' and a directness that encouraged numerous imitations by composers eager to obtain the same forceful impact in the theatre. The tide of *verismo* ran high in Europe, and the most notable French composer to harness it for his own ends was Alfred Bruneau, one of Massenet's pupils. Bruneau quickly established himself with an opera called *le Rêve* based on the story by Émile Zola. (He had, at one time, wanted to set Zola's *la Faute de l'abbé Mouret*, but respectfully withdrew on learning that Massenet was also toying with the idea.) Bruneau's friendship with Zola was very close, and he absorbed much of the writer's naturalistic theories which strengthened his views on 'realism'. Next came *l'Attaque du moulin*, another work from the same source. Few, indeed, of Bruneau's operas had words other than by Zola, and he once remarked that his friend had provided him with enough libretti to keep him busy for the rest of his life. Bruneau's success in this new style of realism was thoughtfully noted by his former teacher, and

Massenet now started looking out for a chance that would enable him to try his own hand at it.

An opportunity soon presented itself in the form of a short story by Jules Claretie. Called *la Cigarette,* it is one of many hundreds Claretie wrote. He belonged to that breed of versatile men, not so rare in the nineteenth-century French theatre, who contrived to double a full-time administrative job with writings of astonishing prolificacy. For nearly thirty years he was manager of the Comédie-Française, where he grappled admirably with the problems of running a great theatre at the same time as he wrote dozens of novels, serials and plays, and kept up a fluent stream of dramatic criticism and newspaper articles. *La Cigarette* is a melodramatic story that takes place during the Spanish civil war of the early eighteen-hundreds. The libretto which Claretie and his collaborator Henri Cain produced for Massenet brought to the stage a heroine of Carmen-like intensity. She is Anita, the girl of Navarre, who is in love with Araquil, a young sergeant who belongs to the troops now being forced into retreat by the Carlist army. Araquil's father, a rich farmer, will not allow her to marry the boy unless she brings a fat dowry with her. When the troop commander offers a reward of two thousand *douros* to whoever will assassinate the Carlist leader, Anita grasps at the chance. She secretly creeps through the enemy lines, carries out the deed, and returns in bloody triumph. But Araquil, puzzled by her whereabouts and inflamed by jealousy, goes in pursuit. Anita is demanding the reward which she intends to be her dowry, when her lover is brought back mortally wounded from his expedition. The girl from Navarre falls weeping on his corpse and goes mad.

Massenet began to score the two-act work during a stay in Avignon. He found the grandiose sun-filled vistas of Provence a congenial background to the story of Spanish passion on which he was engaged. While there he went to visit the poet Frédéric Mistral, whose verse, written in Provençal dialect, enshrines the legends and customs of the region. The poet's *Mireille* had provided Gounod with the subject of an opera, and Mistral's loyal championship of the Provençal literary heritage influenced many writers, among them Alphonse Daudet, who was sensitive to its strange mixture of purity and savagery, that blend which also gives to the landscapes of Provence their unforgettable character. At Maillane, the poet's village home, Massenet was entertained in the drawing-room Daudet knew so well and which remained unchanged, '. . . the sofa with its yellow squares, the two straw-bottomed chairs, the armless Venus and the Venus of Arles on the mantelpiece, the poet's portrait, his photograph by Étienne Carjat, and, in a corner near the window, the desk—the humble little desk of some village postmaster—covered with old books and dictionaries'. Maillane was the scene of religious processions with pink flowered banners and great wooden saints carried on high, crucifixes framed in white silk and altars covered in green velvet, penitents in blue hoods, and saints of coloured faïence. At night, in the village square, '. . . in front of the little café where Mistral goes in the evening to play cards with his friend Zidore, a big bonfire had been lit . . . The farandole was organized. Paper lanterns were lit up everywhere in the darkness; the young people took their places; and soon, at a roll from the tambourines, there began around the flame a mad, noisy dance that was to last all night.' Among the folk tunes they played were doubtless the ones Massenet later utilized in *Sapho* to portray the hero's longing for his native Provence.

La Navarraise was finished in Paris at the end of the year. It was dedicated, as though to make up for the Sanderson diversion, to Madame Massenet. The orchestra required for this short work is a large one and calls for extra percussive instruments including bells. 'It is ESSENTIAL,' [wrote Massenet, underlining heavily]

> that these two BELLS have a very SOLEMN and very DEEP sound—they will be placed off-stage in such a way as to produce, for the audience out front, a *powerful*, *distant* and *melancholy* sound—they must be struck *very hard* with emphasis on the F sharp. If bells aren't available, use powerful sheets of steel (the same deep sound to be obtained)—then strike the F sharp on a low-toned gong to increase the note's vibration.

This effect, which occurs in Act II, was humorously admired by Bernard Shaw, who congratulated the producer on such 'huge and expensive pieces of bell-founding'.

Arrived in London for rehearsals, Massenet put up at the Cavendish Hotel in Jermyn Street. The Cavendish had not yet come under the proprietorship of the fabled Rosa Lewis, and one regrets that Massenet was never acquainted with the *confidante* of Edward, Prince of Wales, and of pretty well half the English aristocracy. By an excellent piece of casting *la Navarraise* was to be sung by Emma Calvé. She had already distinguished herself as Santuzza in *Cavalleria rusticana* and as Carmen, and she was a favourite with London audiences. The men singers included Albert Alvarez, who had sung Nicias in the first production of *Thaïs*, and the bass Pol Plançon, whose career Massenet had taken a personal interest in forwarding. *La Navarraise* was an outstanding event, both social and artistic, in the Covent Garden season. Among the audience who were startled by the 'most tremendous cannonade' with which it opened was the Prince of Wales. The lavishness of the staging was yet another success for the impresario Sir Augustus Harris. Calvé made a tremendous impression, reported Bernard Shaw,

> . . . for before the curtain had been up thirty seconds, during which little more than half a ton of gunpowder can have been consumed, she was a living volcano, wild with anxiety, to be presently mad with joy, ecstatic with love, desperate with disappointment, and so on in ever culminating transitions through mortification, despair, fury, terror, and finally—the mainspring breaking at the worst of the strain—silly maniacal laughter. The opera, which lasts less than an hour, went like lightning; and when the curtain came down there was something like a riot both on the stage and off.

Massenet, as usual, was not in the theatre for the first night, and he was somewhat annoyed to hear that Sir Augustus Harris, replying to the audience's frenzied shouts for the composer, had told them that he had withdrawn to smoke a cigarette but that news of the success would be sent to him as quickly as possible. He also, to his chagrin, missed an introduction to the Prince of Wales, who wanted to offer his congratulations. But the great send-off his opera received made up for the disappointment, and he was further consoled to hear that Queen Victoria had requested a command performance by the whole company at Windsor Castle. The barricade which figures largely in the action of *la Navarraise* was constructed with the aid of pillows and eiderdowns from the royal bedrooms.

It is undeniable that *la Navarraise* is the noisiest opera Massenet wrote. Willy, tongue in cheek, protested his surprise at the composer's limiting himself, apart from two or three arias, to '. . . numerous stage effects such as clapping of hands, rattling of tambourines, clicking of castanets, trumpet calls, ringing of bells, cannon fire, gun shots, pistol shots, etc., etc. It seems to me that a stage-manager would have been equal to the task and that there was no need to disturb, for so small a reason, a Member of the Institut.' In this *Cavalleria española,* as Willy mischievously nicknamed it with a nod to Mascagni, or *Calvelleria española* as another writer called it in homage to Calvé, there were nonetheless some worthwhile pieces of music. Araquil's cantilena, 'O ma bien-aimée, pourquoi n'es-tu pas là?' provides an interlude of quieter emotion, and his love duet with Anita owes less to *verismo* than to the Massenetic tradition. The gentle orchestral prelude to the short second act throws the turbulent climax into greater relief. It is a coincidence of history that only eighteen months afterwards, Lumière's first film show in Paris introduced a medium which used the same technique of brief episodes and concentrated action as *la Navarraise*.

The final judgment on this opera belongs to Shaw. Massenet, he concluded, '. . . has not composed an opera: he has made up a prescription; and his justification is that it has been perfectly efficacious. The drama is simple and powerful, the events actually represented being credible and touching, and the assumptions, explanations, and pretexts on which they are brought about are so simple and convenient that nobody minds their being impossible.' Massenet's own published opinions of the verist composers who had influenced him were, like everything else he uttered, cautious in the extreme. In Milan the following year to supervise the Italian production of *la Navarraise*, he spent many hours with Giordano, composer of *Andrea Chénier*, and Cilea, whose Puccini-esque *l'Arlesiana* was well-known at the time. 'In that great city', Massenet recalled smoothly, 'I had excellent friends, all of them famous, such as Mascagni and Leoncavallo whom I had known before in Paris when they never suspected the magnificent position they were to create for themselves in the theatre.'

Caruso had just revealed his talent in *l'Arlesiana*. 'I remember from my times in Milan,' said Massenet, 'having been present at Caruso's early beginnings. The tenor who has since become famous was then in very humble circumstances. When I saw him a year later, wrapped in an ample fur coat, it was obvious that the size of his fees must have mounted *crescendo!*' Another singer who became a close friend was the soprano Lina Cavalieri, and the Italian performance of *Thaïs* benefited from '. . . her beauty, her admirable physique, her warm and colourful voice, her passionate acting [which] enthralled the audience who praised her to the skies.'

While on the way to Milan for *la Navarraise* Massenet broke his journey and called to see Verdi at Genoa. His reception at the palazzo Doria was amiable in the extreme and the two composers chatted together

> . . . in his bedroom, and then on the terrace of his drawing-room whence you can look out over the port of Genoa and, beyond, to the open sea on the distant horizon. For a moment I had the impression that he was himself one of the ancient Doria

> family who was proudly showing his victorious fleets to me . . . As I was about to pick up the case I had put down in a dark corner of the spacious ante-room with its high gilded chairs in nineteenth-century Italian style, I told him it contained the manuscripts which never left me on my travels. Abruptly seizing the case, Verdi declared that he did exactly the same as me, wishing never to be separated from the work he had on hand. How I'd have preferred my case to contain his music rather than mine!

With maddening discretion the composer of *Werther* never revealed the subject of his conversations with Verdi and left us instead a page of fulsome platitudes.

A short while after Verdi's death Massenet had lunch with Lina Cavalieri. The hotel they chose had been the scene of Verdi's last days.

> The flower-decked table was laid in a large room adjoining the bedroom where Verdi died two years before. The room stayed exactly as it was during the time the famous composer lived there. The master's grand piano was still in position, and on the table he used were the inkwell, pen and blotting paper still marked with the notes he had written. His starched shirt, the last he ever wore, hung on the wall, and you could still trace the shape of the body it outlined! . . . A detail that vexed me, and one that only the avid curiosity of strangers can account for, was that pieces of this garment had been impudently cut out and borne away as souvenirs.

The case of manuscripts which aroused Verdi's approval for Massenet's working habits contained some of the music of the four operas he was writing while touring the capitals of Europe with *la Navarraise*. The first of these operas was *Sapho*, a work based on Alphonse Daudet's novel. 'Do you know of any novel that causes a more incurable wound than *Sapho*?' asked Marcel Proust. Directly inspired by the memories Daudet never forgot of an unhappy love affair in his own youth, *Sapho* is an anguished account of how a vulnerable young man falls victim to his passion and is destroyed by it. Woman is shown as the dominant partner, man as the weak and helpless object of her calculations. Step by step Daudet traces the degradation of the hero as he struggles with lust he cannot overcome. The novel is dedicated to 'my sons when they reach the age of twenty', and although one may at first think of it as a sermon, Daudet is too fine an artist to fall into the trap of preachifying. He makes his point by psychological analysis rather than by melodramatic evangelism. *Sapho* became one of his most successful books, and its popularity, often for the wrong reasons, kept it in print for many years.

Massenet had known Daudet when they were both penniless and obscure young men. They came to the notice of the general public at about the same time, Massenet's *la Grand'tante* being produced a few months after Daudet's *Lettres de mon moulin* appeared in book form. (Passages from the *Contes du lundi,* it will be recalled, inspired the *Scènes alsaciennes.*) A series of stories with the boastful Tartarin from Tarascon as hero won for Daudet a large following who enjoyed his humour, his Dickensian sentimentality and, above all, his gusto. Then he wrote novels satirizing contemporary politics, business life and society, often with a fury that becomes corrosive, especially in *l'Immortel*, an attack on the Académie Française. *Sapho* is proof that Daudet was much more than a best-selling entertainer with an eye for the picturesque and the easy emotional appeal.

The idea of turning *Sapho* into an opera belonged to Henri Cain. He was a busy man of the theatre who fabricated innumerable plays, always in collaboration with other writers and once with the son of Sarah Bernhardt. From *la Navarraise* onwards his name recurs frequently on the title-pages of Massenet's operas. One of his friends, Arthur Bernède, agreed that *Sapho* would be a good subject, and together they called on Daudet for his consent. The novelist accepted their plan, though warning them that the story and its modern setting were likely to upset admirers of the traditional repertory. '*Mais, mes enfants,*' he remarked, 'you'll be looked on as terrible revolutionaries by people who are fond of the old arias and *roulades*!' In answer to criticisms that their version was not particularly faithful to the novel, Cain and Bernède were later able to defend themselves by pointing out that Daudet had himself taken a hand in the libretto.

Massenet probably hoped to repeat his experience with *Thaïs*, where the opera was helped by the popularity of the novel and vice-versa. In any case, he was pleased to renew his association with the genial friend of his youth, and he was a frequent visitor during the period of Daudet's in the rue de Bellechasse between the quai d'Orsay and the boulevard Saint-Germain. There he came under the sharp eye of Léon, Daudet's elder son, already the violent character who was later to emerge as the bitterly brilliant pamphleteer of the extreme right wing in French politics. Even before he gained notoriety he was causing his father much worry, and his marriage to Victor Hugo's granddaughter had just ended, as his parents feared from the start, despite a novel

Alphonse wrote on the horrors of divorce and pointedly dedicated to him.

'Massenet, though he made a great deal of money, had the reputation of being a confirmed miser', grumbled Léon. 'No one ever obtained as much as a smell of his home cooking.' He observed Massenet in his father's home with a malice which, though blatantly unfair, makes highly amusing reading.

> His first task was to compliment everyone present on his or her looks or work, after which he would sink into an armchair and act as if he were a child or a lapdog which must be fed. Milk and cake would be forthcoming, and while he lapped up the one and sprinkled the crumbs of the other, he would relate airy nothings always intended to flatter some of his listeners. Among these there were sure to be several of those old ladies who 'simply adore' music and who smile lackadaisically as they display what are politely referred to as the 'handsome remains' of their former physical glories now fallen into decay. Massenet treated them as though they were still sweet and twenty, covering them with verbal bouquets which, in this instance, might have been funeral wreaths. Meanwhile, his nimble eye, passing beyond these venerable heirlooms, would discover some really young and pretty woman modestly keeping in the background. At once he would leave his chair, get down on his hands and knees, execute a sort of Pyrrhic war dance; in short, he would perform any antic likely to amuse—or annoy—the chosen one who, for the time being, had become his Dulcinea. The musician's shallow but swooning glances seemed to implore, to demand, the prompt satisfaction of his desires. He had all the inflammable sensuality of the lyre-bird or the peacock when it spreads its tail. But social conventions still exist; husbands may be present; in short, life is never as we wish, and Massenet would be obliged quickly to allay his fever. He would go to the piano, and there he would become transfigured, really great—in fact, incomparable.

As soon as the libretto of *Sapho* was ready, Massenet bore it off with him to the country. 'I set out for the mountains with a light heart', he recalled. He asked for nothing better than the joy of writing a new opera amid the austere solitude of Auvergne.

> We lived in a villa where I felt so far away from everything, from the noise, tumult and constant movement of town life and its feverish atmosphere! We went out for walks and long drives

> through that lovely countryside . . . We travelled in silence. The sole accompaniment to our thoughts was the murmur of the rivers that ran along beside the roads with a coolness we could actually feel; sometimes there was the splashing tinkle of some spring or other that interrupted the quiet of the luxuriant scene. Eagles, too, descending from their precipitous rocks, 'the sojourn of thunder' in Lamartine's phrase, came to surprise us in daring flight and made the air echo with their sharp, piercing cries.
>
> As we travelled my mind was busily at work, and on our return the pages of my manuscript accumulated.

He came back to a Paris full of excitement at a State visit from the Tsar of Russia. A million or so people lined the avenues and boulevards to watch the Tsar's progress through the capital. Like everybody else at the time, Massenet had left his home to see the spectacle. Suddenly, as he was standing by a friend's window near the parc Monceau, he thought of his household deserted by family and servants, and offering an open invitation to burglars. As soon as the procession had passed, he rushed to his flat in the rue du Général-Foy. There, on the threshold, he paused in horror at the sound of a whispered conversation from the drawing-room. Convinced that his fear had come true, he threw open the door to confront the burglars . . . and met the surprised glance of Emma Calvé and the librettist Henri Cain. They had come to discuss *Sapho* with him.

After Calvé's triumph in *la Navarraise*, Massenet naturally wrote *Sapho* with her in mind. He was impressed by the versatility which, in certain productions of *Hérodiade*, enabled her to sing either the contralto Hérodias or the soprano Salomé with equal facility. She could even lay claim to four different voices, the third being a head voice and the fourth being produced with the mouth tight shut to create an 'unearthly, disembodied' sound. She had, we are told, learned the trick from a castrato singer, although she never succeeded in teaching the secret of it to her pupils.[1] Her great emotional power and her vocal brilliance were given full expression in the testing part of Massenet's heroine.

The proofs of the score arrived and Massenet took them to play over for Alphonse Daudet. 'I can see Daudet still', he wrote, 'sitting very low down on a cushion and almost brushing the keyboard with his handsome head so capriciously framed with his fine and plentiful hair. He seemed deeply moved.' Daudet's emotion may well have been stirred by this new reminder in music of his youth and also by the

[1] *The Great Singers*. Henry Pleasants. Gollancz, 1967.

knowledge that his death was not far off. He had reached the final and incurable stage of the syphilis he first contracted, ironically enough, at the time of the events which inspired *Sapho*. In Daudet's vague, short-sighted look, Massenet liked to fancy that he could see his poetic soul shining forth. More realistically, Edmond de Goncourt attributed the dull expression of the eyes to the disease that was spreading through him. On the first night of the opera Daudet struggled into the theatre to take his seat. Next day he wrote to Massenet: 'I am happy at your great success. With Massenet and Bizet, *non omnis moriar*. Tenderly yours . . . ' The reference to Bizet, at least, has been justified by time, since *l'Arlésienne* survives for many who would not have known the play but for the music.

A few weeks afterwards the author of *Sapho* was dead. At his funeral in the church of Sainte-Clotilde the introduction to the fifth act of the opera was played during the service. 'When I threw holy water on the coffin', wrote Massenet sentimentally, 'I remembered my last visit to the rue de Bellechasse where Daudet used to live. I gave him news of the theatre and brought him twigs of eucalyptus, one of those trees of the South which he loved. I knew what intimate happiness that meant for him.' Once again Massenet's romantic make-believe annoyed the irascible Léon Daudet. 'I was obliged', Léon fumed, 'to deny formally this ridiculous fable after it had been told to hundreds of people and had found its way into the newspapers.'

On the other hand, there was little romanticism about another incident which occurred just before the staging of *Sapho*. The young composer Henri Busser, a pupil of Gounod's and winner of the Prix de Rome, was due for the performance of a one-act opera to which his prize entitled him. The director of the Opéra-Comique suggested he ask Massenet if it might be put on as a curtain-raiser for *Sapho*. After all, Massenet himself had once been in the same position with his own first opera, *la Grand'tante*, and there was no doubt that, remembering how it too had been taken up as a curtain-raiser, he would look with favour on a similar request from his junior. Busser duly outlined the suggestion to Massenet. The latter jumped from his seat: 'Don't you realize, *mon ami*, that you would get *four per cent out of the total twelve per cent royalties*? *Four per cent*—the figure set by the Société des Auteurs. Yes, yes! It's all very well for them to talk about *la Grand'tante*. But all I got then was *one per cent,* do you understand?' And he marched about declaiming 'four out of twelve per cent! four out of twelve per cent!' *Sapho*, needless to say, did not have a curtain-raiser.

Massenet need not have worried about the takings. *Sapho* was an immediate success, and, in the course of its first twenty performances at the Opéra-Comique, it took nearly a hundred and fifty thousand francs—considerably more than such box-office attractions as *la Bohème, Louise* or *Madame Butterfly* in similar circumstances. It achieved over eighty performances by 1900, though since then the pace has dropped and only an occasional revival brings to the stage once more the fiery artist's model Fanny Legrand and the indecisive youth Jean Gaussin. It is easy to see how Calvé made so much out of the part of Fanny, which is designed for big effects and strong climaxes. Her personality dominates the opera, while Jean, by comparison, strikes one as an even weaker character than he is supposed to be. Jean's dithering as he is torn between his mistress and his family is a further strain on the goodwill of audiences, especially modern ones. Yet when these faults are taken into account, we are left with an opera of genuine passion and superb orchestration.

In some respects *Sapho* is *Manon* brought up to date. It is possible to establish direct parallels between each of the five acts of the two operas so far as the action and development of the plot are concerned. There is even an aria, 'Ah! qu'il est loin, mon pays!' where Jean recalls the charm of his native Provence in the same style as des Grieux' meditative 'En fermant les yeux . . . ' But *Sapho* is undeniably late nineteenth century with its Bohemian artists' studios and assignations in suburban taverns. Some of the music owes a debt to Tchaikovsky, whose influence was already apparent in *Werther*. One of the big love scenes begins with Fanny's aria:

The echo of *Eugène Onegin* is a lingering one.

For Massenet, as for Bizet, Provence was a distant and exotic region that had the same stimulating effect on his imagination as it did on the writers who responded to the literary movement led by Mistral. Although most of *Sapho* takes place in Paris, it is the spirit of Provence that moulds the score and gives to it a clarity and a warmth that belong to the South. The bright sunshine and the luminous air are translated into lucid orchestral writing that is one of the charms of this opera. The themes Massenet uses to convey Jean's feelings for his native home, 'mon pays de clarté, de soleil,' are woven into the texture of the music with skill. One of the Provençal motifs which first appears in 'Qu'il est loin, mon pays!' returns later in 'Chers parents,' so helping to strengthen the idea of Jean's attachment to his roots. Another, and obvious, means to create atmosphere was to use traditional melodies as Bizet had done in *l'Arlésienne*. Massenet chose the old air, 'O Magali, ma tant amado', which Gounod had already used in *Mireille*. It is a bare and poignant little tune which he does not attempt to dress up and which therefore is very effective when he introduces it at just the right moments. The other folk tune used occurs during the fourth act, which is set in Avignon. From the distance comes the rhythmic sound of flageolet and drum beating out a farandole such as Massenet may have heard on his visit to Mistral.

Apart from the folklore elements mentioned above, the rest of *Sapho* is typically Massenetic. A strong feature is provided by the various love duets between Fanny and Jean, for, like *la Traviata,* the opera gives its best opportunities to the pair of lovers. In Fanny's 'Adieu, m'ami', the melody rises and falls in a very characteristic manner, and the prelude to Act V, which was played at Daudet's funeral, has the same sort of languishing melody as the famous *Élégie*.

An interesting documentary fact about *Sapho* is that it was, so far as we know, the occasion of the only gramophone record to be made by the composer. Early in 1903, some five years after the opera's first performance, Massenet was recorded while accompanying the soprano Georgette Leblanc. She had taken part in many provincial and foreign productions of *Thaïs*, *la Navarraise* and other works, and later married the poet Maurice Maeterlinck. The record she made with Massenet was of a scene from *Sapho*. It was never issued to the public since gramophones of the time were judged inadequate to reproduce it properly. At Georgette Leblanc's death a private pressing she had had made of the record was left to a friend, and it eventually came to rest among the Historical Sound Recordings collection at Yale University where it is now preserved. Those who have been lucky enough to hear it played on modern equipment all agree about its great interest and importance.[1] While there exists a comparatively large number of records made by Saint-Saëns and his fellow virtuosi, we have nothing, apart from the *Sapho* record, to illustrate Massenet's acknowledged brilliance as a pianist. It is a tantalizing thought that time and circumstance have prevented us from appreciating the skill which, in his early years, once persuaded him to think of adopting a virtuoso's career.

[1] 'Yale University Historical Sound Recordings Program: Its Purpose and Scope', by Jerrold N. Moore. *Recorded Sound,* No. 16, October, 1964.

IX

A COUNTRY HOME – CENDRILLON – CHARPENTIER – LA TERRE PROMISE – GRISÉLIDIS – MESSAGER – MONTE CARLO AND LE JONGLEUR DE NOTRE-DAME

IN 1896 Massenet was offered the post of Director of the Conservatoire. His seniority there as teacher of composition dated back to 1878. It has been said that he agreed on condition of being elected to the post for life, and that when this was refused he withdrew. Massenet's own reason for resigning was that the theatre was taking up more and more of his time. His absences from class had become frequent, and once, on the eve of examinations, he had dashed off to Aix for an important production without having the time to warn anyone. He was to be offered the post again in 1905, and again he refused for the same reason. 'No Directorship of the Conservatoire, no more classes. I felt younger by twenty years! I wrote *Sapho* with an enthusiasm I'd rarely known until then.'

While his departure from the Conservatoire brought relief, it also brought sadness. The post of Director had become vacant through the death of Massenet's old teacher and protector Ambroise Thomas. He was in his eighty-fifth year. The night before he died he had been at the Opéra to hear the prologue to his *Françoise de Rimini,* one of his best works. The morning dawned pure and cloudless, and the sun shone brightly into the Conservatoire flat where he had lived for so long. 'Fancy dying in such lovely weather as this!' were his last words. Massenet delivered the oration at his grave-side. There were references to the way Thomas mingled 'the honey of Virgil with the sharper savours of Dante', but when Massenet left aside the formal mood and spoke of Thomas as the gentle, attractive person he was, his tears ran freely. More than anyone he had reason to know of the old man's generosity.

In the meantime his daughter Juliette had grown up. Her First Communion, her birthdays and the excursions he took with her were carefully noted in his manuscript scores. She seems to have inherited a certain artistic ability from him, for there is a proud entry in the manuscript of *Werther* to the effect that her first picture, a pastel study of a head, had been accepted at an exhibition. She was nineteen then. Three years later he was bubbling with delight at the prospect of becoming a grandfather and was exchanging excited notes with Juliette's mother-in-law about the layette which doting relatives were preparing. The colour of the little garments was, hopefully, blue . . .

Gradually Massenet ascended the grades of official honours. Just before the death of Ambroise Thomas the Institut celebrated the hundredth anniversary of its creation. Its handsome premises, built by Mazarin, overlooking the Seine, provided the background to a succession of banquets, galas and receptions. The government marked the event by promoting Massenet to the rank of Commandeur in the Légion d'honneur. In 1900 he became Grand-officier. Soon after the news was announced he received a luxurious volume bound in Levant morocco sprinkled with stars. The parchment pages within contained a message of congratulations signed by over a hundred and fifty former pupils, including Charpentier, Bruneau and Reynaldo Hahn. 'Chers amis!' breathed Massenet gratefully.

The newly promoted Grand-officier celebrated the occasion by moving into a very old and very beautiful country home at Égreville. The little town lies on the edge of Burgundy, near Fontainebleau and Sens. In those days it had three hundred inhabitants, was modestly served by a small branch railway line, and went about its business of sowing and harvesting in a manner which had remained unaltered for centuries. The main street, bordered with houses of dazzling whiteness, led into a medieval square containing a Gothic church framed with trees. Ruined by the English in a long-distant war, it had been restored early in the nineteenth century, and once again its spire and slitted turret rose over the town. The walls had become grey with years, while by contrast the interior was kept neatly whitewashed. Wooden joists supported a roof through which, despite hasty repairs of lath and plaster, an occasional chink let in a ray of sunlight. The church threw a pale shadow over the farmers and dealers who met to haggle in the square below. There they would crowd into the seventeenth-century covered market-place which is still standing. It is a homely building, half stone, half timber, with a gable of masonry and roofs that sweep down on either side almost to the ground.

Massenet loved the place. 'There is a gentleness about the little square with its half-shuttered houses, as if they were giving you a sympathetic wink', he said.

> People move about with the calm of wise men who have weighed up their fate intuitively and who spare themselves from adding to inevitable misfortunes the foolishness of useless activity. Their humdrum way of life reminds one vividly of the second act in *Werther*. You remember: a square in front of a church in a little German town one Sunday, where all you notice is the song of three sentimental topers and the church-goers. The passions here take on the pure colours of flowers of the countryside. Albert is badly tormented by jealousy; but a native goodness controls his emotion. In spite of having submitted to her duty, Charlotte still hopes . . .

'Le château de Massenet' was approached over a mossy bridge decorated with stone urns. A Renaissance gate crowned by a salamander opened the way to the gravelled courtyard that lay in front of the house with its elegant twin turrets. Spacious gardens skirted the house and terminated on each side in an ancient moat and ivy-covered walls that circled the property. Everywhere there was a mass of foliage. Giant lime trees provided a background to the vine arbour where Massenet grew his favourite *chasselas*, a superior type of white grape. He loved trees and planted them everywhere, in groves and in lines that marched along the borders of his smooth, sweeping lawns. His grandchildren were instructed never to cut them down.

> These trees [he warned] will remind you that it was the hand of your grandparents, whom you loved so, which planned their foliage to give shade against the rays of the sun and to bring you their sweet and tender coolness in burning summers. With what happiness we saw those trees grow! We thought of you so much as we admired their slow and precious growth! Respect them. Do not allow the axe to strike them. If you do, the wounds you inflict on them will reach us beyond death, would smite us in the grave, and you wouldn't want to be responsible for that . . .

Often he would stroll in the grounds and reflect on his immense good fortune in acquiring this ideal home, the reward of so much hard work and so much exhausting labour. He would walk through a silence occasionally broken by the sound of his gardener raking up fallen leaves, and would sit for a moment on the edge of a wall topped with ornate Renaissance ironwork. Then, armed against the sun with a white parasol lined with green, he might go off into the town to see an old friend. Arrived in the square, he would pat the cheeks of the children who played there. He knew the names of all the dogs that frisked beside the church, even down to the obscurest mongrels. When the local band gave a concert on their usual site near the little cemetery he would stop to listen. Sometimes he invited them to perform in his courtyard at home, where he beat time on the gravel with his walking-stick and offered gentle criticism afterwards. He bought them instruments which their small funds could not afford, and wrote a *pas redoublé*, 'Salut à Égreville', for them to play. (Was it modesty, or a wish to avoid hearing them maltreat it in his lifetime, that led him to deposit the manuscript under seal at the town hall with instructions that it was not to be opened until after his death?)

The site of Massenet's house had been lived on ever since the tenth century, when the lords of Égreville built their château on the spot. It was destroyed and many times rebuilt afterwards by various owners, notably by the duchesse d'Étampes, a mistress of François I. Early in the nineteenth century it was stripped of its front and an attempt was made to demolish the great tower, the oldest part of the building, which dated back to the Renaissance. Fortunately the thickness of the walls prevented this. An artist then took over the abandoned ruin, did some primitive rescue work, and sold it to Massenet. The façade was restored and the old walls were shored up. Massenet turned the wilderness into a shaded retreat, planted a rose garden, and cultivated the rambling acres with a firm but sympathetic touch. When his handiwork was done he had created, among the woods and meadows of an unspoilt countryside, what he described as 'an oasis of peace and tranquility'.

For the rest of his life Massenet regarded Égreville as his true home. 'In Paris, I exist; in the country I compose, ten, twelve, sometimes fifteen hours a day', he told an interviewer.

> I live seven to eight months a year out here, far from Paris. My favourite spot is Égreville, a place as picturesque as you could wish, among ruins and old trees. I go to bed early there and rise with the dawn. I'm often ahead of the sun, which is a great idler at certain seasons, and I go and listen to the song of the woods and the valleys. I am passionately fond of nature and could never tire of its spectacle. A peasant who sings while

> driving his plough, a patch of sky with an unexpected colour that moves me . . . it's from impressions like these that my rhythms are born.

But Paris, dusty and noisy though it was, remained a place where Massenet needed a headquarters. In the same year as he took possession of Égreville he moved from his flat in the rue du Général-Foy to one in the rue de Vaugirard. If he could not have the greenery of Égreville to inspire him, he at least secured the next best thing with a view that looked over the trees and bushes of the Jardin du Luxembourg. The window of his large apartment was shaded by clumps of lilac blossom waving gently outside. A soft light filtered through the tufted branches and gleamed on the pink paint of Massenet's room. On a table stood vases filled with bunches of white lilac. In a corner was the glass-fronted book-case containing the manuscripts of his operas uniformly bound in sheepskin. At No. 48 rue de Vaugirard, Massenet was guarded from interruption not only by his wife but also by a watchful servant. The latter had caught his master's passion for punctuality, and anyone who arrived at ten past eleven for an appointment fixed at eleven was grimly received. This servant was also a music-lover. On the eve of an important first night, he said to Massenet: 'I'm very happy. We're going to have a big success. I've overheard one or two conversations. And, Monsieur, it's probably the first time I've never heard Monsieur swearing!'

Twenty or so years previously, boatmen coming down the Seine at dead of night would be surprised to see the brilliantly lit windows of a villa on the river's edge. 'It's Monsieur Gustave's house', the local people would tell them. Thinking hard about the exact position of a comma, meditating long into the darkness the choice of an adjective, the novelist Gustave Flaubert constructed his elaborate prose while most of his fellow Normans were asleep. In a similar way, belated pedestrians who found themselves in the rue de Vaugirard at four o'clock in the morning would be struck by the sight of a solitary window brightly lit among the sombre façades. It was Massenet's, and he had already begun the day's work. The lamp under whose rays he composed was celebrated in a sonnet addressed to him by Edmond Rostand, author of the romantic play *Cyrano de Bergerac*. The poet imagined that one night a pair of lovers saw the lamp in Massenet's window and murmured: ''Its . . . ' '(For none can be a lover without knowing you.)' The lovers throw a flower up to the window:

Était-il des Grieux? Était-elle Manon?
Qu'importe! Deux amants, l'ombre, un baiser, ton nom,
Ta lampe . . .Ah! que Chénier eût aimé cette histoire!
Aucun laurier ne vaut, si doux qu'il soit au front,
Le salut que toujours, en passant sous ta gloire,
Tes amis les amants à ta lampe enverront![1]

Somewhat different from this lyrical effusion was the view of the writer Paul Léautaud. As a young man he had lived in the same neighbourhood as Massenet. He did not claim to know anything about music, which, in any case, he always found too noisy. In summer, while trying to keep up with his writing, he would be driven mad by the sound of his neighbours practising the piano at open windows, and for this reason alone he was not very enthusiastic about the art. Still, he did not object to Massenet's music.

> You can see, nevertheless, just how it can please. There's something caressing about it, something sensual and languorous. I often used to pass Massenet in the rue de Vaugirard . . . I can see him still very clearly. He must have been very sensitive to the cold, because he was wrapped up in a comfortable petersham overcoat and a white foulard scarf, and wore a hat I've never seen anyone but him wear, a sort of felt top hat, lower and more splayed out than the usual shape. He was small in size and had a rather common face with a moustache like a wine merchant's.

Though in the street Massenet may have looked like a wine merchant to Léautaud's stern eye, the opera which he was about to launch at that period is so far removed from commonness as to be particularly noted for the delicacy of its writing. While in London for the first performance of *le Cid,* Massenet had had long discussions at the Cavendish Hotel in Jermyn Street with his librettist, Henri Cain, about possible future subjects. After several hours' conversation they both came to agree on *Cendrillon,* one of the best-known fairy stories by the seventeenth-century writer Charles Perrault. This was before Massenet had acquired his property at Égreville, and he took an old house for the summer at Pont de l'Arche overlooking the Seine. It was an ideal

[1] Was he des Grieux? Was she Manon?
What does it matter? Two lovers, the darkness, a kiss, your name,
Your lamp . . . Ah! how Chénier would have loved this incident!
No laurel wreath, however sweetly it sits on the brow,
Can equal the greeting which, on passing beneath your glory,
Your friends the lovers will always send up to your lamp!

setting for work on Perrault's exquisite little tale. On the street side a massive gate turned on enormous hinges to give admittance to the house. On the other side a terrace offered a magnificent view of meadows and woods stretching away to the horizon.

In this house the duchesse de Longueville, a contemporary of Perrault and enemy of the statesman Mazarin, had conducted political intrigues and entertained a distinguished series of lovers which included the moralist la Rochefoucauld and the soldier Turenne. So great was the legend of this beautiful woman, described once as the most accomplished actress in the world, that two centuries later the philosopher Victor Cousin dedicated his most important work to her and declared himself her 'posthumous lover'. She was a Bourbon-Condé by birth, and the *fleurs de lys* to which she was entitled were cut in the keystones above the windows through which Massenet looked out while writing *Cendrillon*.

> There was a big white drawing-room [wrote Massenet] with daintily sculptured woodwork of the period, and it was lit by three windows that gave on to the terrace. It was a masterpiece, perfectly preserved, of the seventeenth century. There were three windows, too, that gave light in the room where I worked, and where you could admire a chimney-piece which was a triumph of art in the style of Louis XIV. I'd found in Rouen a big table which dated from the same period. I felt happily at ease laying out the pages of my orchestral score on it.

The four acts of *Cendrillon* were later completed at Nice in the Hôtel de Suède. From there Massenet escaped for a fortnight to Milan where he directed rehearsals of a new production of *la Navarraise*. A little later the costumes and set designs for *Cendrillon* were prepared. These were put aside temporarily to make way for *Sapho*, as Calvé had been unable to sing the name part at any other time in the near future. *Cendrillon* was among the first productions of a man whose new reign at the Opéra-Comique was to cover one of the most flourishing periods in French opera. Albert Carré had learned his craft in the 'legitimate' theatre and for a quarter of a century he directed the Opéra-Comique with a hand of velvet in a glove of iron. Behind his tough exterior lay a personality of great shyness and modesty. It is as good a combination as any with which to manage an opera house. Without being very well up in music—he was always accused by sensitive composers, in fact, of not caring about it—he had the newspaper editor's flair for subjects on which he was not an expert, and in the end even the most reluctant musician had to admit that his suggested alterations were right. Himself a complete man of the theatre, Massenet was delighted with Carré's plans for *Cendrillon* when they were revealed to him. The director's modest little office, hung with red silk and cream stripes, became a place of enchantment for him throughout their debates on the staging of the opera.

The version of the Cinderella story which was presented to enthusiastic audiences at the Opéra-Comique in May 1899 kept close to the original. The chief difference occurs after the ball, when Pandolfe and his daughter Cendrillon decide to leave the town whence all gaiety has flown and return to the farm where they lived before his second marriage. 'Viens, nous quitterons cette ville', sings Pandolfe in a rush of pastoral feeling, while Cendrillon joins in with visions of gathering flowers to the sound of nightingales. The duet is closer, even, than des Grieux' rustic longings to the atmosphere of Marie-Antoinette's model farm at Versailles. The scene moves to the fairies' oak on a moor covered in flowering broom. In the distance is the sea. Night has just fallen, clothing everything in a strange bluish light. Amid the hum of assembled fairies and flittering will-o'-the-wisps, the 'Prince Charmant' is allowed to greet his Cendrillon. But perhaps, it is suggested, all this was a hallucination, because the last act opens with Pandolfe explaining that his daughter has been found unconscious beside a stream, and that after months of illness she has recovered. She is, in fact, restored just in time to try on the glass slipper and to enable the opera to reach its traditional ending.

Although spring may seem an odd time of year, in English eyes at least, to put on an entertainment more suited to Christmas, *Cendrillon* was much appreciated by crowded houses at the Opéra-Comique, and it ran for over sixty performances straight off. Massenet had retired with his wife to Enghien-les-Bains to avoid the excitement of the first night in Paris, and the ritual telegram duly arrived next day with news of his victory. It had been sent by Lucien Fugère, who, as Pandolfe, added new lustre to his growing reputation. The part of Cendrillon was taken by Julie Guiraudon, who improved the occasion by marrying the librettist Henri Cain. 'To Mademoiselle Julie Guiraudon', reads the dedication on Massenet's autograph score, 'the exquisite creator of Cendrillon at the Opéra-Comique (May, 1899)—this manuscript is offered by the grateful composer, J. Massenet.'

Everything about *Cendrillon* was lavishly conceived, from the richness of the costumes and the splendour of the scenery down to the pastel colours of the vocal score and its thick title-page embossed in gold. Inevitably, a comparison arises between Massenet's work and the music with which Rossini nonchalantly gilded the same story. The chief difference of approach lies in Massenet's emphasis on spectacle. This was something Rossini deliberately avoided, since the theatres for which he wrote lacked the mechanical resources necessary to engineer grand transformation scenes and to present the faery fantasies in which Massenet indulged. The clear Latin intelligence of Rossini had not a trace of Massenet's sentimentality, and at his hands Cinderella's Fairy Godmother becomes a wry philosopher employed by Prince Charming.

Elsewhere there are interesting similarities. Rossini's Cinderella, deserted at the fire-side, intones the sweetly mournful ballad 'Una volta c'era un re', while Massenet's heroine has her plaintive 'Reste au foyer, petit grillon', where she admonishes the cricket to stay on the hearth and not to envy the glamorous butterfly. In the *buffo* scenes involving Cinderella's grotesque family Massenet shows a vivacity akin to Rossini's. If he is to be reproached with the echoes from his other works that are to be heard in *Cendrillon*, then we should remind ourselves that the overture to *la Cenerentola* was borrowed from *la Gazetta* and that the concluding aria has an astonishing resemblance to 'Ah, il piu lieto' in the *Barbiere*. The saddest point of comparison between *Cenerentola* and *Cendrillon* is that neither of them enjoys today the revivals they deserve, the former because of the difficulty of finding good enough singers, the latter for the same reason and also because of the elaborate stage machinery required.

There is a great deal of *Manon* in *Cendrillon*. The heroine, in fact, is invested with more of the character of a daughter of Eve than one would expect a simple fairy-tale person to have. The love duets are handled with customary skill, particularly in 'Vous êtes mon Prince Charmant' and in 'Tu me l'as dit ce nom'. Massenet contrives a superb piece of stagecraft when Cinderalla arrives at the ball. The Prince, according to Perrault in the original story, goes to receive the unknown beauty. He '. . . gave her his hand as she stepped down from the carriage and led her into the room where the company was assembled. Then a great silence fell; people stopped dancing and the violins played no more, so rapt was everyone in contemplating the beauties of this stranger.' Here the orchestra falls silent and unaccompanied voices express their charmed surprise at the apparition. It is a perfect moment.

The grace and polish of *Cendrillon* are typified by the waltz from Act

I, long a favourite encore piece with the late Sir Thomas Beecham. The Fairy Godmother gives directions for weaving Cinderella's ball dress from the stars and their rays, from the moonlight and its beams, with colours taken from the rainbow. Her attendant fairies harness moths and butterflies to draw the coach. The jewellery will be provided by lady-birds and glow-worms, with fireflies and scarab beetles for diamonds and rubies. The following tune, all wedding-cake glitter and melting modulations, accompanies the Fairy Godmother:

Dances and ballets succeed each other with bewildering brilliance. A consort of lute, viola d'amore and *flûte de cristal* greets the entry of the Master of the King's Pleasures and his train. The pastiche of ancient dances has a command of seventeenth-century idiom as intuitive as that shown by the eighteenth-century minuets in *Manon*. The 'Florentine' and 'Rigodon du Roy' are preceded by an *entrée* cleverly evoking the archaic mandola. There is not a trick Massenet forgets to draw on from his considerable store of theatrical and musical legerdemain. Even the critic Willy, surrounded by an applauding first-night audience, could scarce forbear to cheer;

> It would have been impossible to understand if, with so many aces in his hand, M. Massenet had lost the game: he has won it triumphantly. To deny it would be dishonest. The clever composer has spared nothing to make this operetta of apparitions successful—neither the iridescent polychrome of fairies' wings, nor humming choruses, nor castanets, nor the Mustel organ, nor the abundance of fourths and sixths, nor real turtledoves, nor the pizzicati of mandolas, nor *buffo* ensembles in the Italian manner, nor the archaic prettiness of imitation minuets brought into fashion by *le Roi l'a dit,* nor the technique of fairy *galanterie* inaugurated by Messager in *Isoline* . . .

The presence of Willy, bearded, squat and stove-pipe hatted, at an entertainment involving dew-drops and fairies, cannot have been among the least engaging of the spectacles offered by *Cendrillon.*

Among the notes of congratulation Massenet found on his desk was one from his pupil, Gustave Charpentier, a former winner of the Prix de Rome. The following year Charpentier himself was to have his moment of glory with the opera *Louise.* It was an isolated moment. Apart from *Julien* he produced no successor to *Louise*, and although there were from time to time rumours of other masterpieces in preparation, Charpentier spent the rest of his long life in vaguely socialistic enterprises intended to bring music to the people by way of popular festivals, and in running an establishment which provided free music lessons for the working girls of Paris. He died as lately as 1956 in his ninety-sixth year, more than half a century after his one great triumph. His career raises the question whether it is more rewarding to have written an opera which is a landmark in French musical history, than to have produced a string of competent but minor successes. For *Louise* is undoubtedly a turning-point.

Charpentier knew well the working-class life of Montmarte in which his opera is set. During the winter that preceded his opera's appearance he lived in wretched poverty and kept himself alive with the cheese and eggs supplied on credit by an obliging dairyman who had a liking for music. *Louise* adds to the picturesque *vie de bohème* popularized by Henri Murger a note of social realism. A later generation may question the artistry of *Louise* and deplore its facile concentration on those aspects of the Paris scene most likely to attract the tourist, but its influence on the development of French opera was potent. Massenet was at the first night in February 1900, a grand occasion attended by the President of the Republic, and he wrote to Charpentier:

> I want to tell you again of *our* deep emotion. (My wife and family are passionate admirers of Louise!) You are an admirable artist, and my heart was filled with happiness on hearing the cheers of the whole audience! Thank you once more for the score and the words that show yet again the very touching and kindly affection you have for your old friend, an enthusiast from the beginning . . .

Massenet's pleasure was genuine, as it never failed to be when a former student of his was successful. Yet there was irony in the fact that two of his best pupils unwittingly contributed to the developments which were to give his own operas a dated air, even in his lifetime. First it was Bruneau with his realism, and now here was Charpentier carrying on the work. This change of circumstance was unconsciously emphasized only a few weeks after *Louise* by the performance of an oratorio, *la Terre promise*, which, except for several minor features, was a curious return to the style of religious works Massenet was writing in the 'seventies and 'eighties. He took his text from the Bible and spent several years composing the score. It includes an episode describing the fall of Jericho, embodied here in a stately march seven times interrupted by trumpets which, distributed throughout the church of Sainte-Eustache where it was first played, combined with the great organ to produce a stirring sound. The oratorio is distinguished for two fugues, both of them worked out with a loftiness and rigour that surprised admirers of *Manon*. They had forgotten that Massenet once gained a first prize in fugue at the Conservatoire. 'Do you want to judge what his marvellous technique was like?' the composer, Charles Koechlin, used to say. 'Then look again at the fugue that won him the prize.'

Little more was heard of *la Terre promise* and it shared a sudden obscurity with the oratorio Saint-Saëns wrote a few years later, also called *The Promised Land* and performed in Gloucester Cathedral, whence it never emigrated to France. Saint-Saëns' flirtation with oratorio was largely due to his love of Handel and his frequent visits to England, where the form was much cultivated at the time. Massenet's interest may have been reawakened by the recent concerts of religious music by Handel and Bach. Together with the new prominence given to Palestrina and others, they supplied a novelty in Parisian musical life at the turn of the century. *La Terre promise* was given on the same occasion as Wagner's *Das Liebesmahl der Apostel.* The latter piece, according to Willy, carried within it the germ of *Parsifal,* yet even a keen Wagnerian such as he could listen to it with little more than respect. In these circumstances poor Massenet received shorter shrift than usual. The fugues that had impressed everyone else reminded Willy of a notorious definition: 'A fugue is a piece of music in which all the players set off one after another and the audience sets off all together.' And the gentle pastoral sections of *la Terre promise*? 'Latrina Christi!' he replied with blasphemous wit.

A production of *Phèdre* at the Odéon towards the end of 1900 brought a request for incidental music. Massenet took out the overture he had written for Pasdeloup twenty-five years before and added to it several entr'actes, an 'Athenian' march, and a charming idyll entitled 'Hippolyte et Aricie', played by clarinet, horn and violin solo. 'Let *Phèdre* commence!' exclaimed Willy, adding in annoyance at the long applause that greeted the overture: 'Allons, Phèdre, Thésée-vous!' In his notice he raised the old problem of incidental music: if it is too good it distracts attention from the play, and if it is bad it irritates. For instance, he said, the measured thirds in G minor on the woodwind militated, by their very precision, against the evocative atmosphere of Racine's verse. As we have already seen, this was one of the few works of Massenet to earn Debussy's approval, and Willy conceded, with a smile: 'Racine's reputation now lacks for nothing.'

Nineteen-hundred was not, on the whole, a happy period for Massenet. While hundreds of thousands of visitors streamed into Paris for the Universal Exhibition, and the Belle Époque blossomed in a flourish of extravagant pavilions beneath the shadow of the Eiffel Tower, the composer lay in bed with a serious illness. The cause, doctors found, was the onset of uraemia. It was all he could do to attend the hundredth performance of *le Cid* at the Opéra, where he had to be helped on the stage to acknowledge an ovation from the audience. Then he went back to his bed. While he convalesced he had the feeling, he said afterwards, that '. . . the path from life to death is so easily travelled, the slope had seemed so gentle, so restful, that I regretted having retraced my steps, as it were, to see myself once more in the midst of life's hard and bitter anxieties.'

An illness, however grave, was no excuse for keeping Massenet from his work so long as he had strength to hold a pen in his fingers. Propped up in bed, with a stock of manuscript paper at one side, he forced himself on despite pain and inconvenience, and speedily piled up the pages of orchestration that formed a sizable mound at his other side. The opera he completed in this fashion was *Grisélidis,* a 'conte lyrique', which had occupied him on and off for some ten years. The bulk of it was written during his travels in the Midi and while staying at a villa lent him by a friend at cap d'Antibes. The villa, its white walls bathed in the hot sun of the south, stood on a hill surrounded by groves of eucalyptus, myrtle and laurel. As he laboriously traced the music of the final scenes, Massenet remembered how he used to leave the villa and go down to the sea along shaded paths through air heavy with the scent of flowers. The recollection helped to lighten the dreariness of the sick-room.

The subject of *Grisélidis* came from Boccaccio. It is one of the stories in the *Decameron.* English readers were introduced to it by Chaucer, who gave 'The pleasant comedy of patient Griselidis' to the Clerke in the Canterbury Tales. Thomas Dekker made it into a comedy, *Patient Grissil,* and many other writers were attracted by the tale. So were musicians, and during the eighteenth century it was the source of a baker's dozen of operas. At one time Bizet planned to use the story and wrote a certain amount of music for it. In the end the Opéra-Comique deemed it too expensive to put on, and the thrifty composer is believed to have utilized his material for other stage works. The original plot as Boccaccio told it concerns a haughty nobleman who has married a beautiful girl of lowly station. To test her devotion he tells her that their two children have been killed. Then he rejects her and, as a further trial, forces her to enter the service of a noble lady, there to work at the meanest tasks. Her devotion remains unfaltering, and she is reunited with her husband. He declares himself satisfied and explains that it was all in fun. The story is not an attractive one, and it is difficult to see why it appealed to such a number of authors, unless, since they were all men, it flattered their vanity. One does not know which is the more unappetizing: the crass conceit of the husband or the weakly submission of *Grisélidis.*

Massenet's librettists, happily, softened the more brutal aspects. Grisélidis becomes a gentle shepherdess whom the marquis de Saluce falls in love with and marries. She gives birth to a son, Loys. The marquis is called away to the Crusades. Enter the Devil, more comic than diabolic, who plans to tempt her while the husband is absent. His own domestic situation is, it appears, unsatisfactory, and he has sworn to visit on all other husbands the humiliations which his shrewish wife puts him through. He conjures up the handsome Alain, a former suitor of Grisélidis; he blackmails her by abducting her son; he teases her with all sorts of cunning tricks in the attempt to shake her fidelity. She remains unmoved. When the marquis returns from the wars he refuses to believe the slanders with which the Devil approaches him. In the end Saint Agnes intervenes and rescues Loys from the Devil's clutches, and the curtain falls to the strains of the Magnificat intoned by seraphs.

This mixture of unsophistication, buffoonery and poetry gave an excuse for creating what amounts almost to a jolly pantomime. Lucien Fugère, as the Devil, sang his jaunty couplets with relish and displayed a rich comic talent in his various disguises as a pirate and as an old Jew from Byzantium. The role of Grisélidis was sung by Lucienne Bréval, who had temporarily deserted the Wagnerian and classical opera in which she made her name to bring an attractive simplicity to the music written for the heroine. A little three-year-old girl appeared as Loys. In the second act, while lying on Grisélidis' lap, she had to fall asleep, and in order to give an impression of weariness she suggested that she let her arm fall as if overcome with fatigue. 'Oh delightful little ham actress!' said Massenet with admiring approval. The opera was played in settings of elaborate beauty. The forest of the prologue, airy and translucent, featured a pool in which the sky was mirrored. In the second act the castle was seen from a terrace at sunset, framed with slender umbrella pines and shrouded in blue evening mists. The last act presented a golden altar at which Grisélidis and her husband pray for the return of Loys. It gradually became lit with a bright blaze and the leaves of the triptych slid open to reveal the boy sleeping at Saint Agnes' feet.

As for the music, it is nicely attuned to the mixed moods of the action. Grisélidis' oath of fidelity is prefaced with some strange dissonances—strange, that is, for Massenet—which help to create the other-worldly air of the scene. When Grisélidis' lady-in-waiting reads to her from an illuminated manuscript, she does so to the ghostly sound of hunting horns fading in the distance. Grisélidis' aria, 'Il partit au printemps', has the sweet melancholy of a medieval 'complainte' which is paralleled in Bertrade's *chanson*, 'En Avignon, pays d'amour'. The marquis' farewell to Loys contains a passage which quotes momentarily from the prelude to Act II of Massenet's next opera, *le Jongleur de Notre-Dame*. Indeed, quite a lot of music, especially the duet 'L'oiselet est tombé du nid', has the same quality as that of *le Jongleur*. It is the style of *Esclarmonde*, lucid and simple but purified of the self-consciousness which sometimes mars the earlier opera. By contrast, the

Devil provides interludes of bouncing drollery with his scurrying pizzicati and malicious trills.

The conductor of the orchestra at performances of *Grisélidis* was André Messager. He was in his third year as musical director of the Opéra-Comique, where Carré had put him in charge of new productions. Reynaldo Hahn, an excellent conductor himself, once declared that neatness was Messager's distinguishing characteristic on the rostrum.

> M. André Messager has it to an exceptional degree, and shows it as much in his way of writing and orchestrating as in his manner of dressing, speaking and playing the piano. But it is when he conducts an orchestra that his neatness, which you might call organic, shows itself most notably . . . He seems to use his bâton less to conduct the orchestra than to enlighten the public. His movements are those of a connoisseur, who, with great delight, remarks one after another on all the beauties of a piece of music, pointing them out, savouring them, analysing them with a delicate and methodical eloquence. All pomposity, all exaggeration, is banished from his commentary; here we have a brilliant, precise and satisfying improvisation by a well-informed mind.

Messager's path to the Opéra-Comique had been long and difficult. His parents, like Massenet's, had known financial hardship, and his early interest in music as a hobby was necessarily turned into a means of earning a living. He took lessons from Gabriel Fauré at the École Niedermeyer, where Saint-Saëns initiated them both into the forbidden delights of Wagner and Liszt.

> As I saw him then, [Fauré recalled] so I have seen him at every stage in life: familiar with everything, knowing it all, fascinated by anything new, provided the music was worthy of his attention. He had been one of the first pilgrims to Bayreuth and could play Wagner by heart at a time when the latter was still unknown in Paris . . . His orchestration is clear, full-bodied, rich in happy inventions, and full of piquant sonorities; you will never find in it the indifference and careless oversights which have so often spoilt works of light poetry.

It is worth quoting the opinion of Fauré, since Messager is often unjustly dismissed as a simple fabricator of musical comedy. That he was a considerable musician is proved by his membership, with Saint-Saëns and the song-writer Henri Duparc, of an informal committee to which Fauré was in the habit of submitting his latest music for advice and criticism.

After various appointments as church organist and a string of odd jobs in the musical world, Messager achieved his first success with the ballet *les Deux pigeons,* which was produced at the Opéra through the friendly intervention of Saint-Saëns. He went on to write many light operas which justified Fauré's high opinion and showed a superb gift for the theatre. (Look again at *Véronique* and you will see a good example of the technical mastery and harmonic freshness which characterize his work.) A famous incident in his crowded life, which included the direction at various times of the Opéra, the Opéra-Comique and Covent Garden Opera House, was the first night of *Pelléas et Mélisande.* On the morning of this historic occasion he had attended the funeral of his beloved elder brother, yet there could be no more convincing proof of his excellence than the professional way in which he conducted the opera, after rehearsals at which he had shown a rare insight into the new and difficult music. Debussy, with good reason, dedicated the score of *Pelléas et Mélisande* to the memory of his publisher Hartmann and 'as a mark of deep affection to André Messager'.

The rehearsals of *Grisélidis* were not such a trying time for Messager, though there were moments of strain nonetheless. To the distraction of the conductor, Massenet was in the habit of moving agitatedly from singer to singer as they went through their parts. There was not a detail that Massenet failed to check or to revise if need be. Messager was relieved that the composer followed his usual custom and did not inflict his disturbing presence on him at the first night. At eight o'clock that evening Massenet wrote to a friend: 'At this very moment . . . the curtain is about to rise . . . and here we are, my wife and I, in the tranquillity that "*ignorance* and *oblivion*" bestow. What's going on over there? . . . At this moment . . . what excitement on one side—*here . . . what calm.*' He came with his wife to the second performance. Cheered by the news that the box office had taken maximum receipts of over nine thousand francs, he toured back-stage lavishing tremendous compliments on everyone he met.

Grisélidis was the last of Massenet's full-length operas to receive a first production at the Opéra-Comique. At least half a dozen of his works, including *Manon* and *Werther*, were still played regularly there, and he was always welcomed whenever he looked in to supervise a revival or to see how a production was faring. It could not, indeed, be otherwise, since he had contributed a great deal to the prosperity of the Opéra-Comique, and no other French composer could boast so many operas in the current repertory. But there was a change of atmosphere in the place. Although Messager always carried out his duties with scrupulous musicianship, he had little personal enthusiasm for such popular successes as *Grisélidis, Manon, Carmen, Louise, Werther* and *Lakmé*, which could be relied upon to please the box-office manager and fill the house. He much preferred the opportunities that came his way to conduct Mozart and to satisfy his taste for novelty with Rimsky-Korsakov and Mussorgsky. The arrival of Debussy was another element that darkened the horizon at the Opéra-Comique for Massenet. His silence about his revolutionary junior is instructive, and nowhere in his published writings did he refer to Debussy with the exaggerated praise which he usually accorded to his great contemporaries. The composer Henri Busser was then acting as Messager's deputy at rehearsals of *Pelléas et Mélisande,* and he wrote in his diary for the 12th April 1902:

> I met Massenet in the theatre corridors and persuaded him to come and listen to *Pelléas* which was being rehearsed in the auditorium. He watched the last two tableaux with me, without saying a word. Debussy caught sight of him, came up to greet him, and Massenet told him of the great emotion he felt in the presence of a work that was so new, so unexpected!

The tone was one of diplomatic ambiguity.

Several months before *Grisélidis* appeared at the Opéra-Comique, Pierre Lalo, the music critic and son of Édouard, came across Massenet walking down the rue de Vaugirard. They went into the Jardin du Luxembourg to get away from the noise of the traffic. Lalo asked Massenet what he was writing at the moment. 'Oh!' replied the composer in one of his youthful bursts of enthusiasm, 'something very remarkable. In fact, "remarkable" is a very weak word to describe it. I want to say, like Madame de Sévigné in her famous letter, the most astonishing, the most surprising, the most unheard-of, the strangest, the most unbelievable . . . Guess. No, you'll never guess. I'm writing a play, a legend, a tale with music, call it what you like, *in which there's not a single woman's role!* Not one, do you understand, not the smallest role for a woman. What do you say to that?' After enjoying Lalo's surprise, Massenet went on: 'I'm getting towards the end, and for several days I've felt, I've *known* with certainty that *le Jongleur de Notre-Dame* will be my masterpiece.'

Now Massenet was not the best judge of his own works. At one time or another he declared at least half a dozen of his operas to be his 'masterpiece'. In the excitement of the moment, stirred by admiration for a particularly good performance or moved by the beauty of a leading lady, he was apt to grant the accolade indiscriminately. In some respects he was like the actor who inevitably claims that his latest production is his best. It can be said, however, that *le Jongleur de Notre-Dame* has qualities which give it a place on its own in the body of Massenet's work.

In the Spring of 1901 he had gone to Égreville bent on convalescence from his illness.

> I took with me a great load of correspondence made up of letters, pamphlets, files, which I'd not yet opened. I planned to look at it on the way to take my mind off the slowness of the journey. I undid several letters. I'd just opened a package: 'Oh no,' I said, 'it's too much!' I'd discovered, in fact, yet another play . . . Did the theatre have to pursue me like this still? I thought. When I didn't want to have any more to do with it! So I threw aside the intruder. While the journey continued I picked up the manuscript again, rather to kill time than anything else, as the saying is, and began to look over the contents of that famous package, however unwilling I might have been.
>
> My attention, superficial and absent-minded at first, gradually concentrated—I began to take an unconscious interest in my reading, so much so that I ended by feeling genuine surprise—which became, shall I admit, amazement even.
>
> 'What!' I cried, 'an opera without a woman's role except for a silent appearance by the Virgin Mary?'

Where now were Manon, Thaïs, Sapho, and all the other seductive ladies his public expected of him? It was true, as he could argue, that the Virgin Mary was the sublimest of all women.

The medieval legend on which *le Jongleur de Notre-Dame* is based was published in a learned journal early in the eighteen-seventies. Anatole France, who had a flair for this sort of thing, turned it into an exquisite short story which he included in the volume entitled *l'Étui de nacre*. He tells how the humble juggler Barnabé earns his bread travelling the country from town to town on fair-days. He lays down his threadbare carpet in each market square and performs his tricks, juggling with copper balls that flash in the sun, and adding to them a dozen knives that fly in a perfect circle. His life is cruel and laborious. Yet he does not complain, for he is a pious man of simple religion. He never passes a church without entering and praying to the Virgin Mary. One rainy day, when his usual cheerfulness deserts him, he takes shelter in a monastery. Impressed by his goodness the monks accept him as one of themselves. At first he is happy, but when he looks around him and sees the clever ways in which his new companions serve the Virgin—writing books, painting miniatures, sculpting, tracing elegant calligraphy—he despairs of his ignorance and lack of talent. 'Alas! alas! I am a crude fellow and without art, and you I can serve, Madam Virgin, neither with edifying sermons, nor treatises well drawn up according to the rules, nor delicate paintings, nor statues accurately chiselled, nor verse counted in feet and marching in rhythm. I have nothing, alas!' One day an idea comes to him, and from then onwards he is no longer sad. He spends hours in the chapel at times when it is empty. The Prior, curious to know what he does there, comes and watches him unobserved. He sees Barnabé lying before the altar juggling with the six copper balls and the dozen knives. Thinking that Barnabé has gone mad, the scandalized Prior steps forward to stop this sacrilege. At that moment the Virgin Mary herself comes down the steps of the altar and wipes the sweat off the juggler's forehead with the lappet of her blue robe. At last he has found his own way of glorifying her. 'Blessed are the pure in heart', cries the Prior on his knees, 'for they shall see God!'

The story is told with a deliberate simplicity that adds much to its charm, and it is one of the best things Anatole France ever wrote. (Agnosticism, it seems, is a good qualification for writing beautifully on religious subjects. France is an example of this, and another is Ernest Renan, author of the classic life of Jesus.) Massenet's libretto was the work of Maurice Léna, a professor of philosophy at Lyon university. His close acquaintance with the medieval atmosphere enabled him to give his text a genuine feeling for the period and an attractive flavour of archaism. Massenet did not take long to compose the music. One day in August he met his collaborator at the little railway station in Égreville, hurried him over to his house, and there displayed to him the four hundred pages of manuscript orchestral score, together with the vocal score which he had already had engraved.

The exuberance of composer and librettist gradually faded as month followed month without any sign of *le Jongleur* being accepted for production. Theatre managers were uneasy about this new departure. They thought it foolish of Massenet to have written an opera not only on a religious subject, which was ill-advised enough to begin with, but also one without a heroine to please the large audiences he had always attracted with his portrayals of frail but fascinating women. So *le Jongleur* languished on the shelf until one day Massenet had a visit from the director of the Théâtre de Monte Carlo. His name was Raoul Gunsbourg, and he was for many years a colourful and noisy figure in the theatrical world of Paris and the Principality of Monaco. As late as the nineteen-twenties he was to be seen on the boulevards, toothless but swash-buckling as ever, the assiduous squire of very young girls. Though his talent lay in production and theatrical administration he fancied himself as a composer, and in 1906 an opera he concocted, with the aid of God and the conductor of the Monte Carlo orchestra, was put on in Monaco.

'You cannot be unaware', he proclaimed to Massenet, who was himself an adept at grandiloquence and appreciated it in others, 'that the capital of His Highness Prince Albert I now possesses, thanks to Him, an opera house built, like yours, by Charles Garnier. As an informed music-lover he is an enthusiastic admirer of you, a master of French music, and he would be honoured if new works of your inspiration were to be performed upon this stage; everything would be done to ensure that the production is worthy of them.'

Hastening to pay due tribute to his visitor's genius as a producer, his charm as a friend, his brilliance as a composer, Massenet quickly handed over the score of *le Jongleur*. A private performance was arranged at the house of the publisher Henri Heugel, in the avenue du Bois de Boulogne. His Serenest Highness came in person and expressed his satisfaction. The opera was forthwith put into rehearsal. In February, 1902, Massenet and his wife gratefully left the snow and ice of Paris for the sunshine of Monte Carlo. They stayed in the Palace, where they were treated like visiting royalty. 'The dream had begun', said Massenet. 'Need one emphasize the wonder of those days we spent as in a trance, in that Dantesque paradise, in the midst of that splendid scenery, in that luxurious and sumptuous palace where everything breathed the scent of tropical flowers?' This was the beginning of Massenet's Indian summer. Paris may have been a little less responsive to his advances lately, he may have felt that younger men were contesting the eminence he had enjoyed unchallenged up to now, but in Monte Carlo the sun was always shining and he could look forward to a welcome unqualified by the reserve which had crept in elsewhere. The ornate little theatre which Charles Garnier had built there, embodying as it were an overflow of the rococo fantasy which inspired his Paris Opéra, was to be the scene of half a dozen gratifying triumphs for Massenet from his sixtieth year onwards.

Le Jongleur de Notre-Dame, so piquant a contrast in subject with the rakish atmosphere of Monte Carlo, was applauded warmly. At the end of the performance Massenet was summoned to the Prince's box and there, in full view of the audience, decorated with the ribbon of the Order of St Charles. Although no one rushed from the gaming tables to demonstrate card tricks at the altar, there was no doubt that Massenet's opera, despite its absence of pretty women, had been a success. Two years later, by which time Massenet's faith in it was seen to be not misplaced, Albert Carré, 'mon cher directeur', at last put it on at the Opéra-Comique in Paris, where its third revival in 1939 testified to an active life spread over more than three hundred and fifty performances.

The scene is the square in front of the abbey of Cluny in Burgundy during the fifteenth century. Jean, a wretched juggler, tries to squeeze a few coins out of an indifferent audience who have seen all his tricks before. They persuade him to sing a sacrilegious drinking chorus. The Prior of Cluny emerges to rebuke Jean for endangering his eternal soul. Softened by Jean's repentance, he invites him to enter the monastery and expiate his sin against the Virgin he has offended. From then on the action follows the plot of the old story, except that after performing before the altar and being visited by the Virgin Mary, Jean dies happily haloed with glory.

> Among the many libretti which gave Massenet's tremendous activity the opportunity of writing operas more important, bigger, and of keener or deeper feeling, [wrote Fauré] I know of none that gave him a more constantly sustained or more charming inspiration than the lovable poem of *le Jongleur de Notre-Dame*. Massenet has transcribed and exalted the youthful dash, fine temper, serene emotion and tenderly religious perplexity which it contains with a uniformly happy touch, and, I will add, the rarest frankness, the clearest artistry and the most precious care.

The chief impression is, as Fauré remarked, one of uniformity throughout. There are not many other operas in which Massenet achieved such a happy balance of musical interest. He moves with smoothness from the boisterous couplets of Jean's 'Le vin, c'est Dieu le Père' to the serenity of Friar Boniface's 'Pour la Vierge d'abord', and there is no feeling of incongruousness at the quick transition from the hearty teasing of the monks to the gentleness of the 'Légende de la Sauge', where Boniface tells the old story of how the common sage gave the hospitality of its calyx to the infant Jesus while the proud Rose disdained to help. The changing moods of the action are imperceptibly fused together, and the whole work is unified by a remarkable evenness of inspiration.

Simplicity is the tone of *le Jongleur*. It is a simplicity, though, which could only have been achieved by the most cunning art. The motto of the work is a chorale theme which finally emerges to the Prior's words, 'Heureux les simples car ils verront Dieu', during the juggler's apotheosis. Another element is the tune of the 'Légende de la Sauge' which appears again, passing through some enchanting modulations, in the *Pastorale mystique* linking Acts II and III. It was the thrifty habit of medieval troubadours to use the same song for quite different purposes, and a *chanson* addressed to the pretty eyes of a shepherdess would do service also as a hymn to the Virgin Mary by the simple substitution of a different name. So Jean, having laid his carpet before the altar, preludes on his viol and treats his divine audience to the patter with which he was accustomed to attract the fairground crowds. Then he bursts into a lively war song, only to realize half-way through that the din may well frighten Mary. He switches to a little ditty about 'Belle Doette', but forgets the words, to music which perfectly shadows his comico-pathetic embarrassment. After singing *le Jeu de Robin et Marion* he asks Mary if she is ready now for his juggling tricks, a little magic, griffins or flying devils even? ('Forgive me . . . it's habit! Between you and me I'm pitching it a bit too strong. As you know, patter is never completely sincere.') While the horrified monks intone imprecations against his sacrilege he kicks his heels in the air and dances a clumsy *bourrée*.

The scene at the altar is the centre-piece of Act III, much as the episode where the monks exalt their different ways of serving Mary is the focal point of Act II. This latter is introduced with a music lesson which the musician-monk is giving to his colleagues. The pleasant humour of the passage leads naturally into a good-tempered contest between the monks as they vaunt their different pursuits. 'Juggling?' says the sculptor-monk, 'it's a shabby craft, you ought to be a sculptor.' His painter colleague elbows him aside: 'Inanimate marble cannot give life, but under the all-powerful brush you see creation throbbing and quivering.' They are both dismissed by the poet-monk, who emphasizes the crudeness of their art compared with his. The musician-monk intervenes in the quarrel with soothing talk of harmony. None of them will agree, and it is perhaps Friar Boniface who has the last word as cook when he hymns the Virgin Mary in an aria which unites gastronomy with mysticism. Is not the sage blessed by Mary a valuable aid in cooking? he asks. Did not Jesus accept with equal grace the gold, frankincense and myrrh of the three kings as well as the shepherd's modest reed-pipe tune? At which point Jean conceives his great idea.

Besides giving Jean his inspiration, Boniface is also responsible for some of the high lights in an opera by no means sparing of good things. It is Boniface who, in the first act, brings for Mary the flowers she loves —carnations, lilacs, myosotis, eglantine, lilies, anemones, helianthus and periwinkle. For her humble servants, he adds, here are fresh onions, ripe pears, cress from the meadows, velvety cabbage and flowering sage:

The witty turn of this aria excuses the deliberate Handelian anachronism which Massenet allows himself. In the Paris production the role was sung by Fugère, who, excellent alike as singer and actor, played it, so people said, with perfect naturalness and geniality. Another, and later, piece of casting gave the lie by a curious twist to the description of *le Jongleur* as an opera without women. For the production at the Metropolitan Opera House which followed soon afterwards, Mary Garden decided to play the Juggler herself *en travesti*. Massenet was horrified at the idea and for a long time struggled to make her change her mind. He was unsuccessful. 'My feelings are somewhat outraged, I confess, at seeing the monk throw off his robe after the performance so as to put on an elegant dress from the rue de la Paix', he gently remonstrated later. 'Still, I bow before the artist's triumph and applaud.'

Le Jongleur de Notre-Dame is lit by the rosy glow of stained-glass windows. Its characters are like those primitive figures depicted in glistening colours on the pages of illuminated manuscripts. In creating the atmosphere he wanted Massenet used his material shrewdly. The monks' 'Ave coeleste lilium' at the beginning of Act III, in the chapel where Jean is shortly to pay tribute after his fashion to Mary, comes from a sequence formerly sung at Assumption, the source being Saint Bonaventura. Jean's impious *Alleluia du vin* in Act I was written after close study of the *chansons farcies* which used to be a speciality of the old minstrels. All these elements are featured with skilful judgment and blended into a satisfying unity with the rest of the work. By comparison with the 'bondieuseries' of the oratorios and the stiff stateliness of

Esclarmonde, the emotion in *le Jongleur* is much warmer, more alive and that much more natural.

Le Jongleur was also to have an influence on Puccini. With his customary reserve, Massenet never expressed a public opinion about the rising young composer sixteen years his junior who was now a formidable rival in a field which he had previously dominated. The only reference he makes in his memoirs is when, speaking of a dinner with his Italian publisher Ricordi, he says: 'There is little need to add that we drank to the health of the famous Puccini.' (He must have studied Puccini's music with guarded and respectful interest.) It was *Manon* which had decided Puccini to write his own *Manon Lescaut,* so called to distinguish it from Massenet's version. Massenet, said Puccini according to his biographer Mosco Carner, felt the subject as a Frenchman, 'with powder and minuets'. He, as an Italian, went on Puccini with endearing *grandiosità*, would feel it 'con passione desperata'.[1] There are many traces of Massenet in Puccini's music, and not only in *Manon Lescaut.* Both textually and musically Puccini's *Suor Angelica* is the most directly affected by a work of Massenet. Written some fifteen years later, it has in common with *le Jongleur* a single-sex cast, (Puccini, understandably, chose women), a convent as the setting, and a miracle in which the Virgin Mary appears and blesses the transgressor. But Massenet, by then, was in his grave, and we shall never know what his reaction to Puccini's opera might have been.

[1] Mosco Carner: *Puccini.* Duckworth, 1958.

X

CIGALE - CHÉRUBIN - ARIANE - LUCY ARBELL - THÉRÈSE

IN the third year of this century, a young composer called on Massenet in the rue de Vaugirard and brought a score for him to look at. After Massenet had read it and offered some kindly advice, the conversation took a general turn. Why, asked the visitor, had *Esclarmonde* never been revived? Massenet's expression changed abruptly. There were personal reasons, he explained evasively, behind his decision not to authorize a revival of *Esclarmonde*. It was the opera in which Sybil Sanderson had scored her great triumph, and when she died in 1903 at the age of thirty-eight, he could not bring himself to confide to another the role which was for ever associated in his mind with the singer whose beauty and talent had made such a poignant impression on him. The high-lying tessitura which the opera's heroine has to encompass was, of course, a factor which limited the choice of singer, but his chief motive remained the affectionate memory of Sanderson. The opera was only revived, long after he himself died, in 1923 and in 1931. He always maintained that *Esclarmonde* was as much her creation as his, and he persisted in giving it a quite disproportionate place of honour among his works.

Her death was a harsh blow to him. In the early days of his grief he would pour out his misery to everyone he met, even to the most casual acquaintances. He never forgot the long brown hair, the ivory complexion, the violet eyes that rivalled the flash of diamonds in Thaïs' head-dress, the soft Californian accent that had given her voice a charm no other woman could equal for him. After he discovered her she had sung in other operas than his. At the Opéra she was a lovely Juliette and in *Rigoletto* a frail Gilda. Towards the end of her life she was an enchanting Phryné in the first performance of Saint-Saëns' witty operetta. It is for her connection with Massenet, though, that she will be remembered. 'You have justified my faith in you', Massenet wrote to her in the first glow of their relationship, 'because it was for you that I wrote *Esclarmonde*, and you have proved in today's rehearsal, Saturday, the 11th May 1889, that I entrusted this role, unique on account of the difficulties of every sort which it involves, to an artist who is herself unique. It is your début, but I predict a future for you that will be unique also. In time to come, when people talk about the glories of the theatre, they will speak the name of Sanderson.'

Despite Massenet's enthusiasm, Sybil Sanderson never completely won the approval of critics. Though struck by her beauty and her talent as an actress, they nearly always found some reservation to make on the subject of her vocal performance. 'Mademoiselle Sanderson has not confirmed the splendid promise she showed', said one reviewer; 'strange in *Esclarmonde,* she was only pretty in *Manon*, and she endangered the success of *Thaïs* at the Opéra.' This was an exceptionally stern judgment, yet even the most favourable opinions were usually mingled with qualification. It seems that she had great natural gifts which she could not wholly succeed in developing as well as she might have done. Her top G, according to the best judges, was a phenomenal achievement, and a wit nicknamed it the 'sol Eiffel' after the tower which at that time astonished Parisians with its vertiginous height. Her impressive range of three octaves was given full scope in the operas Massenet wrote for her, and he 'produced' her, Pygmalion-like, with all the considerable musical and stage-skill at his disposal. Since, however, she did not depend on the stage for her living and was able to lead a comfortable social life with the money her father left, she probably did not give so much time to her professional career as she ought to have done. She was rumoured to have spent four hundred thousand francs on launching the Belgian dramatist Francis de Croisset in the world of letters. He wrote adaptations for the stage of novels by Maurice Leblanc, Octave Feuillet and Somerset Maugham, and light comedies of which the best are those he wrote in collaboration with the talented Robert de Flers. Croisset, wrote someone maliciously, '... has the face of a footman, though admittedly one in a high-class establishment. The mysteries of love! It looks as though she launched him badly, however, because he never went very far.' Whether Massenet knew of this supposed liaison has not yet been discovered. Either way, a few years later he raised no objection to setting de Croisset's play *Chérubin* as a musical comedy.

Whatever the critics' opinion might be, Sanderson was for Massenet an 'ideal' Manon, an 'unforgettable' Thaïs, and 'one of the most superbly gifted people I have known... *Esclarmonde* was, in spite of everything, to remain the living memory of that rare and beautiful artist whom I had chosen to create the work in Paris; it enabled her to make her name famous for all time.' In May 1903, enveloped in a cloud of sadness, he was at the funeral of the woman '. . . who had been cut down by pitiless death at the height of her beauty and in the full bloom of her talent'. The crowd that pressed around the funeral procession was silent and numerous. With Albert Carré, director of the Opéra-Comique, Massenet headed the mourners behind the coffin which contained

> . . . the pathetic and beloved remains of what had once been beauty, grace, generosity, talent with all its attractiveness; and, as we experienced a common feeling of emotion, Albert Carré, interpreting the mood of the crowd and its sentiment for the lovely creature now vanished, said these words, so eloquent in their brevity and so unforgettable: '*She was loved!*' What simpler, more touching and more deserved praise could have been paid to the memory of she who is no more?

Massenet was sixty-one years old. His illness of three years before, and now the death of Sybil Sanderson, were severe tests of a constitution which, though schooled by a lifetime of discipline, had begun to show signs of strain. Unusually for him, that year of 1903 remains a blank so far as new productions were concerned, though any composer of lesser industry than Massenet would have taken pleasure in the fact that four of his operas were currently being played. In the spring of the year, which marked Berlioz' centenary, he went to Monte Carlo as the Institut's representative at the inauguration of the Berlioz monument. As one who had known every success while he was still alive, Massenet commiserated with a musician who had received so little applause during his career. Did Massenet suspect that in his own case the tables were eventually to be turned with almost mathematical precision?

> One might say [he observed of Berlioz] that his present reputation is built of his past sorrows. He was misunderstood and knew little but disappointments. Nothing was seen of the genius in that vigorous artist's face, no one was dazzled by the halo which already crowned him. Is it not, then, a miracle indeed to see this man who, while alive, had the appearance of a vanquished fighter, an unfortunate and tormented being, a seeker after an ideal which always seemed to be elusive, a breathless pioneer in art whose thirst was eternally unquenched, a musician of wretchedness who was often stoned, is it not, I say, remarkable that he should draw

> himself up after his death, pick up those stones which had been thrown at him, and use them to make himself a pedestal and dominate the world?

Massenet's success in Monte Carlo, where *le Jongleur de Notre-Dame* brought him local celebrity, had not gone unremarked by his sharp-eyed rival Camille Saint-Saëns. Though he was now approaching his seventies, the composer of *Samson et Dalila* remained as fertile in music as he was pugnacious in advancing the cause of his own works. He wrote, with frenzied determination, a dozen or so operas, yet none of them, except the one already mentioned, held the stage for long. The theatre was the one domain in which this extravagantly gifted musician failed to enjoy the easy triumphs that came his way elsewhere. Moreover, the fame which had been his for over half a century was now being overshadowed by younger composers more in sympathy with contemporary musical developments, and he chafed irritably at the uncomfortable experience of having become a legend in his own lifetime. If Paris would not have him, he decided, then Monte Carlo would be allowed the privilege. So he let it be known, with discretion but with firmness, that he would not be averse to writing an opera for that gracious and munificent patron of the arts, Prince Albert I of Monaco.

The hint was not ignored, and once again Raoul Gunsbourg set out for Paris in search of a new opera for His Serenest Highness. After a little decent hesitation, Saint-Saëns allowed himself to be won over. He had always wanted to write something about the classical Helen. Undeterred by his irreverent predecessor Offenbach, whose satirical operetta would seem to have taken the bloom off the subject for anyone else, he wrote his own libretto which presented Helen as the slave of destiny, the victim of Aphrodite, a tragic heroine whose fall should provoke a sacred fear rather than mockery. While travelling through Egypt on one of those restless wanderings to which he was addicted, he completed his libretto, so he modestly said, with the aid of Homer, Theocritus, Aeschylus, Virgil and Ovid. The music was dashed off on a boat travelling slowly up the Suez Canal, and the finishing touches were added in various hotel rooms in Biarritz, Cannes, and Aix-en-Savoie. The nomad *Hélène* finally came to rest in Monte Carlo during the season of 1904. Being a one-act piece, it needed a companion to furnish out the evening's entertainment. It would be diverting to know what Saint-Saëns' reaction was when he learned that Gunsbourg had decided to pair *Hélène* with *la Navarraise*.

Hélène was given a splendid launching with Melba in the cast. Next day the *Journal de Monaco* predicted that it would doubtless be the outstanding triumph of the season. But *Hélène,* which pleased the Monégasques, soon withered in the sharper air of Paris, where even the efforts of Mary Garden and of a lady unpromisingly called Madeleine Bugg failed to save it from the oblivion into which it swiftly, though not quite deservedly, vanished, Saint-Saëns was not put off. His double billing with Massenet was the opening skirmish in a competition between the two men which, formerly confined to Paris, was now transferred to the more exotic setting of Monte Carlo. Saint-Saëns was to have two other new productions to his credit there, besides revivals of his earlier works, while Massenet was easily to outdistance him with a score of seven. On the occasion of *Hélène* Massenet stayed at home in Paris and left Saint-Saëns to glory undisturbed in the applause, his beard twitching with delight and his great parrot's beak of a nose sniffing happily as the cheers thundered out in the auditorium.

Massenet's excuse for not appearing at what might have been a piquant confrontation was the fact that *Hélène* coincided with one of his own first nights in Paris. It was not an important one, but Massenet supervised its preparation with the care which he always gave to anything in which he was involved. The piece was a two-act ballet he had written for a charity bazaar which eventually was cancelled. Rather than let it go unproduced, he allowed it to be staged at the annual benefit performance on behalf of the employees of the Opéra-Comique. It was called *Cigale,* and, with a few pretty flourishes added by his librettist Henri Cain, it told the fable of the grasshopper and the ant as recounted by La Fontaine. The wordly old fabulist would have been discomfited at seeing his grasshopper, now a true Massenetic heroine, dying of hunger in the snow surrounded by angels and the murmur of a celestial choir, but the audience, conscious that charity was the purpose of the evening, professed its satisfaction. Massenet himself derived an innocent pleasure from writing the score, and his treatment of an old carol and some deft variations on *Au clair de la lune* showed clever touches. A few months later he brought a similar lightness to the incidental music for a production of *le Grillon du foyer* at the Odéon. Here Charles Dickens' cricket chirruped a *Chanson du grillon* which put everyone into a good humour and was succeeded by a song from another member of the hearth, the kettle, and by a symphony of Christmas bells. The story's popularity in France dated from one of Dickens' visits to Paris, when he gave a public reading of it while sitting for his portrait by Ary Scheffer. (It was on this visit that Dickens saw and admired Auber's *Manon Lescaut*. Auber, he found, was 'rather petulant in manner', though eager to talk about his youthful experiences in England when studying the language at a place called "Stock Noonton"—which Dickens, no mean linguist, was able to translate as Stoke Newington.) The production, with its music, was revived in 1921, on which occasion an over-enthusiastic producer sought to embellish the Anglo-Saxon spirit of the tale by adding movements from the *Scènes alsaciennes*.

The five-hundredth performance of *Manon* at the Opéra-Comique in 1905 showed that if Parisian audiences had cooled in their attitude towards Massenet's later works, they remained faithful to the old ones. This gala performance was conducted by Alexandre Luigini, one of Massenet's former pupils at the Conservatoire. He is, alas, notorious for his *Ballet égyptien*, a piece of Wardour Street flummery whose claim, if any, to serious consideration was long ago dissipated by a famous music hall trio who used it to hilarious effect as the 'vamp till ready' accompaniment of their soft-shoe shuffle. Despite the mockery that now surrounds his name, Luigini was an excellent musician. He had been conductor at the Opéra-Comique for several years and had just become its musical director. Soon after the gala performance of *Manon* he died at the early age of fifty-six. The part of des Grieux' father was taken by the ever-reliable Fugère, who was for long identified with the role. The date chosen for the performance was 13th January. Massenet's superstitious fears were amply confirmed. On that very afternoon occurred the death of his elder sister, the 'bonne et grande soeur' who had taken him in and given him shelter when he first came back to Paris as a penniless but hopeful student at the Conservatoire. At the same time an irony of chance brought him, once again, an offer of the post of director at the Conservatoire. He once more refused it.

It was on a rare outing to the theatre that Massenet came across the subject for the next opera. One evening at the Odéon he saw *Chérubin*, the play by Francis de Croisset which has already been mentioned. The light amorality of Croisset's plays had gained him the reputation of being an efficient entertainer on the boulevard, and *Chérubin* was a typical exercise in an atmosphere of eighteenth-century libertinage. What, Croisset asks, became of Cherubino after Beaumarchais and Mozart had finished with him? That such a question should be asked is a tribute to the powers of imagination that created him. As Sacha

Guitry used to say, when a bad actor leaves the stage he vanishes from the audience's mind, but when a good actor has made his exit we know that he is only in the next room. Croisset's answer is to show Cherubino at the age of seventeen, no longer a mischievous page but a mature, and much more dangerous, junior officer whose uniform only serves to increase the havoc he spreads among his women admirers. He is torn between the rival charms of four women: the Baroness and the Countess, who are carried over from Beaumarchais; l'Ensoleillad, star of the Madrid opera and royal favourite; and Nina, the Count's ward. There is also a character known as le Philosophe who is ever at hand to offer worldly reflections on life—

'Petit, le mal qui te dévore,
Je l'ai connu voici longtemps.
Je voudrais souffrir encore,
Car on n'en souffre qu'a vingt ans' etc.

—in the best manner of disillusioned boulevardiers. By curtain-fall it is, of course, Nina who has won the doubtful privilege of ensnaring Cherubino, and yet another great problem in dramatic literature is solved.

Massenet started on the composition of his new opera with the energy of a man thirty years his junior. He spent more than twelve hours a day at it, and when friends expressed surprise at such vigour he replied: 'It often happens to me like this. I've just finished *Chérubin* and I worked on it for two hundred and ten hours straight off, with only intervals for meals and a few hours' sleep each night. When I start work I just don't feel tiredness . . . ' The result was described as a 'comédie chantée en trois actes', which is perhaps another way of saying that Massenet had written not an opera, not even an operetta, but a sort of hybrid which, despite the recitatives, is best described as a musical comedy.

Chérubin had its first performance in Monte Carlo with a strong cast which included Mary Garden as Cherubino and Lina Cavalieri, an old friend of Massenet's, as the fiery Ensoleillad. It was saluted with much enthusiasm, and Gabriel Fauré went to the extent of declaring that the music had something of Mozart's grace and spirit. Few people seem to have agreed with him. After the Paris production, in which Mary Garden repeated her role and Fugère sang le Philosophe, *Chérubin* crumbled abruptly and evaporated as quickly as the scent which pervades the score. There are practical reasons for its disappearance—it calls for a very large number of performers and is too long to feature as part of a double bill—but the real cause of its failure is the music.

Massenet's craftsmanship was as shrewd as ever, and, in its contrapuntal ingenuity, pastiche gavottes and well-found harmonies, it succeeded in creating a charming illusion of youthfulness. The clever score, nonetheless, cannot disguise a lack of melodic invention, and the pink tints of *Chérubin* have faded beyond revival.

No sooner had Massenet returned from basking in the hospitality of his royal host at Monaco than he was busy with another opera. At Égreville that summer, on a July afternoon (it was half-past three, he noted in his score, at the same time as he entered a marginal comment on the swallows circling around the ancient tower of his house), he wrote the first page of *Ariane*. Less than three months afterwards the five-act opera was complete. Ariadne, so ungratefully abandoned on Naxos by Theseus after she had helped him destroy the Minotaur, is a heroine whose plight has inspired at least thirty composers and as many poets. None of them, for all the ink they expended, has ever touched the majesty of Racine's simple couplet:

Ariane, ma soeur, de quel amour blessée
Vous mourûtes aux bords où vous fûtes laissée!

Massenet's enterprise was doomed from the start, for the poet who wrote his libretto was Catulle Mendès. This prolific versifier, described in his fair-haired, bright-eyed youth as '. . . a Northern Christ, but a Christ who was not born for the Cross', loomed large in journalism of the nineteen-hundreds. An early member of the Parnassian group of poets, a champion of Wagner without really knowing much about music, the irrepressible Catulle had by now exchanged the role of poet for that of editor, publicist and drama critic. His Silenus-like figure, globular eye, flabby cheek and greedy mouth were a familiar presence in the boulevard cafés, where he trumpeted his judgments in a voice hoarsened by perpetual draughts of champagne. The novels he wrote under such titles as *Folies amoureuses,* the plays he scribbled in profusion, the poetry that flowed from him as from a tap, are all as dead and cold as if they had never been. Only a circumstantial fame attaches to him as the son-in-law of Théophile Gautier. One night, not long after he had confected the libretto of *Ariane*, he stepped out of his carriage in the tunnel of Saint-Germain and was mangled by an oncoming train.

'That great man of letters', as Massenet described his new collaborator, provided him with a libretto whose quality may be judged by the following extract. One is not being unfair to Mendès. There are many others which are even more horrendous:

Pour le beau héros,
Le désir, bitume
Fluide, consume
Ma chair et mes os.

Mendès, commented Massenet suavely, '... appreciated with delight the respect I had brought to the delivery of his beautiful lines. In our work together and during rehearsals at the theatre, I loved those demonstrations of devotion and affection he showed me, and the admiration in which he held me'. The reader will by now have realized that in his public utterances Massenet very often meant the exact opposite of what he said. The fact is that he and Catulle Mendès detested each other. They met hardly at all during the preparation of *Ariane*, and when they did they found it difficult to repress their mutual hatred. As an enthusiastic Wagnerian Mendès had frequently and savagely attacked the composer of *Manon*. These attacks were not forgotten. Why, then, did they agree to collaborate? On Mendès' side the reason was money. He lived on such a grand scale and incurred debts of such magnitude that he grasped at every chance of earning a royalty. Massenet, for his part, was genuinely moved by the legend of Ariadne. The opportunity of adding yet another heroine to his gallery overrode the animosity he felt for his collaborator.

One afternoon at Égreville Massenet was strolling beneath his pergola when he heard a distant and unfamiliar honking. A Horatian line about Jupiter thundering in the heavens came to mind, but before he had time to pursue the classical reminiscence a new-fangled automobile emerged from the cloud of dust. Out of it jumped Pedro Gailhard, director of the Opéra, and Charles Garnier, the architect of that portentous building. They had come to ask whether *Ariane* was finished and whether it could be performed at the Opéra. Massenet put on a bland front. 'We went upstairs to my big room, which, with its yellow tapestry and antique furniture, might well have been taken for the home of a general during Napoleon's Empire. I showed them, on a black marble table supported by Sphinxes, a heap of manuscript. It was the completed score.' Later, under the cool shade of Massenet's vines, they decided on the casting of the new opera. Then Gailhard, cutting off a twig from a eucalyptus tree, declaimed: 'Here is the pledge of the promises we've exchanged today. I'm taking it with me!' Whereupon the visitors piled back into their machine and vanished anew into a whirl of dust.

The laboured merriment of the scene masked feelings of rancour. It was more than ten years since the Opéra had put on a new work by Massenet, and he bore Gailhard a hearty grudge. In the meantime he had had his successes at the Opéra-Comique and in Monte Carlo, where the Casino-controlled local newspaper was always kind to him. But the Opéra's neglect still rankled. He did not let Gailhard forget. Waiting with him in a box at the first rehearsal, Massenet pretended to catch the eye of the orchestral players in the pit below. 'Good evening, mon bon ami! How nice to see you again here!' he said to one of them. 'You haven't changed a bit. And yet it's a long time ago, so many years since I set foot in the place . . . You'd never believe it . . . No, mon bon ami! it's longer than that . . . How the time flies! You don't always appreciate it. Look, I was at the Opéra-Comique yesterday . . . How nice they are to me over there! By chance I looked at the poster and I saw: *Manon*, hundred and fiftieth performance . . . *Werther,* hundred and twenty-third . . . and *le Jongleur,* eighty-fourth. Here it's only my poor *Thaïs* that's put on from time to time . . . But at the Opéra-Comique, what activity! How nice they are over there, how nice . . . ' And so on, while Gailhard sat in his chair with a face of stone.

By the time of the dress rehearsal Massenet's nerves were at their tautest. So were Mendès', and the two men prowled the auditorium with agitated expressions. In an argument with the Secretary of the Opéra Massenet lost his usual smoothness and let fly with Cambronne's famous swear-word. A little later, wishing to apologize, he sent a note asking if he might have a word with the Secretary. 'I know, I know', replied the latter, 'he's already said it to me!'

Ariane made her bow on the vast stage of the Opéra in the autumn of 1906. The production was a spectacular one, and in the matter of scenery at least Massenet had no reason for complaint. He looked at the great deck of the ship that bears Ariadne and Theseus towards Athens, at the towering halls of the palace of Naxos, and at the vivid flickering set that represented the Shades, and he thought back to his early days when he had to be content with cobbled-up bits of scenery left over from other productions, and when the stage-manager would say to him: 'For the first act we've found an old back-drop from *la Favorita*; for the second, two flats from *Rigoletto* . . . ' His pleasure was confirmed by the reception *Ariane* was given. At the point where Ariadne pleads with her jealous sister Phaedra, who also covets the favours of Theseus, a short violin solo accompanies the words, 'Ah! le cruel! Ah! la cruelle!' On the first night this touch was greeted with applause and encored, an incident which was repeated at all the subsequent performances.

There was, however, nothing new in *Ariane*. It had a good run of sixty performances, chiefly, no doubt, as a result of the loyalty Massenet's admirers felt for him. Ariadne's pretty little air, 'La fine grâce de sa force', is the same sort of thing as Manon's wistful musings, and her 'Tu lui parleras, n'est-ce pas?' is a simple re-statement in the tone of *la Vierge*. There is a neat passage in the prelude to the second act which evokes, in a wavering oboe solo, Ariadne's ship riding on the waves, but soon Massenet is falling back again on self-plagiarism and reminders of Gluck and Rameau. At the climax, where Theseus and Ariadne declare their passion for each other, he also repeats the thirty-year old theme of his overture *Phèdre*. One notes, sadly, that there is even a salon waltz in the fourth act. *Ariane* is an inflated and pretentious creation which lost all hope of real success the moment its composer agreed to saddle himself with Mendès' ghastly libretto. So the opera floated off down the years, most of the time hidden from sight but surfacing on occasions for a revival, the last being in 1937 when it reached its seventy-fifth performance at the Opéra. Audiences then were able to ponder for themselves Fauré's unusual remark, '*Ariane* is a great, noble and moving work.'

For Massenet, *Ariane* signalled the start of a new episode in his private life. According to his memoirs it was his little granddaughter who inspired him to make an important change in the structure of the opera before it was produced. He recounted the plot to her, so he says, and ended at the point where Ariadne sets off for the Shades to find the soul of her sister Phaedra. In her 'silvery winning voice', so the legend runs, the little girl persuaded her granddaddy to restore the fourth act which takes place in the Shades, despite his earlier decision to leave it out. If, for the silvery tones of Massenet's granddaughter, we substitute those of the beautiful singer Lucy Arbell, who took the role of Persephone, the account is largely correct. It so happens that the fourth act is dominated by the character of Persephone, who is on stage nearly all the time and has four big arias, while Ariadne is given little more to do than suffer, with an occasional chirrup, in the background. In the other acts, of course, Ariadne most decidedly has the leading role. Lucy Arbell was determined not to lose this big chance, and Massenet was not unwilling to be convinced by her arguments. 'I wanted the fourth act to be for Mlle. Arbell alone', he blurted out to an acquaintance—and then regretted his impulsive confidence.

The reference books are coy on the subject of Lucy Arbell's birth date. All we know is that she was born Georgette Wallace somewhere in the closing decades of the last century. She made her début in 1903 at the Opéra in *Samson et Dalila* and was soon remarked for her acting talent. She also sang there in *Aïda* and *Rigoletto,* with an occasional foray into Wagner. Then, for a dozen or so years, she played the lead in numerous Massenet operas, both new productions and revivals. She began to occupy in Massenet's circle something like the position Sybil Sanderson had once held. Impressed by her gift for tragedy and her strong contralto voice, the aging Master gave her the role of 'la sombre et belle Perséphone' in *Ariane,* and, as related, preserved the fourth act on account of her. Lucy Arbell was at the same stage in her life and her career as Sybil Sanderson had been when she first encountered Massenet. Her eyes were dark and deep-set, her hair was sable. From this point onwards she played an increasing part in his life, and for several years after his death she was, as will be seen later, to cause problems for his executors. She brought a welcome element of youth and beauty into an existence that had begun to be marred by professional disappointments and the ills of advancing age. For her Massenet wrote his next opera, *Thérèse,* in which the embers of his inspiration, lately dulled in *Chérubin* and *Ariane,* took on a new and brighter glow.

One summer morning in 1905, accompanied by Lucy Arbell, Massenet joined a friend to visit the former Carmelite convent a few steps away from his home in the rue de Vaugirard. During the September massacres of 1792, when angry crowds, incited by the virulent Marat, burst into the prisons and murdered over a thousand of the inmates, the convent itself had not escaped. The 'septembriseurs' smashed their way into the cells of the ancient cloister, dragged out the occupants, killed them, and threw their bodies into the wells. As Massenet and his friends wandered through the silent garden and past the sinister wells, an imaginative member of the party evoked the figure of Lucile Desmoulins, wife of the Revolutionary hero and, like him, to be a victim on the scaffold. The sensitive Lucy Arbell retreated in tears. A few days later Massenet was dining at the Italian Embassy in the rue de Grenelle. The building, he was told, had once been the home of an old and noble family. At the Revolution some of them had been guillotined, others had escaped abroad. The new régime decided to sell the house for the benefit of 'the people'. A faithful old servant of the family opposed them. 'I am the people', he said, 'and you shall not take away from the people what belongs to them. This is my home here.' Years later one of the survivors of the family went back to look at the house out of curiosity. To his surprise the old servant greeted him at the door. 'Monseigneur', he declared, 'I have been able to look after your possessions. Now I return them to you.'

Much preoccupied with thoughts of the September massacres and of persecuted noble families, Massenet went that November to Brussels, where he was to supervise one of his productions. The sun was pale and sent out autumnal gleams. He strolled in the Bois de la Cambre looking at the fallen leaves, yellowed to a delicate gold, and he walked through them with a feeling of pleasure at the sound of their brittle crackling. The framework of *Thérèse* was complete. Now he started to find out everything he could about the reign of terror during the Revolution, turning up old prints and looking out all the books on the subject. Throughout the next fourteen months he was busy setting the text provided by Jules Claretie, his librettist for *la Navarraise*. They had long telephone conversations to discuss the development of the plot. The following dialogue which took place one morning shows that even in those days, when the telephone was a novelty enjoyed by few subscribers, it was possible to be the victim of a crossed line:

Massenet: Have Thérèse's throat cut and all will be well.
Unknown Voice: Ah, if I knew who you were, you rascal, I'd tell the police about you.
Claretie: Once she's been done in she'll join her husband in the tumbril. I prefer throat cutting to poison.
Unknown Voice: It's too much! Now the criminals are going to poison her! Operator! Operator!

Finally, on a visit to a house built near the Bois de Boulogne by the comte d'Artois during the reign of Louis XVI, Massenet discovered the perfect setting for *Thérèse*. The house, embowered among trees, stood, and is still there today, in the parc de Bagatelle. The steps led up to an arched doorway framed in a classical portico whose austerity was softened by wreaths of tangled ivy. Immediately in front there was a fountain embellished with statuary, its channels filled with leaves and twigs. Into the distance rolled misty avenues of slender trees. The leaders of the Revolution had made a pleasure park out of it. When the comte d'Artois entered into possession of his home again, he restored it and called it 'Bagatelle'. Then it was bought by Richard Wallace, a member of the Hertford family who created the Wallace Collection and after whom the nearby boulevard is named. He died shortly before Massenet's visit, and the house, empty and a little forlorn in the spring sunshine, had precisely the atmosphere Massenet imagined for his opera. (There was also the pleasant chance that Lucy Arbell, née Wallace, had a close link with the Hertford family.) Massenet's designer received instructions that '... the scenery in the first act of *Thérèse* should resemble it exactly'.

The score of *Thérèse* was completed 'on Sunday, 20 May 1906, at 5.47 in the morning' noted Massenet. The words were written out in the same clear but unknown hand which had also filled in the vocal line. Perhaps because a second party, wife or amanuensis, had become involved in preparing the score, there are none of the intimate remarks which crowd upon each other in the manuscripts of the earlier operas. What comments there are relate to strictly technical matters, among them a great concern for the correct tempo to be followed, exact notation of metronome markings, and the injunction: 'The tempo must be set according to a new metronome.' Massenet's handwriting had always been square and pointed. Here it is crabbed, and the notes have almost a gnarled appearance.

Thérèse had its first rehearsal on New Year's Day 1907, in the flat which Raoul Gunsbourg owned in the rue de Rivoli and which the expansive occupant had filled with luxurious tapestries and valuable pictures. It was bitterly cold outside, but a vast fire and regular libations of champagne inspired both cast and composer to work from eight until midnight. Next month they were all in Monte Carlo where the opera was to be unveiled. Massenet bustled into the theatre, which was still hung with grey dust sheets, to take the final run-through. Under his arm he carried a plump brief-case, filled not with papers, as one might have imagined, but with the spare shirt and flannel waistcoat into which, like Sir Henry Wood, he preferred to change after the exertions of conducting.

A mistake by one of the players made him shiver with anguish. A slip was corrected and the orchestra resumed. Sometimes while they played he would hand over to an assistant and wander about the darkened auditorium to listen intently, or to mount on stage and check the positions of the singers. A particular phrase would catch his fancy, and, with unaffected enjoyment of his own work he would beat time happily to himself. At the end of the act, when soldiers were heard singing in the distance, he could not get the effect he wanted. Expressing a profound theatrical truth to the stage-manager, he cried: 'People must *think* they can hear them!' And when an oboe solo introduced the second act, he said: 'Ah, the smell of spring!' and mimed, with voluptuous pleasure, the action of smelling a flower. The opera terminates in a roll of drums and fortissimo passages depicting the fury of the mob. Anxious to watch over the percussion at this important stage, Massenet found his way barred by a heap of cushions. He screamed and swore like a spoilt child in his excitement.

'You've done it deliberately! You've piled up these cushions here just to annoy me!' he bellowed. A sweating stage-hand scrabbled to clear the way for him. Standing by the drums and encouraging them to still greater efforts, Massenet was rewarded with an ear-splitting climax. As the last echo of the brass died away: 'Gentlemen,' he addressed the orchestra, 'I love you when you're deafening!' While the players applauded him in turn, he rushed off to Gunsbourg's office to change his dripping garments for those which he had prudently brought with him.

At the first night of *Thérèse*, unable for reasons of protocol to absent himself as he usually did on such occasions, Massenet compromised by withdrawing to the Prince's private room next to the Royal box. As the evening went on and he heard through the heavy drapes the acclamation his opera was enjoying, he realized that Monaco had not lost its high opinion of him. He emerged from his retreat to salute what the *Journal de Monaco* described as 'a unanimous shout of victory greeting the distinguished Maître of *Manon* and *Werther*'. The success of his opera was made doubly sweet by the personal triumph of Lucy Arbell, who was praised for her lovely voice and acting. The only cloud over Massenet's happiness was an unguarded remark by Alfred Bruneau, his former pupil. Bruneau was then in Monte Carlo for the performance of one of his own operas. He also wrote music criticism, and in the course of an article referring to Lucy Arbell's voice he had called her a 'pallid contralto'.

Sweeping through the vestibule of the theatre with Lucy on his arm, Massenet espied Bruneau coming up to them.

'Look, here she is, your pallid contralto!' hissed Massenet, gesticulating at Lucy's pale cheeks, his face contorted with anger. Though pained at having annoyed Massenet, Bruneau could not help feeling a certain pride at his achievement in piercing for once the determined blandness with which Massenet normally faced the world. It was not to last. Next day he received a touching and deeply repentant telegram of apology couched in the smoothest terms. The mask had slipped, but only for a fleeting second.

The atmosphere of *Thérèse* can be judged from the minuet which accompanies one of the key scenes:

In the Monte Carlo production this was played off-stage on a harpsichord by the virtuoso Louis Diémer, with an accompaniment of pianissimo strings. It perfectly expresses the autumnal mood which impregnates the whole opera. In the leaf-strewn grounds of a house near Versailles, in a setting that recalls Verlaine's 'Dans le vieux parc solitaire et glacé', we meet the Revolutionary politician André Thorel and his wife Thérèse. The property once belonged to the marquis Armand de Clerval. Confiscated, and put up for auction, it has been bought by André Thorel, who, a childhood friend of Armand, intends secretly to look after it so that one day he may restore it to the rightful owner. A strange figure prowling through the grounds turns out to be Armand himself, returned to see once again the place of his boyhood. André and Thérèse take him under their wing for his own safety. The trio move to Paris where André is called by political duties. Thérèse, having fallen in love with Armand, decides to betray her husband and flee with her lover. It is June 1793, and the Terror is in full spate. The Revolution, in Danton's words, has begun to devour its own children, and André is condemned to death. Ignoring the passionate pleas of Armand, Thérèse now decides that her fate lies with her husband. She opens the window, shouts 'Vive le Roi!' and is seized by the mob. She goes to the guillotine, and, like Lucile Desmoulins, is executed with her husband.

It is interesting to see how Massenet and his librettist took the facts from the various sources which real life had provided, and how they tailored them into a theatrical whole. Although Jules Claretie was in his time a writer of importance and authority, it was Massenet who controlled and developed the action according to his shrewd sense of the stage. The opera is a tightly constructed dramatic unity with strong situations. Sympathy is aroused for the aristocratic Armand and the plight in which he finds himself after being stripped of his family possessions and forced to become an *émigré*. André, despite his Revolutionary beliefs, shows himself a generous man, and his noble action in protecting Armand is contrasted with the latter's heartless seduction of Madame Thorel. The curtain falls on the first act with the dilemma of the three characters well and truly posed. During the second act Thérèse wavers just enough between her husband and Armand so as not to tire the patience of the spectator. The tension never slackens and reaches a natural climax when Thérèse looks out of the window to see André riding by in a tumbril on his way to the guillotine. Her problem, established in the first act, is inexorably solved. Marital duty triumphs, the mob drag her off, and she goes to her death amid the triple fortissimo that Massenet was so anxious to squeeze from his orchestra. In addition to Massenet's theatrical skill, it should be noted that he was careful to respect the social and political attitudes of his audience. It is hardly necessary to enlarge on the opinions of bourgeois opera-goers so far as the French Revolution was concerned. The topic served as a dramatic excuse for inducing an atmosphere of terror and bloodshed, with a hint of compassion for dispossessed noble families. Neither were moral considerations flouted. As in *Manon*, the heroine is allowed to titillate the audience with the spectacle of forbidden love, but she pays for it in the end with her death.

The music of *Thérèse*, like that of *le Jongleur de Notre-Dame,* represents a high level in the concluding period of Massenet's career. Its tone and treatment are on the lines of *Werther*. It has the same intimacy and the same unified conception. The orchestration expands and comments on the action with satisfying versatility. (As Tristan Bernard once observed, an audience likes to be surprised, but only with what it has come to expect.) Massenet's 'fingerprints', as Ernest Newman would have called them, are sprinkled throughout the score, yet with such discretion that they do not degenerate into mannerisms. His fondness for a melodic line that rises only to be paralleled by a corresponding fall is shown in Thérèse's invocation, 'Jour de Juin! Jour d'été!, which, though it is comparable with Thaïs' plea to her mirror, 'Dis-moi que je suis belle', is saved from monotony by a swift change of key. At the point where André becomes aware of the danger that threatens his life, 'Le danger s'accroît, l'heure presse . . . Je vous aimais . . . ', a cello solo accompanies him with a melody in a minor key, similar to the over-exposed tune from the incidental music to *les Érinnyes*. Here, however, the inspiration is richer, more discreet, and has a justified dramatic significance. Another characteristic present in *Thérèse* is the composer's tendency to brief, irregular phrases. Elsewhere this sometimes becomes a failing, but in the present opera it is an advantage, since the music illustrative of Revolutionary mob scenes is all the more effective for the violent, short-breathed bars in which it is expressed. A particular example is the urgent three-note phrase which, first appearing in the prelude as a suggestion of mob violence, returns at the climax with redoubled poignancy as Thérèse is dragged away by the crowd.

Fast-moving and direct, *Thérèse* makes its point by sudden switches from turbulence to tenderness and back again. To the rough march of soldiers bound for war succeeds the gentle tone of the heroine as she expresses anxiety for her husband, 'Sais-tu quelle est ma crainte?' Echoes of the charming old song 'Il pleut, il pleut, bergère', the best-known piece by Fabre d'Églantine who himself perished under the guillotine, are heard for a moment, only to be blotted out by the howls of demagogues and snatches from the *Marseillaise*. The most effective stroke of all is the harpsichord passage noted earlier. The minuet is, of course, a trifle and a pastiche. Yet its placing within the context of the opera and the presentation it receives bear witness to an unerring gift for theatrical effect. It is one thing to write a dainty pastiche, but quite another to know how to exploit it so cunningly within the conventions of the theatre.

Thérèse is one of Massenet's shortest works—it takes barely an hour and a half to perform—and one of his best. In spirit and emotion it is as far removed from such 'grandes machines' as the portentous *Ariane* as it is from the equally short opera *la Navarraise* with its overdone cacophony. '*Thérèse* is my heart and *le Jongleur* is my faith', said Massenet. Even making allowance for his infatuation with Lucy Arbell, it is probable that he spoke with more sincerity than he usually employed. She, of course, was '. . . a wonderful interpreter! Without Lucy Arbell *Thérèse* would no longer be *Thérèse* . . . She is not only a singer, she is an artist in the most exalted and purest meaning of the word . . . ' When, four years later, *Thérèse* made its way to Paris and the Opéra-Comique, Lucy Arbell again appeared in the title role. Another new work was featured with it on the double bill and received its first performance at the same time. Neither Massenet nor the composer of the companion piece ever exchanged their impressions of each other's opera. The occasion must have been a piquant one. The name of the younger man was Ravel, and in the title of his opera, *l'Heure espagnole,* posterity may discern yet another sign that the reign of Massenet was coming to an end.

XI

ESPADA – BACCHUS – DON QUICHOTTE – AMADIS – PANURGE – CLÉOPÂTRE

In the last decade of his life Massenet divided his year into three periods as unvarying in their regularity as the seasons. Between October and February he lived at his Paris home in the rue de Vaugirard. Then he was off for a month or so to Monte Carlo, where he usually had a new work to introduce for the season. The rest of the summer he spent in his country house at Égreville, which, in a flash of poetic enthusiasm, he christened 'la Solitude des étés'. He made a further subdivision of his day, again inspired by the mystic figure of three, into the hours reserved for work, duties and friendship. Under the heading of duties came the large and demanding correspondence with which he had to deal. Conscientious over everything, he never employed a secretary and himself opened the bundles of letters which arrived in shoals each day, wrote his reply, and then sealed, addressed and stamped the envelopes. Letters sent to close friends were distinguished by the triple, sometimes quadruple underlinings of particular epithets in red or blue pencil. Only towards the end did he lighten the burden by allowing his wife to sort out the letters.

At one time he worked on his correspondence first thing in the early hours of the morning before settling to composition. This habit was abruptly checked on a day when, having as usual cleared off his mail and started writing musical notes rather than words, he heard a strange rumble that filled the house and set the china dancing. His pen quivered and blotted out a vital triplet. He sprang to the window and saw the cause of the disturbance. The first motor bus to run in the streets of Paris was thundering down the rue de Vaugirard, and the peace of what had once been a quiet and exclusive district was shattered for ever. Henceforward the early dawn hours of tranquillity were reserved for composing, and the writing of letters, a much easier task, was assigned to the period when the vile splutterings of the motor buses had begun.

Later in the day he would receive his friends, and especially the young whose company he savoured. He sat behind a little oak table, fingering from time to time the ornate bindings on his shelves with a hand that had assumed the tint of old ivory. He treasured these moments of intimacy. Although a master publicist and an expert at handling journalists, he sought publicity not for himself but for his work. The slightest reference to his private life made him furious. 'I forbid people to meddle in my private life, to talk about my home, to say a single word about my wife, who is a saint—a saint, do you understand?' he once exploded. The cause of the outburst was a harmless mention in a gossip column of Madame Massenet's gardening pursuits at Égreville.

The time he had to spend in travelling away from his home he referred to with a sigh as 'being held in custody', and for weeks ahead the date of the journey hung heavy in his mind. Hotel life depressed him too, and only when he had begun the work of rehearsals did he recover his cheerfulness. His annual trip to Monte Carlo in the February of 1908 was made more acceptable by excursions in a motor car over the border into Italy and as far as San Remo. The distracting clatter of the engine was, he felt, a small price to pay for the delight of seeing that beloved country again.

The reason for Massenet's presence in Monte Carlo that year was the first performance of his new ballet *Espada,* which accompanied a revival of *Thérèse.* The heroine of this Spanish version of *Pagliacci* is a beautiful and popular dancer. Just as she is about to respond to the clamour of her admirers in the *posada* where she dances, news comes that her lover has been killed in a bull-fight. She makes her appearance, nonetheless, dances with a frenzy she has never shown before, and then drops dead. For this scenario, which recalls Serge Lifar's adaptation of Ravel's *Boléro,* Massenet provided a score complete, it too, with a bolero, as well as a slow waltz and a breathless fandango, the whole being seasoned with a sprinkling of castanets and local colour à la *Cid.* Unlike *le Carillon,* which is a simple *divertissement, Espada* is a genuine ballet and represents Massenet's only venture in the form. It has not been heard since its first performance.

The palm trees and gleaming terraces of Monaco gave way to the softer outlines of Égreville, and Massenet found himself happily once more in his own territory. He chatted with his labourers, urged them to remain faithful to the countryside, warned them against the horrors and treacheries of Paris, and indulged in all the rustic fancies to which innocent city-dwellers are prone. The spectacle of Massenet enlarging with fervour on the pure delights of country life is an amusing one, and his view of an existence which, even now, is hard and laborious, had more in common with the idylls of a Marie-Antoinette than with reality. His approach was typical of a mind which always took the romantic view, which always invested the commonplace with a facile poetry, and which was admirably suited to the improbable world of opera. He was, in fact, engaged at that moment upon one of the most wild and fantastic of all his stage-works. This peculiar hotch-potch was *Bacchus* and had been put together by Catulle Mendès.

Henri Heugel, Massenet's publisher, hoping to capitalize on the success of *Ariane*, had persuaded Mendès to write a sequel to that misshapen work. Hard-up as ever, Mendès concurred and knocked off the libretto at speed. He and Massenet came together in Heugel's office, each sitting at his own table with the publisher in between as if to see fair play. Massenet was determined to have his own way, and, before even the second page was reached, he demanded a cut. Mendès protested. 'Out!' said Massenet curtly. 'But look . . . ' Mendès began, only to be answered with: 'Out! . . . Let's go on.'

At the end of it Massenet's anger boiled over. 'I'm not going to have the *Ariane* business all over again,' he swore. 'I didn't make enough cuts in that filthy poetry! What vile stuff, what perpetual spewing it all was! And those blasted poet's notions gave me a hell of a time! I had to work like mad to fit in all that stuff! Damned nonsense, it was! It gave me quite enough trouble . . . I'm not standing for it again!' And fixing Mendès with a sharp look: 'I loathe it!'

Mendès, beside himself, spluttered: 'Muck about with it as much as you like, then!'

The composer threw the libretto into his brief-case as if it had been a poisonous snake and marched out. Mendès staggered, red-faced, on the verge of apoplexy, and managed to stutter at Heugel: 'Now you've got to give me the cash!' Massenet, no doubt, experienced a malicious pleasure when he wrote later of Mendès and ' . . . the inspiration, ever warm and colourful, of his poetic muse'.

The result of this prickly collaboration was a mishmash of ungainly proportions. *Bacchus* is taken from a Sanskrit epic. It appears that Ariadne, who was last heard of descending into the Shades, has changed her mind, as all women are entitled to do, and has popped up in India. The god Bacchus has incarnated himself in the body of Theseus, and his adventures with the unlucky Ariadne in the shadow of Buddha form the plot of the opera. At last—and there is no need whatever to explain how the situation comes about—Ariadne perishes at the stake and disappears for good, to the relief of the audience and, in all probability, of everyone who has ever had to grapple with the score. One of the set pieces in this grotesque fantasia is an interlude picturing a battle between monkeys of the Indian forest and Bacchus' army. While writing it Massenet paid several visits to the Paris zoo to document himself on the behaviour of the monkeys there, and the material he gathered was incorporated in the score to imitate the cries of those interesting mammals as they hurled blocks of stone at the unfortunate Bacchus and his army. This Kiplingesque sortie, which prefigured Charles Koechlin's *les Bandar-Log* of some thirty years later, was undertaken with the painstaking care Massenet devoted to the whole opera. Despite his execration of Mendès' libretto, he took endless pains in the writing of it. His disappointment at the resounding failure of *Bacchus* was proportionately acute.

The lustreless opening night at the Opéra in the Spring of 1909 was overshadowed by the death some weeks previously of Catulle Mendès. On the second night there was, Massenet noticed hopefully, applause for the ballet, and on the third night Bacchus' triumphant entry was greeted with cheers. After six performances *Bacchus* was taken off. It was the greatest setback of Massenet's career. Even the operas he wrote as a tyro had gained more success. When he read the critics' articles he burst into tears. The only other work of his to be mentioned on theatrical posters at the time was the incidental music he had written for a quaint little piece called *Perce-Neige et les sept gnomes,* whose coy title seemed to mock him as he reflected on his fallen glory in the echoing corridors of the Opéra. The frustration of *Bacchus* never left him, and until his death he railed painfully at its fate. That month he was a judge on the Prix de Rome committee, and the candidates saw before them a man overwhelmed, leaden of face and with features that seemed ten years older. Beneath the charming small talk they expected from him there ran a current of chill resentment.

Massenet's experience with *Bacchus* was a vivid example of the hazards of theatrical life. In any other profession he could justifiably have expected, at his age and with his experience, to enjoy the respect due to a long and honourable career. In the world that he had chosen, on the other hand, the merest beginner and the seasoned craftsman alike are vulnerable to the same swift judgment of chance. It did not matter that he had behind him a dozen triumphs, years of public favour, and a mastery of technique laboriously achieved. At the first night of a new work all men are equal, and none can expect the advantages which in other spheres are granted by seniority and a record of past success. To the emotional distress Massenet suffered at the time was added the torture of excruciating physical illness. A severe attack of rheumatism confined him to bed for many weeks, and the lancinating pains that shot through his body gave a foretaste of the uraemia that was to prove mortal. Yet his reaction was typical. He had a sort of desk ingeniously constructed so that he could write while in bed, and in this way he was able to go on composing regardless of malady or inconvenience. The work that occupied him through the months of illness was *Don Quichotte*.

The subject came to him from Cervantes' masterpiece by way of a verse drama written by Jacques Le Lorrain. The son of a shoemaker, Le Lorrain had arrived in Paris from the country dreaming of independence as a poet. Haughty, unworldly, absorbed in the visions of his private world, he led a wretched existence and lacked entirely the gifts for intrigue and diplomacy which would have helped him on a career in the salons. Fortunately he attracted the notice of such influential men as the poet François Coppée, the critic Ferdinand Brunetière, and the dramatist Eugène Brieux. With much tact they persuaded the touchy poet to accept their assistance. Then, a little later, he suddenly renounced all hope of literary fame and set up as a cobbler in the Latin Quarter to follow his father's trade. For a time the cobbler poet's shop was patronized by curious sightseers. The nine-day wonder passed, Le Lorrain's poetic urge triumphed over his cobbler's vocation, and he was penniless again. He fell dangerously ill and friends arranged for him to convalesce in the Midi. Meanwhile, his play *Don Quichotte* had been accepted for production. In Cervantes' hero he had seen a reflection of his own character, and the play is in effect a self-portrait, foolhardy to the point of nobleness, eccentric to a degree of genius. *Don Quichotte* was produced and caused a sensation in 1904. Determined to see the realization of his dream, Le Lorrain gave his doctor the slip and dragged himself to Paris. There he lay in a coma for three days. He was carried to the theatre and forced himself, through sheer will, to sit out the performance. A few days later he died.

Le Lorrain's version of the knight of the doleful countenance inspired a late flowering of Massenet's art as mellow as it is attractive. The crabbed notation of the score, angular as a manuscript of Bach's, was jabbed on to paper by a hand contorted with rheumatism. The bar lines were no longer neatly drawn as they once had been, but were shakily sketched by a quavering pen. The crossings-out were feverishly hatched in red and blue crayon. Yet the music the composer had translated into his jerky handwriting was rich with serenity and beautifully matured.

Don Quichotte was intended for Monte Carlo. The role of Dulcinea offered no problem since obviously it would be taken by Lucy Arbell. As for the doleful knight himself, Massenet had decided, even before he started on the score, that the part would be Chaliapine's. When Massenet's intention was made known, the great Russian bass declared that his breath was taken away at the thought that 'a big Siberian bear like me' should have been chosen. He went to call on Massenet and found him '. . . an elderly man with grey hair and such eyes as I have never seen, before or since. It always seemed to me that when he went to bed he must take his eyes out and leave them all night standing in a bowl of oil, they were so lustrous and shining.' The score was finished and already printed. Massenet began playing it over to Chaliapine, and by the time he reached the last act the singer was in tears. Somewhat embarrassed by the supercharged reaction he was inducing, Massenet played on to the end with occasional interjections of: 'Chaliapine, please, please! Calme-toi!' When it was over, Chaliapine retired to another room in the attempt to compose himself.

'By degrees I grew calmer,' he recalled. 'When I came out, however, I was still too much under the spell of this work, so touchingly, so immortally beautiful, played by Massenet himself, in the sanctity of his own home, to be able to talk very much.' Wordlessly, the two men embraced each other. 'There are many composers, of course, that I could mention who have written more profound music than Jules Massenet,' Chaliapine wrote, 'yet I must confess that I never remember being more intensely moved than by his interpretation of the score as he played it to me that day for the first time.'

Chaliapine had for several years been a familiar and popular guest in Monte Carlo, where the delights of the place were enhanced by the noisy good fellowship of Raoul Gunsbourg with his 'enormous nose and the shrewd eyes of a business man,' his explosive amiability, and his insistence on showing everyone the scar in his groin which, so he claimed, was the result of a bayonet wound while serving in the Russian army—though others who knew him better would have ascribed it rather to some battle of the boudoir than to any martial encounter. Their friendship even survived a disagreement over that opera of Gunsbourg's which has been mentioned earlier. 'Heaven only knows what was not included in it,' said Chaliapine. 'There was a conflagration, a hunting scene, a Bacchanalian orgy in a church, dances, battles; Ivan the Terrible rang church bells, played chess, danced, and died . . . It was a truly colossal production of ignorance and audacity.' Such, however, was Gunsbourg's genius as a producer, that in performance this monumental absurdity almost carried conviction.

The 'comédie héroïque' that Massenet and his librettist Henri Cain evolved presents a Don Quixote rather different from Cervantes' creation. The doleful knight becomes a champion of goodness and idealism. Dulcinea is transformed from a tavern servant into a sophisticated lady who might be a distant cousin of Manon. She is serenaded by Don Quixote, who, undaunted by a scuffle with a rival and by the jeers of the crowd, swears eternal love and begs to play the paladin on her behalf. He is overjoyed when she charges him to recover from a gang of brigands the pearl necklace they have stolen from her. The famous windmill episode is brought over from Cervantes and occurs while Don Quixote is setting off on his gallant errand. Disregarding the sensible advice of Sancho Panza, he gallops blindly at the anthropomorphic machines, locks them in combat, and is last seen being carried aloft, his lean shanks waving, on one of the sails. Eventually he falls in with the bandits and is at first roughly treated. But his blessed simplicity so affects them that they hand over Dulcinea's necklace and beg his forgiveness. The lady of his heart, overjoyed at the return of her bauble, grants him a nonchalant kiss. His offer of marriage is rejected amid peals of laughter, and although Dulcinea repents of her cruelty and tries to make amends, the old man realizes his futility. Alone in the forest with Sancho Panza at his side, he dies, lance in hand, leaning against a tree. (The idea was Gunsbourg's: 'A knight ought to die standing up!' he declared.)

In February 1910, Massenet and his wife arrived in Monte Carlo and put up at the hôtel du prince de Galles. It was his favourite. Unusual among hotels, it offered an atmosphere quiet and peaceful enough to enable him to work in comfort. From his window he looked out on to olive groves and lemon trees. Beyond them, on the horizon, stood the old palace on a rock dominating the blue waves. He had brought with him eight hundred pages of the orchestral score of a new opera to be called *Roma*, and in between rehearsals of *Don Quichotte* he completed the overture. After the miserable failure of *Bacchus* and the disabling illness which accompanied it, Massenet found the gentle climate of Monte Carlo and the flattering attention he received there a balm to the soul. He was heartened by Gunsbourg's perpetual optimism and the loving energy with which the producer mounted *Don Quichotte*. It was impossible to feel depressed while the eupeptic Chaliapine dominated rehearsals, superbly confident of his great talent, believing wholeheartedly in his role, and overcoming problems with easy disdain. And there was always Lucy Arbell with her dark eyes and darker voice.

'O la belle, la magnifique première!' cried Massenet after *Don Quichotte* had appeared on the stage at Monte Carlo and been greeted with unanimous acclaim. His happiness was unalloyed and the rebuffs of past months were forgotten. The opera had the unique privilege of being played five times during the season, and reports filtered back to Paris that Massenet's touch was as sure as it had ever been. The manner of *Don Quichotte* follows that of *le Jongleur de Notre-Dame* rather than the

earlier works which established Massent's fame. The glitter and the airiness are replaced by a more relaxed and contemplative mood. The theme of Don Quixote's mandoline serenade, which returns effectively at various points throughout the action, is a tender statement of his romantic idealism. [See example, page 181.]

Dulcinea replies, 'Vous êtes, Monseigneur, plus que compromettant', in a tune that exquisitely conveys ironic politeness mingled with just a dash of true feeling. Here Massenet largely avoids the usual formula he employed when constructing his heroines' melodic lines, and indeed the whole of Dulcinea's music represents an advance on his earlier technique. This is particularly noticeable in the plangent minor tones of her lament, 'Lorsque le temps d'amour a fui', which gains still more from the contrast it makes with the bright festival music immediately before and after it. Only in the fourth act, where she gently disabuses the amorous knight and tells him 'Oui, je souffre votre tristesse,' does the inspiration seem slightly out of place. The melody has warmth and an expansive bloom, but its provenance hints suspiciously at operetta and is the sort of idea that Reynaldo Hahn would have used as the basis of a whole act.

Don Quichotte is full of a good humour that expresses itself in various different ways. One such example is the earthy boisterousness of Sancho's diatribe against women, 'Comment peut-on penser du bien/ De ces coquines, ces pendardes'. Generally, though, the comic vein is subtler. Don Quixote blandly hopes that happiness may perfume his path and the sun always shine, in an aria that has Molièresque undertones of sadness. His assault on the windmills, 'Géant, Géant, monstrueux cavalier' reaches a plane where idiocy becomes sublime. By the fifth act, where Quixote dies in the starry night, sympathetic amusement at him has turned into pity. The faithful Sancho addresses him, 'O mon maître, O mon Grand!' in a few bars of pathetic *grisaille*, and the knightly apotheosis takes place to a flowing accompaniment which repeats the fourth-act motif of Dulcinea's regret that the time of love has flown.

Le Jongleur de Notre-Dame, Thérèse and *Don Quichotte* form a trinity of Massenet operas which prove that the composer had more than one string to his lyre. Though posterity chooses to remember him as the creator of *Manon* and of *Werther*, he shows in these later works that, despite having been persuaded by early success into over-emphasizing one aspect of his genius, he was capable of other things as well. The humanity of *le Jongleur de Notre-Dame,* the deep feeling of *Thérèse,* and the genial warmth of *Don Quichotte* are achievements too often ignored for the sake of the more immediately noticeable quality of *Manon* and *Werther*.

By the end of the year *Don Quichotte* reached Paris. It was played at the Gaïté-Lyrique with Lucy Arbell again as Dulcinea, the illustrious Vanni Marcoux as Quixote, and Lucien Fugère as Sancho Panza. The role of squire to the unworldly knight was one of Fugère's last 'creations' in a career which flourished all the way from the rakish days of the Second Empire down to the mid nineteen-twenties of the Third Republic. The eighth child of an artisan father, he early became a star of the café-concert and sang popular songs each night to the clinking of glasses on drink-stained tables. He acted in sketches and pantomimes, and provided his own music, props and costumes, all for a hundred francs a month. Nightly contact with a hard and demanding audience sharpened his actor's talent and enabled him to perfect his craft. From this he graduated to Offenbach, and within a few years he was a much-loved attraction at the Opéra-Comique, where his Papageno, his Figaro and his Bartolo delighted a large following of admirers. At the hundredth performance of *Manon* he took over the part of the Count and made it difficult for his successors to outdo him. His contributions to *Grisélidis* and *le Jongleur de Notre-Dame* had figured importantly in the success of those operas. Massenet's dedication of *Don Quichotte* to Fugère was not only an appreciation of his past work but also a tribute to his performance as Sancho Panza, a role to which he brought his subtle gift for comedy mingled with pathos. *Don Quichotte,* in fact, was always lucky in its various casts. The title part was sung by Vanni Marcoux innumerable times in France and abroad, and when he introduced it to America his partner was Mary Garden. Having been performed in nearly all the capitals of the world, (including even musical London, where, at its twelfth and last representation, it played to a house worth £51), *Don Quichotte* finally entered the portals of the Opéra-Comique in 1924. Marcoux was in the cast once more together with Fugère, and so was the tenacious Lucy Arbell, who blossomed again for the 1931 revival. The last new production there was in 1945.

The events at Monte Carlo left the composer with precious memories. He sought to preserve them by having the manuscript score magnificently bound and lettered in illuminated capitals. With it were bound in a sketch of Don Quixote by Chaliapine, who was rather good as an artist, and self-portraits by Caruso, who was not. There were also half a dozen pages of photographs and press cuttings about the triumph, and a florid inscription by Raoul Gunsbourg in praise of woman's love. But the joys *Don Quichotte* had granted were spoilt for Massenet by another attack of uraemia. Once back in Paris he was taken by ambulance to a clinic. Forbidden to give interviews or to see anyone but his close relatives, he lay wrapped in ice. To a letter inviting him to collaborate on a new opera, he replied that he was already tied by contracts up to 1914. 'And afterwards . . . shall I still be working? . . . shall I even be able to finish the work I have in hand? . . . at my age, it's madness to take on commitments!'

Madness it may have been, but he was, nonetheless, engaged in writing four operas at the same time. One of these was actually a revision of an earlier work entitled *Amadis* which he had written some twenty years ago in the eighteen-nineties. At the time of *le Jongleur de Notre-Dame* he had taken the score out again and touched it up. Now, in the spring of 1910, he returned to it once more. Based on an old Breton legend, the opera told the medieval tale of Amadis, a chivalrous knight, and his twin brother Galaor who is his rival for the hand of the beautiful Floriane. The action includes a tournament during which Amadis, ignorant of his relationship with Galaor, slays him in combat. There are magical confrontations in sylvan glades, interventions by the wizard Merlin, and festive set-pieces in royal palaces. The music is an amalgam of sonorous pageantry from *Esclarmonde* and wistful medievalism from *Grisélidis*. Massenet was oddly indecisive about *Amadis*, and, while he was alive, vacillated perpetually about releasing it for production. Eventually he sealed up the score in a parcel and wrote on it: 'To be opened after my death in the presence of my friends Jules Claretie and Heugel', naming his librettist and his publisher. His instructions were honoured. *Amadis* was performed, long after his death, at Monte Carlo in 1922. It was little known in France, where it made a brief appearance at the Grand Théâtre de Bordeaux in the same year.

Another work that occupied Massenet while he lay on his sickbed was a version of Rabelais' *Pantagruel* which he had begun a few months before the Monte Carlo production of *Don Quichotte*. The notion of transferring Rabelais to the stage is at best a daring one. In the case of Massenet it was foolish. His libretto, entitled *Panurge* after the sly rogue who becomes Pantagruel's lieutenant, was not uninventive and made quite skilful use of the original rumbustious masterpiece. Yet this 'haulte farce musicale' was from the start unsuited to Massenet's temperament. The open-air vulgarity of Rabelais, his gigantic roars of laughter, his broad, belching satire and his excremental jesting had little in common with the musician's tastes. The best things in the score are those which do not try to adapt the Rabelaisian spirit. Among them are Panurge's 'Touraine est un pays au ciel bleu', which has struck more than one listener as a decided echo of Boniface's Légende de la Sauge in *le Jongleur de Notre-Dame*, and a setting of Charles d'Orléans' exquisite rondeau, 'Le temps a laissé son manteau'. Otherwise *Panurge* is chiefly an exercise in the reconciliation of that which stubbornly refuses to be reconciled. It was performed in the year after Massenet's death by a cast which included Vanni Marcoux and Lucy Arbell. The final verdict must be Alfred Bruneau's. He observed that the epic humour and the violent *gauloiserie* of the libretto called not for a Massenet but for a Chabrier.

By the midsummer of 1910 Massenet was well enough to go home to the rue de Vaugirard. Reunited with his books, his music and his familiar surroundings, he wept the tears that came so easily now. Supported by his wife and his brother, he went out for slow, cautious walks in the Jardin du Luxembourg. 'How happy I was to convalesce walking through those shady paths in the Luxembourg gardens amid the gay laughter of children and the young who were playing there, among the bright songs of the birds that hopped from branch to branch, content to live in that lovely garden, their charming kingdom!'

He was already far advanced on the third opera of the four which kept him busy that year. It was strange that he, who specialized in seductresses, should not yet have written a *Cléopâtre*. He sought to repair the omission with a four-act opera on the subject. Alas, the sultry heroine, from her first note to her last, turns out to be a paler shade of Thaïs. Her melodic line follows, with almost the same intervals, the sinuous pattern of the courtesan's vocalizing. Having anticipated Debussy in some of his early operas, Massenet here pays his younger rival the compliment of imitating him. In certain passages the astonished listener finds himself abruptly transported from the mood of *Thaïs* into episodes of sub-Debussy pastiche. For this reason *Cléopâtre* is an unsettling experience. The whole opera is cloaked in an atmosphere of that ambiguity which surrounded its fate on the stage and gave rise to posthumous legal battles in which Lucy Arbell figured determinedly.

The last of the quartet of operas which belongs to 1910 is *Roma*, a work Massenet completed early in the year. When Raoul Gunsbourg asked him for a new opera to be produced during the 1912 season at Monte Carlo, the score and parts of *Roma* were all to hand. Autumn brought with it official duties that fell to him by reason of his seniority as a member of the Académie des Beaux Arts. He was now automatically qualified to act as President of the whole Institut, and in September he was called upon to deliver a funeral oration for the sculptor Emmanuel Frémiet, whose daughter Gabriel Fauré had married. Occasions like these caused Massenet spasms of foreboding which his basic shyness tended to magnify. He detested speaking in public, and his nervous delivery robbed the sentences he had so laboriously prepared of much of their effect. In September he mounted the rostrum with hesitant tread and evoked the sculptor of the famous *Jeanne d'Arc* which stands in the place des Pyramides. His speech contained the graceful compliments which are normally required, but he could not help a tinge of personal bitterness when he spoke of the decorations Frémiet had received. 'He lacked none of the honours awarded to living artists, except perhaps the Grand-croix of the Légion d'honneur, of which he was only a Grand-officier. But if this supreme honour was missing, it had long since been awarded to him by public opinion . . . ' remarked Massenet, only too conscious that he also was denied the highest rank in the Légion d'honneur. For some reason neither had Gounod ever received the honour, and when the less distinguished Reyer was elevated instead to that dizzy peak the reaction of his colleagues was sharp with venom. Saint-Saëns, as was to be expected, flavoured with a plentiful malice his observations on the incident. Once having made this disastrous false judgment, the officials at the Chancellery decided to avoid upsetting anyone else and made no further awards for some time, with the result that Massenet died a Grand-officier still and Saint-Saëns had to wait a little longer before it came his way at last.

A few weeks later Massenet had again to address the Institut on the occasion of its annual public session. The unwilling President followed custom by paying tribute to the various distinguished members who had died in the past year. 'It is a heavy task for an unfortunate composer who has always been deeply interested in scientific and literary problems, but whom the tyranny of semiquavers has not allowed the leisure to increase his knowledge of them,' he warned his listeners. A sprinkling of classical references helped him through the ordeal of celebrating a defunct Hellenist, and he dwelt on the pleasing fancy of a vanished philologist opening the gates of Paradise with his tome on the epic of Homer. Pausing to note, rather wistfully, that members of the Académie des Inscriptions rarely took leave of this world before the excellent age of ninety, Massenet started bravely on a consideration of the ravages death had made in the ranks of the other Académies which comprise the Institut. Engineers, explorers, astronomers and even a stray zoologist came beneath the vigilant gaze of the President, who also spared a few noble words for William James, Henry's brother and an associate member, who escaped with the description of '. . . the most illustrious thinker America has produced since Emerson'. By the time he sat down Massenet had, with the dignity and mellifluousness expected of his office, despatched on their way some twenty of the Institut's departed glories.

Next month he appeared once more in his Academician's uniform. This time he felt a little easier since his audience was the Académie des Beaux Arts. Here again he was obliged to keep up the necrological tenor of his earlier discourses, as if the spirits of newly dead composer and artist members were likely to remain unquiet unless they had been lauded both to the Institut in full session and to their own Academy. Speaking, as it were, to his own, he made a sly reference, which few initiates could miss, to the failure of *Bacchus*. It occurred in his remarks on a late member who had been concerned with sponsoring the newly invented telephone at an Exhibition in 1881. Patrons had been linked direct to the Opéra by this modern marvel and were astonished to hear a performance in progress. 'From a distance that's really something,' observed Massenet in his driest tone. Old wounds never healed, and although the pleasure of success was not forgotten, the pain of failure was always deep enough to torture a sensibility which knew neither calm nor resignation.

XII

MEMORIES – ROMA – CURTAIN

AUTUMN went out in a tiring round of academic solemnities. Wearied by the effort his speech-making and ceremonial duties cost him, Massenet had a relapse and took to his bed again. He cheered up at the first and successful Paris production of *Don Quichotte,* and in the spring of 1911 another distraction arrived to take his mind off the boredom of illness. The music editor of the *Écho de Paris* had asked Saint-Saëns, who was then in his late and combative seventies, to write his memoirs for the paper. Massenet soon heard the news and hastily intimated that he, too, was prepared to grant a similar favour to the *Écho de Paris.* The unfortunate music editor saw himself caught between two lines of fire. He dared not refuse such a famous musician. On the other hand he did not wish to offend Saint-Saëns. His solution to the problem was a masterpiece of diplomacy. Instalments from the respective autobiographies were printed on alternate weekends, and neither composer, for whom this occasion was the last and perhaps the strangest manifestation of their rivalry, was able to protest at favouritism.

When Massenet wrote *Mes souvenirs* he chose to see his past life in the gentlest of colours. None of those whom he knew is described as anything but loyal, kind, charming and wholly delightful. Even his enemies appear to be lovable folk whom he really adores. In chapters with such expansive headings as 'Chères émotions', any suggestion of darker tones is deliberately suppressed. The total impression is one of overpowering sweetness. There is no mention of the distress Massenet suffered or of the disappointments he experienced during his career. *Mes souvenirs,* with their frequent omissions and impenetrable gloss, comprise what may well be the least informative memoirs ever written. Massenet was determined to preserve his optimism to the last, and he thought perhaps that by this turning of the other cheek he would finally convince those who hated him that he deserved in fact to be liked. The pathos of these memoirs comes not from the events they recount but from Massenet's obvious desire for affection.

The manuscript of *Mes souvenirs* was contained in a well-bound volume of large thick sheets of the same de luxe quality as the famous 'papier Massenet' which the composer used for his scores. It had been finished some time before he offered it to the *Écho de Paris*. To provide the material for each instalment, he neatly cut out the appropriate chapter and handed it to the editor with flattering deference. 'I've complete confidence in you', he would murmur benignly, 'I leave myself entirely in your hands.' After which, of course, few men would have had the heart to tamper with the manuscript. Saint-Saëns approached the matter differently. He improvised his contributions just in time to meet the deadline. They were scribbled hastily on odd pages torn from exercise books, and, in a way that would have appealed to Stendhal, reproduced the tone of his conversation without attempt at literary elegance. In the nineteen-hundreds Sunday sales of newspapers were usually lower than at other times. While Saint-Saëns' articles attracted lively interest among the intelligentsia and abroad, they had no effect on circulation. On the Sundays when Massenet was announced, however, sales increased, especially in the richer districts of Paris. A theatrical figure is, by the nature of his trade, a strong public draw; large crowds rushed to buy their copies of the paper in the hope of stories about their favourite actresses, backstage gossip about their idols, and revelations of the glamorous world behind the curtain.

As early as 1907 the author of a study of Massenet had been told by his subject: 'Your book is incomplete: it lacks the chapter about my death!' And now, when people spoke to him of *Mes souvenirs*, he would reply: 'Yes, yes, *Mes souvenirs* are all right so far as they go, but they're not finished yet: the chapter on my death still has to be written.' In his seventieth year the notion of death haunted him. Under the title of 'Pensées posthumes' he added an appendix to *Mes souvenirs*. This bizarre passage visualizes his own death and the effect it has on those who knew him. He sees himself leaving this world and dwelling among the splendour of stars big as millions of suns. (Even here his professionalism does not desert him. He regrets never having been able to obtain '. . . lighting like this for my sets on the great stage of the Opéra, where the back-drops are often too dark'.) Here, he says, there are no more newspapers, no tedious dining out, no restless nights. He looks down and sees how his family and his friends take the news. In theatrical circles, he reports with a wry knowledge of the milieu, the talk goes something like this:—

'Now he's dead they won't put on so many of his works, will they?'

'Did you know he's left yet another opera? He'll never stop boring us!'

'Ah, I was very fond of him! I was always so successful in his operas!' And, adds Massenet, it was '. . . a woman's pretty voice that made that remark'.

For an interview which was to be the last he gave a newspaper, Massenet sat in front of his window overlooking the trees of the Luxembourg and delivered his views on love and music as seen by different nationalities. The Germans? For them love has an atmosphere of eternal betrothal, said Massenet. The suitor is racked for years by the anxiety and nervousness which characterize the music of Schumann and which had to be borne in mind while *Werther* was being written. As for the Italians, there was only one way of being Italian: to love in Italian and sing of love in Italian. The English and Americans wrote music very correctly, their composers were professors at universities, and they produced chaste and tender music worthy of Mendelssohn, their patron saint. 'Mais l'amour français et la musique française, Maître?' 'A woman who is loved by three Frenchmen can say that she's loved in three different ways,' declared the Maître, his eyes lighting up as he hit on this typical piece of *marivaudage*. He was always good with journalists when he could choose his own ground.

Nowadays, when he tried to write, his hands were too shaky and his pen trailed blots over the paper. He looked in the mirror, and a gaunt, haggard face stared back. The silence of Égreville no longer charmed him with its promise of tranquillity but terrified him with thoughts of death and its empty spaces. Students at the Conservatoire saw a bent, emaciated figure shuffle away from the rooms of the examining committee and hoist itself clumsily into the old-fashioned carriage waiting at the door. Somebody said that he bore a ghostly resemblance to Houdon's statue of Voltaire, with the high forehead, sunken cheeks, prominent jaw, and shining eyes . . . but without the irony that sparkles in those macabre features. A colleague guided his stumbling feet down a treacherous stairway. 'Do you recall what Rameau said—Rameau, that great musician you admire so much—when he'd reached my age?' asked Massenet. 'He said: "As each day goes by my judgment improves; but my genius is no more".'

A gala evening at the Opéra in Massenet's honour drew a packed house anxious to show its affection for him. A scene from *Manon* was inevitable. As a just acknowledgment of the later years Lucy Arbell appeared in the second act of *Thérèse* and Vanni Marcoux died magnificently in *Don Quichotte*. Then Mounet-Sully came forward and spoke Rostand's sonnet to the composer. For weeks Massenet had lain awake at night worrying that he would not be able to attend his apotheosis. When the evening arrived he somehow screwed up the strength necessary to get into his carriage, to walk through the dazzling lobbies of the Opéra where the lights glinted dully on his parchment skin, and to lean thankfully on the sill of his box. Then it was back to bed and the frustrating inaction of the rue de Vaugirard.

In the last weeks of 1911 rehearsals began for the new opera *Roma*. Massenet followed them by telephone. Each evening, between five and seven o'clock, he was put through to Raoul Gunsbourg's flat in the rue de Rivoli so that he could hear for himself how the production was shaping. Once he was assured that it was developing well, a new torment presented itself: would he be fit enough to get to Monte Carlo for the première? His doctor, cajoled and pleaded with, finally allowed the patient to travel. Massenet and his wife started from the gare de Lyon on a frozen January evening. As their carriage rattled through the night he forgot the tedium of the journey in thoughts of work and the rehearsals to come. When they arrived at the hôtel du prince de Galles he was struck down by a chill. Two days later, indomitable, he was up again and declaring that he felt better than ever. On the day of the dress rehearsal he went out strolling in the parc Saint-Roman where he caught the distant gleam of the sea through the leaves of the olive groves. A stray cat attached itself to him and he tried to calm his first-night nerves in the company of the discreet but friendly animal.

At its first performance the victory of *Roma*, said a journalist, was 'one of the most complete we have had to report in these columns for fifteen years'. The tremendous ovation that greeted Massenet overwhelmed him. It was too much for his exhausted frame. He collapsed into the arms of Prince Albert, who, royally prepared for every occasion, supported the unexpected burden with as much grace as if it had been a somewhat over-large bouquet presented by a loyal subject. Then there followed a banquet in the Prince's marble dining-room where the guests sat at tables strewn with silver baskets of cyclamen and Raoul Gunsbourg intoned a homage to their host. His Royal Highness 'spoke, amid a respectful silence, of the deep impression M. Massenet's new work had made upon him', reports a chronicler, 'and expressed a wish that the Maître should continue to inspire in us, for a long time to come, new and like emotions'.

What was there about *Roma* that caused such enthusiasm in the opera house at Monaco over half a century ago? The cast, which included some of the best singers from the Paris Opéra, was good. The production by Raoul Gunsbourg was yet another example of his inventiveness. The plot was taken from a play which, tailored by an expert, was closely associated with Sarah Bernhardt. It was the story of a Vestal virgin who falls in love with an army officer, draws down the wrath of the gods, and is sentenced to be walled up alive as the penalty for her impious act. Moments before the sentence is carried out she is stabbed by her blind grandmother, that venerable person being anxious to spare her the agonies of a long-drawn-out death. (For years elderly playgoers remembered Sarah's thrilling hiss as she buried the poniard in the Vestal's heart.) The sacrifice is justified soon afterwards, for the gods are appeased and they smile on Roma once more. Without Sarah's magic to stun us into a suspension of disbelief, however, the elderly relative with her poniard is shrouded not in terror but in the faintly risible atmosphere linked with those ancient jokes in which grandmothers have suffered only a little less than mothers-in-law. The music works hard, very hard, to evoke a mood of direness, but it fails to convince. The prelude to the 'Bois sacré', which was heartily encored at the first night, reads like a first sketch of the Méditation from *Thaïs*. Flute and harp dialogue together in a melody which, in point of figuration and key changes, is almost a twin of the earlier piece. For good measure a self-plagiarism from the prelude to *Werther* is thrown in. Even the Vestal's 'big' aria, 'Je ne regrette rien, rien! près de toi', looks to Tchaikovsky for inspiration. A descending theme, intended to represent the Vestal and to serve as the motto of the work, is used almost ad nauseam and does not develop in a way either interesting or novel.

If, though, *Roma* is to be counted among the more resistible of Massenet's operas, it deserves a place in an account of his life as being the last occasion, and that a happy one, on which he was concerned in the production of a new work. From Monte Carlo he went on to take a cure at Vichy. By the sort of non-coincidence which governed the life of this indefatigable worker, he was able to supervise there another performance of his opera. *Roma*, at Vichy, was, he wrote to his friend the editor of *Figaro*, 'an unforgettable success', and he promised that a review would be sent for insertion as soon as possible. This was part of his usual tactic in preparing the ground for the launching of a new production, and he practised it with all the old vigour. Snippets of news about *Roma* began to appear in the Paris newspaper, hints of its remarkable triumph were allowed to leak through in chosen publications, and tantalizing but blameless anecdotes were broadcast to arouse curiosity on the eve of its Paris début. On the way home from Vichy Massenet broke his journey to spend a few days rehearsing *Thérèse* in a small casino just outside Paris. *Thérèse* was due at the Opéra-Comique a few weeks later, and in the faded suburban theatre, on a stage thick with dust and brooded over by the mournful shreds of last month's scenery, Massenet impressed his colleagues by the way he directed the proceedings 'with such liveliness and enthusiasm that no one would have suspected his days were numbered'.

He continued to amaze people with his unfaltering appetite for work. 'How do you still manage to get up at five o'clock every morning and compose?' they would ask.

'Oh, it's easy,' he would reply with a sad smile. 'I go to bed with the sun . . . and anyway, at my age, who else do you expect me to sleep with?'

A few days after his seventieth birthday he was very ill again. Even before his doctor arrived he had prepared instructions authorizing Lucy Arbell to take the leading role in the eventual production of *Cléopâtre*. This was in addition to a letter written earlier that year making similar arrangements for her to star in *Amadis*. None of these letters was posted. They were handed over personally to Lucy Arbell. The urgency with which they were written and the fact that, in his letter on *Cléopâtre,* Massenet repeated his earlier statement about *Amadis*, gives a hint of the strange circumstances which inspired them. It seems that Lucy Arbell, having secured for herself the unusual privilege of 'creating' the heroines in no less than half a dozen successive Massenet operas, was anxious to preserve the same rights for *Amadis* and *Cléopâtre*. The wording was such that she was granted an exclusive hold over these two operas. She alone was to sing the principal role both at the first and at all subsequent performances. Her stubbornness in pursuit of these rights was hardened by the attitude of the composer's family, who, when they realized what she was about, opposed her designs with suspicion and hostility. Gradually Massenet himself began to understand her tactics. He saw with bitter clarity how, at each of his illnesses, she had taken advantage of his weakness and played upon the confusion of a sick man to fulfil her increasingly exorbitant demands. One day he was speaking to a friend in the presence of Lucy Arbell. The latter, with a proprietorial air, gave an unasked opinion about some private matter. 'Massenet was furious,' said the friend later, 'shut her up abruptly and threw her a look of hatred such as I had never associated with him before.' He quickly recovered and treated her from then on with elaborate politeness. But his feeling for Lucy Arbell, whom once he had adored as another Sybil Sanderson, was now changed into malevolence. He never forgave her. Soon after his death she was to pursue Madame Massenet with the same vigour she had shown in attaching herself to the composer. The operas were to be kept on the shelf while she fought tedious and involved lawsuits. Both the Opéra and the Opéra-Comique were denied Massenet's last works because of her obstinacy. She won her case, only to see it rejected by a court of appeal. *Cléopâtre* was sung at Monte Carlo in 1914 by another, and in 1919 it came to Paris with Mary Garden. *Amadis*, again without Lucy Arbell, made its appearance at Monte Carlo in 1922. By that time war and violent change had swept away Massenet's world and there were few left with strong opinions about the affair.

Massenet spent the early days of August, 1912, at Égreville. It was over forty years ago that he had settled in Fontainebleau, and, by an unwelcome twist of chronology that may not have escaped the superstitious composer, exactly thirteen since he bought the house with its ancient tower and ivied colonnades. Had a career of more than fifty years' incessant labour and perpetual anguish been worth it? Even as he crept painfully through his quiet domain, supported at every feeble step, there was not the slightest doubt that he would have replied with a triumphant affirmative. He could not have accepted any other life than that of the theatre. Though every nerve of his febrile temperament had been scraped raw in the process, he forced himself on in the cruel world of the stage with a resolve that overcame the most painful emotional torment. If a new opera happened to fail, his reaction was to start work immediately on yet another. He never gave up hope while he remained alive. The deference, the flattery, the often cloying sweetness with which he armed his personality were the reaction of a sensitive man who knew the world is a harsh and envious place, but who nonetheless tried to comfort himself by pretending it was otherwise. That there was a genuine good-heartedness beneath this facile exterior is proved by the trouble he took with his pupils, the sympathy he offered and the encouragement he freely gave.

Massenet has often been accused of opportunism. It is true that he sometimes took his subjects from best-selling novels, that he was apt to be influenced by the more effective of his contempories' musical ideas, and that he did everything in the way of publicity to ensure the success of his operas. It should be remembered, though, that he also found his subjects among ancient stories and novels long forgotten, that while he may have benefited from other men's discoveries he also contributed something new of his own, and that an artist who really believes in his work is entitled to do all he can to see it presented under favourable circumstances. No mere opportunist would have had the dedication necessary to write twenty-eight works for the stage and innumerable orchestral, instrumental and vocal pieces. Nor would he have taken the endless pains Massenet took to get every detail right. The money, the possessions and the celebrity that fell to Massenet were simply regarded as a material acknowledgment of his success. He was pleased that he was able to provide comfortably for his family, but he disliked going out into society, he entertained little, and he saw holidays as just an excuse for working in different surroundings. Apart from his country retreat at Égreville and his pleasant flat in the rue de Vaugirard, his daily life remained as abstemious and hard-working as it had been when he was a student.

Manon, of course, is the opera by which he is today best remembered. It was the ideal libretto for him. He was not a man of profound emotion. In his portrayal of a heroine whose feelings do not go very deep, he created a recognizable type with which he himself had affinities. Both he and Manon were affectionate creatures, easily moved and quick to react. The element of 'prettiness' in his music, that quality of pleasing immediately which Massenet, in his work and in his life, always aimed at, was bound to harm him when his time had passed. Yet it was the result of such a skilful technique, such an impressive mastery of craft, that even those who disliked it were forced to admit his superiority as a musician. Saint-Saëns, an unlikely defender, dealt with the charge that Massenet lacked depth. The accusation, he said, was unimportant.

> The Greek artists whose work fills us with admiration were not 'deep'. Their marble goddesses were beautiful. Beauty alone was enough for them. Are our sculptors of time past, such as Clodion and Coysevox, to be considered 'deep'? Are Fragonard, La Tour, Marivaux, 'profound'? Each individual has his value, each is necessary. The rose with its fresh colours and scent is, in its own way, as precious as the haughty giant oak. Are smiles and graces to be ignored after all? . . . Happiness is disapproved of in the music of our time. Haydn and Mozart are to be reproached with it. We modestly turn away our faces at that giant explosion of joy which ends the Ninth Symphony so triumphantly. Long live sadness! Long live boredom!

The opera that brought Massenet his greatest fame is only one side of the story. When one has acknowledged his originality in evolving a new style and approach which were personal to him alone, as he did with *Manon*, there still remains something to be accounted for. He is too complex a figure to be pigeon-holed as a writer of pretty tunes and as an after-dinner entertainer for Opéra audiences. Even in the least considerable of his works there is usually some neat piece of invention or some clever technical device to admire. He worked his talent with infinite care and made it yield all that could be harvested. The operas leading up to *Manon* show him perfecting the unique style for which he became famous. *Werther* represents a new departure and demonstrates how he could adapt his gifts so that he moved with complete naturalness from the eighteenth century of Fragonard to early German Romanticism. His 'brilliant' period comes to an end with *Thaïs* and *Cendrillon*. In *Grisélidis* can be heard the mellower notes which develop into the heartfelt tones of *le Jongleur de Notre-Dame*, become reflective in *Thérèse*, and then broaden out into the sunset splendour of *Don Quichotte*.

There is bound to be unevenness in the output of a man who had the courage to be prolific. Massenet believed that the way to artistic achievement lay in the production of a solid body of work amassed on the grand scale over years of steady concentration. This was the method of the great creators. It is impossible to conceive of a Balzac or a Dickens endlessly polishing a single novel in the time it would have taken them to write half a dozen. For all the faults and flaws in which their work abounds it has a vitality that triumphs over everything else. 'If the artist who produces little has merit as well, then he may become an interesting artist,' Saint-Saëns wrote, 'but he will never be a great one . . . [Massenet] had the supreme gift of vitality, a gift that cannot be defined but one that the public never mistakes and that guarantees success for works often inferior to Massenet's'. With his resourcefulness as a composer, his versatility as a man of the theatre and his thorough knowledge of the genre he had made his own, Massenet embodies an aspect of the French character which, though it may be unfashionable and even obscured at the moment, is an enduring Gallic trait. The desire to please is, after all, a feature of civilized society, and a delight in the immaculate surface of things does not necessarily imply ignorance of what is underneath. In historical terms Massenet is the inheritor of Gounod. Although he was maliciously nicknamed 'la fille de Gounod', the tradition which he carried on is important in French music and one whose influence neither Ravel nor Debussy was able to escape.

Massenet's fecundity as a writer of opera is apt to distract attention from the large quantity of other work he produced. He composed, for instance, some two hundred songs. His early discovery of Schumann left an abiding mark, and he deserves credit as being among the earliest, if not the first, of French composers to utilize the song cycle as a form in his country. He was also the first to set Verlaine. These songs of his were written for an age of musical literacy when people sang and played at home, an age when they made their own music and could not rely upon the convenient but atrophying aid of the gramophone record. It was not for virtuoso performers that Massenet wrote, but for modest amateurs of the drawing-room. Even within these limits his artistry is sure, and the vocal line, thanks to his feelings for words, is sensitively matched to the piano accompaniment. From the Schumannesque series of *Poèmes* to the shorter trifles there runs a vein of effortless charm which evades sameness by ringing deft changes on rhythm and harmony. As a popular composer for the salon he might also have been expected to write an equal amount of piano music. This he did not, since the voice was his chief interest. Yet there exists a reminder of his youthful virtuoso ambitions in the piano concerto which he wrote in 1902. It took him over three months to complete from sketches he had made while a student during the Prix de Rome years, and he approached what was for him an unfamiliar form with workmanlike thoroughness. The first movement, an allegro non troppo, opens with a long cadenza against a background of strings in the approved Lisztian manner. It develops into a jolly Hungarian dance thrown off in a plethora of wild, darting octaves, and the rushing passage work is accompanied by an attractive theme from the orchestra which does more than hint at Hummel. The largo is, characteristically, marked 'bien chanté'. The last movement lives up to its somewhat daunting title, 'Airs slovaques', by plunging straightway into a highly rhythmic allegro with much ornament, and then by dissolving into an unmistakable Hungarian Rhapsody. The concerto, dedicated to Louis Diémer, was first played by him in 1903. The tepid welcome it received inspired few revivals.

Among the last things Massenet wrote was *la Vision de Loti,* a choral setting of a poem addressed to the novelist Pierre Loti. He was able also to complete the incidental music for a play called *Jérusalem*, the result of a final commission from Monte Carlo. Early in August 1912, he left Égreville and went back to his flat in the rue de Vaugirard. He wanted, he said, 'to work . . . ' The capital, at that holiday time of the year, was deserted, and he came home through streets oddly quiet. The atmosphere was close. Sudden storms blew up and lightning flickered on the horizon. He sensed that the end was near. He did not know that, with a timing almost perfect, he himself was to disappear only a short while before the events of 1914 destroyed the society which had made him. In a moment of premonition he wrote to a friend: 'The Paris theatres are forgetting me. You'll be the only person who won't.'

The tango was all the rage that year. Energetic couples who traced its ungainly steps among the potted palms of Cannes and the Edwardian elegance of Le Touquet were agreed that the Season had never been more enjoyable. Beneath Massenet's window the trees of the Luxembourg stood damp and lifeless. On 12th August, his seventieth birthday, he felt very ill with uraemia. When Lucy Arbell called to see him he forbade his servant to tell her how grave his situation was. He was at least entitled to peace and quiet on his deathbed. In the evening he arranged notes and music paper on his desk ready for the next day's work, a ritual he had performed for over fifty years and which had become a fixed habit. Early in the morning, at a time when normally he would have been at work, he lay restless and disturbed. At four o'clock he died surrounded by his family. It was 13th August. The figure which he avoided so nervously all his life had triumphed at last.

He was buried, as he wished, in the little cemetery at Égreville. On 17th August a small group of people gathered in the old church to hear low Mass. Madame Massenet and the immediate family took their places around the austere catafalque. The rest of the congregation was made up of local people and friends from Paris, among them Reynaldo Hahn, Gustave Charpentier and Raoul Gunsbourg. There was, by Massenet's request, no music. Then a single white horse drew the funeral carriage to the cemetery. The heavy rains which until that morning had soaked the countryside ceased abruptly. The sky turned blue again. The sun came out and glinted on a silver palm which Raoul Gunsbourg placed on the coffin.

Two years later the bust of Massenet was unveiled in the gardens at Monte Carlo on the occasion of the first performance of *Cléopâtre*. The composer's *Suite théâtrale* was played. It consisted of three movements symbolizing tragedy, comedy and the dance, and was a posthumous tribute to the art which Massenet had followed with such tenacity. Less than a decade afterwards Prince Albert was dead too, leaving behind him a musical tradition which is not the least of Monte Carlo's glories. He died at his Paris residence. A mourner who wished to pay his last respects arrived at the house. Surprised at the absence of servants, he walked through empty corridors that resounded to the noise of workmen's hammers. In a large room scattered with odd pieces of furniture and piles of carpenters' tools he found the ceremonial bier. Upon it, dressed in a uniform plastered with medals and decorations, reposed the grey-faced corpse of Prince Albert, no less alone in all his glory than Massenet in his plain tomb at Égreville.

Massenet's successor at the Institut was his old pupil and friend Gustave Charpentier. He chaired a committee which was formed to raise a monument to the composer. The members included such irreproachable figures as the Prime Minister, Anatole France, and Saint-Saëns, who, having seen himself immortalized by statuary in his own lifetime, could hardly grudge Massenet the same privilege after death. By the time the monument was ready quite a few members of the committee had died. It was finished at last in 1926 and took the form of an imposing obelisk set up in a leafy, tree-shaded corner of the Luxembourg gardens. On the front is a medallion of the composer, who looks out over a full-size statue of a woman in eighteenth-century dress with a suggestion of Manon about her. The other three sides of the obelisk bear sculptures among which may be distinguished Werther, Don Quixote, Grisélidis and Esclarmonde. 'À Massenet, ses élèves, ses admirateurs' reads the inscription, which is now almost hidden by straggling undergrowth. From bushes nearby there slyly peep the statues of Flaubert, Baudelaire, and a surprisingly benign Stendhal. On the day when Massenet's monument was inaugurated a vicious rainstorm pelted from lowering skies, cut through the gardens, and sent guests scuttling for the shelter of the Senate. There Gabriel Pierné, another of Massenet's pupils, directed a concert of his music.

But statuary was powerless to halt the fulfilment of the pessimistic vision Massenet had had shortly before his death. The theatre soon forgot him. Only *Manon*, with help from *Werther*, remained to keep his memory fresh among the general public. His daughter Juliette, who had divorced her husband after the birth of a son and taken again the name of Massenet, died in 1935. His wife lived on until she reached the age of ninety-seven. When she died in 1938 her husband's glorious reputation had dwindled near to oblivion. Several decades were to elapse before the wheel turned again and a new generation began to discover the pleasures that lie at the centre of Massenet's subtle art.

BIBLIOGRAPHY

Unpublished sources.

With the exception of *la Grand'tante* and *Don César de Bazan*, all the manuscript full scores of Massenet's published operas are held in the Bibliothèque de l'Opéra, Paris. They were bequeathed by him to the Bibliothèque. The manuscript score of *Don Quichotte* was later given by Henri Cain. The Bibliothèque also holds a quantity of correspondence. Other material is in the possession of Monsieur Pierre Bessand-Massenet and of Madame Alice Cavaillé de Codrika, the stepdaughter of Massenet's sister. The author has also made use of his own collection of Massenet manuscripts, correspondence and documents.

Published sources.

Among the books and articles consulted are the following. Dates given are those of the edition used.

Bellaigue, Camille. L'année musicale, 1889. Delagrave, 1889.
—— L'année musicale, 1891. Delagrave, 1892.
—— L'année musicale, 1893. Delagrave, 1894.
Boschot, Adolphe. Maîtres d'hier et de jadis. Plon, 1944.
—— Portraits de musiciens, vol. 1. Plon, 1946.
Brancour, René. Massenet. Félix Alcan, 1931.
Bouilhol, Éliane. Massenet. Heugel, 1969.
Bouvet, Charles. Massenet. Laurens, 1929.
Bruneau, Alfred. Musiques d'hier et de demain. Fasquelle, 1900.
—— La musique française. Fasquelle, 1901.
—— Musiques de Russie et musiciens de France. Fasquelle, 1903.
—— Massenet. Delagrave, 1935.
Bruyr, José. Massenet, musicien de la belle époque. E.I.S-E, Lyon, 1964.
Busser, Henri. De Pelléas aux Indes Galantes. Fayard, 1955.
Carel, A. Histoire anecdotique des contemporains. Paris, 1885.
Chaliapine, Fédor. Pages from My Life. (Trans. and ed. by H. M. Buck and K. Wright). Harper, 1927.
Clément, F., & Larousse, P. Dictionnaire des opéras, supplément par A. Pougin. Larousse, 1904.
Colson, Percy, Massenet: *Manon*, Heinemann, 1947.
Cooper, Martin. French Music. O.U.P., 1951.
Coquis, André. Jules Massenet, l'homme et son œuvre. Seghers, 1965.
Dandelot, Arthur. Petits côtés amusants de la vie musicale. Dandelot, 1932.
Daudet, Léon. Fantômes et vivants. Plon, 1920.
Debussy, Claude. '*D'Ève à Grisélidis*'. Revue blanche, 1 Dec. 1901.

Debussy, 'La reprise de *Werther*'. Gil Blas, 27 April, 1903.
—— Monsieur Croche, antidilettante. Gallimard, 1926.
Delmas, Marc. Massenet. Sa vie, ses œuvres. Jeune Académie, 1932.
Destranges, É. Consonnances et dissonnances. Fischbacher, 1906.
Dukas, Paul. Écrits sur la musique. S.E.F.I., 1948.
Fauré, Gabriel. Opinions musicales. Rieder, 1930.
Fétis, F. J. Biographie universelle des musiciens. Supplément par A. Pougin. Didot, 1880.
Finck, H. T. Massenet and his Operas. John Lane, 1911.
Fournier, C. Étude sur le style de Massenet. Yvert et Tellier, 1905.
Gregh, F. Étude sur Victor Hugo suivie de pages sur Massenet. Fasquelle, 1905.
Hahn, Reynaldo. 'Autour de Massenet et d'Alphonse Daudet'. 'Autour de Massenet et de Marcel Proust'. 'Mort de Massenet'. Candide, Aug-Sept., 1935.
—— Thèmes variés. Janin, 1946.
Harding, James. Saint-Saëns and His Circle. Chapman & Hall, 1965.
—— *Massenet* in: Dictionnaire de la musique, Bordas, 1970.
—— 'Massenet's "Werther",' *The Listener*. 30th June 1966.
Haward, Lawrence W. *Massenet* in: Grove's Dictionary of Music and Musicians, vol. V. Macmillan, 1954.
Hervey, Arthur. Masters of French Music. Osgood, McIlvaine & Co. 1894.
—— French Music in the Nineteenth Century. Grant Richards, 1903.
Hostein, Hippolyte. Historiettes et souvenirs d'un homme de théâtre. Dentu, 1878
Imbert, Hugues. Profils d'artistes contemporains. Fischbacher, 1897.
Jullien, Adolphe. Musiciens d'aujourd'hui, 2 vols. Librairie de l'Art. 1892/94.
—— Musiciens d'hier et d'aujourd'hui. Fischbacher. 1910.
Lalo, Pierre. De Rameau à Ravel. Albin Michel, 1947.
Léautaud, Paul. Journal littéraire, vols. I, II and XIII. Mercure de France, 1955, 1956, 1962.
Leroux, Yves. Hommage à Massenet. Gosswiller, 1963.
Loisel, Joseph. *Manon* de Massenet. Mellottée, 1924.
Malherbe, Charles. Notice sur *Esclarmonde*. Fischbacher, 1890.
Mendès, Catulle. L'art au théâtre, vol 3. Fasquelle, 1900.
Mesnard, Léonce. Essais de critique musicale. Fischbacher, 1892.
Maupassant, Guy de. Notre cœur. (1890). Éditions du Grand Passage, 1945.
Musica. Numéro double consacré à Massenet. September, 1912.
Newman, Ernest. Opera Nights. Putnam, 1943.
—— More Opera Nights. Putnam, 1954.
Noël, E., & Stoullig, E. Les annales du théâtre et de la musique. Charpentier, 1875–1895. Berger-Levrault, 1896.
Pougin, Arthur. Massenet. Fischbacher, 1914.
Reyer, Ernest. Quarante ans de musique. Calmann-Lévy, 1909.
Rigné, Raymond. Le disciple de Massenet, vols. 1 and 3, Renaissance Universelle, 1920 and 1923. (Other volumes in this projected 5-volume series do not seem to have appeared.)

Romain, Louis de. Essais de critique musicale. Lemerre, 1890.
Rosenthal, Harold. Two Centuries of Opera at Covent Garden. Putnam, 1958.
Saint-Saëns, Charles Camille. École Buissonnière. Lafitte, 1913.
Schneider, Louis. Massenet, l'homme et le musicien. Carteret, 1908.
—— Massenet, 1842–1912. Charpentier, 1926.
Séré, Octave. (Jean Poueigh). Musiciens français d'aujourd'hui. Mercure de France, 1911.
—— Ibidem, revised edition, 1923.
Servières, Georges. La musique française moderne. Havard, 1897.
Shaw, Bernard. Music in London, vols 2 & 3. Constable, 1956.
Solenière, E. de. Massenet. Bibliothèque d'art de 'La Critique'. 1897.
Stoullig, E. Les annales du théâtre et de la musique. Charpentier, from 1897 onwards.
Willy. (Henri Gauthier-Villars). Lettres de l'ouvreuse. Vanier, 1890.
—— Voyage autour de la musique. Vanier, 1890
—— Bains de sons. Empis, 1893.
—— La mouche des croches. Fischbacher, 1894.
—— Entre deux airs. Flammarion, 1895.
—— Notes sans portée. Flammarion, 1896.
—— Accords perdus. Empis, 1898.
—— La colle aux quintes. Empis, 1899.
—— Garçon, l'audition! Empis, 1901.
—— La ronde des blanches. Librairie Molière, 1901.
Wolff, Albert. La gloire à Paris. Havard, 1886.
Wolff, Stéphane. Un demi-siècle d'opéra-comique. Éditions André Bonne, 1953.
——. L'opéra au Palais Garnier, 1875–1962. 'l'Entracte', 1962.

APPENDIX

The Works of Massenet
OPERAS

1. LA GRAND'TANTE

Opéra-comique in one act
Libretto by Jules Adénis and Charles Granvallet
Opéra-Comique, Paris, 3rd April 1867

Le comte Guy de Kerdrel . . . . . Victor Capoul
Alice de Kerdrel . . . . Marie Heilbronn
La Chevrette. . . . . Mlle Girard

Conductor: Théophile Tilmant
14 performances

2. DON CÉSAR DE BAZAN

Opéra-comique in four acts
Libretto by Adolphe d'Ennery, Philippe-Pinel Dumanoir, and Chantepie
Opéra-Comique, Paris, 30th November 1872

Don César de Bazan . . . . . Jacques Bouhy
Charles II . . . . Paul Lhérie
Don José de Santarem . . . . . Neveu
Le Capitaine des Gardes . . . . Bernard
Maritana . . . . Priola
Lazarille . . . . Marie Galli-Marié

Conductor: Deloffre
13 performances at the Opéra-Comique until 1873

3. LE ROI DE LAHORE

Opéra in five acts and seven tableaux
Libretto by Louis Gallet
Opéra, Paris, 27th April 1877

Alim . . . . Marius Salomon
Scindia. . . . . Jean Lassalle
Timour . . . . Auguste Boudouresque
Indra . . . . Menu
Un chef . . . . Auguez
Sita . . . . Joséphine de Reszke
Kaled . . . . Jeanne Fouquet

Conductor: Ernest Deldevez
57 performances at the Opéra until 1879.

4. HÉRODIADE

Opéra in four acts and seven tableaux
Libretto by Paul Milliet, Henri Grémont and Zamadini
First performance, Théâtre de la Monnaie, Brussels, 19th December 1881
First performance in France, Théâtre Italien, 1st February 1884
First performance at the Opéra, Paris, 24th December 1921

	Théâtre de la Monnaie	Opéra
Salomé	Marthe Duvivier	Fanny Heldy
Hérodiade	Blanche Deschamps	Lyse Charny
Jean	Edmond Vergnet	Paul Franz
Hérode	Manoury	Édouard Rouard
Phanuel	André Gresse	Marcel Journet
Vitellius	Charles Fontaine	Romain Carbelly
Conductor	Joseph Dupont	Philippe Gaubert

192 performances at the Opéra until 9th November, 1947

5. MANON

Opéra-comique in five acts and six tableaux
Libretto by Henri Meilhac and Philippe Gille
Opéra-Comique, Paris, 19th January 1884

Manon	Marie Heilbronn
Poussette	Molé-Truffier
Javotte	Esther Chevalier
Rosette	Remy
Servante	Lardinois
Des Grieux	Talazac
Lescaut	Taskin
Le comte	Cobalet
Guillot	Grivot
Brétigny	Collin

Conductor: Jules Danbé
2,133 performances until 30th May, 1959

6. LE CID

Opéra in four acts and ten tableaux
Libretto by Adolphe d'Ennery, Édouard Blau, Louis Gallet
Opéra, Paris, 30th November 1885

Chimène	Fidès-Devriès
L'Infante	Rosa Bosman
Rodrigue	Jean de Reszke (début)
Don Diègue	Édouard de Reszke
Le Roi	Leon Mélchissedec

Le comte de Gormas	Pol Plançon
L'ombre de Saint-Jacques	Lambert
L'envoyé maure	Balleroy
Don Arias	Girard
Don Alonzo	Sentein

Conductor: Ernest Altès
152 performances until 1919.

7. ESCLARMONDE

Opéra romanesque in four acts and eight tableaux
Libretto by Alfred Blau and Louis de Gramont
Opéra-Comique, Paris, 14th May 1889
Opéra, Paris, 24th December 1923

	Opéra-Comique	Opéra
Esclarmonde	Sybil Sanderson	Fanny Heldy
Parseïs	Nardi	Yvonne Courso
Roland	Gibert	Paul Franz
Phorcas	Taskin	Charles Delmas
Évêque de Blois	Bouvet	Édouard Rouard
Énéas	Herbert	Gaston Dubois
Cléomer	Boudouresque fils	Albert Huberty
Un envoyé sarrazin	Troy	Charles Guyard
Un héraut byzantin	Cornubert	Soria

Conductor: Jules Danbé (Opéra-Comique); Philippe Gaubert (Opéra).
27 performances at both houses until 1934

8. LE MAGE

Opéra in five acts and six tableaux
Libretto by Jean Richepin
Opéra, Paris, 16th March 1891

Zarastra	Edmond Vergnet
Amrou	Charles Delmas
Le roi d'Iran	Jean Martapoura
Un prisonnier	Agustarello Affre
Un héraut	Douaillier
Un chef iranien	Voulet
Un chef touranien	Ragneau
Varedha	Caroline Fierens
Anahita	Maria Lureau-Escalais

Conductor: Augusto Vianesi
31 performances until October, 1891

9. WERTHER

Drame lyrique in four acts
Libretto by Édouard Blau, Paul Milliet and Georges Hartmann
Vienna Opera, 16th February 1892
Opéra-Comique, Paris, 16th January 1893

	Vienna	Opéra-Comique
Werther	Ernest van Dyck	Ibos
Albert	Neidl	Max Bouvet
Le bailli	Mayerhofer	Thierry
Schmidt	Schlittenhelm	Barnolt
Johann	Felix	Artus
Bruhlman	Stoll	Éloi de Roqueblave
Charlotte	Renard	Marie Delna
Sophie	Forster	Laisné
Katchen	Carlona	Domingue

Conductor (Paris): Jules Danbé
1,342 performances to February, 1969, and still in the repertory.

10. THAÏS

Comédie lyrique in three acts and seven tableaux
Libretto by Louis Gallet
Opéra, Paris, 16th March 1894

Athanaël	Charles Delmas
Nicias	Albert Alvarez
Palémon	Delpouget
Un serviteur	Euzet
Thaïs	Sybil Sanderson
Crobyle	Marcy
Myrtale	Meyrianne Héglon
Albine	Laure Beauvais
La Charmeuse	Mendès

Conductor: Paul Taffanel
683 performances until 1956.

11. LE PORTRAIT DE MANON

Opéra-comique in one act
Libretto by Georges Boyer
Opéra-Comique, Paris, 8th May 1894

Le Chevalier des Grieux	Lucien Fugère
Tiberge	Grivot
Jean, vicomte de Mortcerf	Elven
Aurore	Laisné

Conductor: Jules Danbé

12. LA NAVARRAISE

Épisode lyrique in two acts
Libretto by Jules Claretie and Henri Cain
Covent Garden Opera House, London, 20th June 1894
Opéra-Comique, Paris, 8th October, 1895

	Covent Garden	Opéra-Comique
Anita	Emma Calvé	Emma Calvé
Araquil	Albert Alvarez	Jérôme
Garrido	Pol Plançon	Max Bouvet
Remiggio	Gilibert	Mondaud

Conductor: Jules Danbé
187 performances until 1928.

13. SAPHO

Pièce lyrique
Libretto by Henri Cain and Arthur Bernède
after Alphonse Daudet's novel
Opéra-Comique, Paris, 27th November 1897

Fanny Legrand	Emma Calvé
Divonne	Charlotte Wyns
Irène	Julie Guiraudon
Jean Gaussin	Leprestre
Caoudal	Marc-Nohel
Césaire	André Gresse
La Borderie	Maurice Jacquet
Le patron du restaurant	Dufour

Conductor: Jules Danbé
126 performances until 1935.

14. CENDRILLON

Conte de fées in four acts and six tableaux
Libretto by Henri Cain after Charles Perrault
Opéra-Comique, Paris, 24th May 1899

Cendrillon	Julie Guiraudon
Madame de la Haltière	Blanche Deschamps-Jéhin
Le Prince Charmant	Émelen
La Fée	Bréjean-Gravière
Noémie	Jeanne Tiphaine
Dorothée	Marie de Lisle
Pandolfe	Lucien Fugère
Le Roi	Dubosc

Le Doyen de la Faculté	Gourdon
Le Surintendant des Plaisirs	Troy
Le Premier Ministre	Huberdeau

Conductor: Alexandre Luigini
77 performances until 1909.

15. GRISÉLIDIS

Conte lyrique in three acts and a prologue
Libretto by Armand Sylvestre and Eugène Morand
Opéra-Comique, Paris, 20th November 1901

Grisélidis	Lucienne Bréval
Fiamina	Jeanne Tiphaine
Bertrade	Daffetye
Petite Suzanne	Loys
Le Diable	Lucien Fugère
Marquis de Saluces	Hector Dufranne
Alain	Nicolas Maréchal
Le Prieur	Jacquin
Gondebaud	Huberdeau

Conductor: André Messager
73 performances until 1942.
Transferred to the Opéra, 29th November 1922
Revived at the Opéra-Comique, 30th October 1942.

16. LE JONGLEUR DE NOTRE-DAME

Miracle in three acts
Libretto by Maurice Lena
Opéra de Monte Carlo, 18th February 1902
Opéra-Comique, Paris, 10th May 1904

	Monte Carlo	Opéra-Comique
Jean le Jongleur	Nicolas Maréchal	Nicolas Maréchal
Boniface	Maurice Renaud	Lucien Fugère
Le Prieur	Soulacroix	André Allard
Un moine poète	Berquier	Ernest Carbonne
Un moine peintre	Nivette	Étienne Billot
Un moine musicien	Grimaud	Guillamat
Un moine sculpteur	Cuperninck	Huberdeau
Deux anges	Buck and Girerd	Argens and Cortès

Conductor: Léon Jéhin (Monte Carlo), Alexandre Luigini (Paris)
356 performances until 1952.

17. CHÉRUBIN

Comédie chantée in three acts
Libretto by Francis de Croisset and Henri Cain
Opéra de Monte Carlo, 14th February 1905
Opéra-Comique, Paris, 23rd May 1905

	Monte Carlo	Opéra-Comique
Chérubin	Mary Garden	Mary Garden
Nina	Marguerite Carré	Marguerite Carré
L'Ensoleillad	Lina Cavalieri	Aline Vallandri
La Comtesse	Doui	Jane Guionie
La Baronne	Blanche Deschamps-Jéhin	Mathilde Cocyte
Le Philosophe	Maurice Renaud	Lucien Fugère
Le Comte	Lequien	André Allard
Le Duc	Nerval	Maurice Cazeneuve
Le Baron	Chalmin	Chalmin
Le Capitaine Ricardo	Paz	de Poumayrac
L'hôtelier	Poudrier	Huberdeau

Conductor: Léon Jéhin (Monte Carlo), Alexandre Luigini (Paris)
14 performances.

18. ARIANE

Opéra in five acts
Libretto by Catulle Mendès
Opéra, Paris, 31st October 1906

Ariane	Lucienne Bréval
Phèdre	Louise Grandjean
Perséphone	Lucy Arbell
Cypris	Marcelle Demougeot
Eunoé	Berthe Mendès
Chromis	Antoinette Laute-Brun
Thésée	Lucien Muratore
Pirithous	Francisque Delmas
Le chef de la nef	Triadou
Phereklos	Stamler

Conductor: Paul Vidal
75 performances until 1937

19. THÉRÈSE

Drame musical in two acts
Libretto by Jules Claretie
Opéra de Monte Carlo, 7th February 1907
Opéra-Comique, Paris, 19th May 1911

	Monte Carlo	Opéra-Comique
Thérèse	Lucy Arbell	Lucy Arbell
Armand de Clerval	Édouard Clément.	Édouard Clément

André Thorel	Hector Dufranne	Henri Albers
Morel	Chalmin	Belhomme
Un officier	Gluck	Andal

Conductor: Léon Jéhin (Monte Carlo), François Ruhlmann (Paris)
31 performances until 1930

20. BACCHUS

Opéra in four acts and seven tableaux
Libretto by Catulle Mendès
Opéra, Paris, 5th May 1909

Ariane	Lucienne Bréval
La reine Amahelli	Lucy Arbell
Kéléyi	Antoinette Laute-Brun
Bacchus	Lucien Muratore
Le Révérend	André Gresse
Silène	Marcelin Duclos
Mahouda	Triadou
Pourna	Nansen
Ananda	Cerdan

Conductor: Henri Rabaud
6 performances in same year.

21. DON QUICHOTTE

Comédie héroïque in five acts
Libretto by Henri Cain, after Jacques Le Lorrain
Opéra de Monte Carlo, 24th February 1910
Gaîté-Lyrique, Paris, 29th December 1910
Opéra-Comique, Paris, 7th October 1924

	Monte Carlo	Gaîté-Lyrique	Opéra-Comique
Dulcinée	Lucy Arbell	Lucy Arbell	Lucy Arbell
Don Quichotte	Fédor Chaliapine	Vanni Marcoux	Vanni Marcoux
Sancho Panza	André Gresse	Lucien Fugère	Lucien Fugère
Pedro	Brienz	Brienz	Marthe Coiffier
Garcias	Brielga	Dehaye	Lucienne Estève
Rodriguez	Warnery	Gilly	Goavec
Juan	Delmas	Delmas	De Creus
Chef des bandits	Delestang	Alberti	Willy Tubiana

Conductor: Léon Jéhin (Monte Carlo), Amalou (Gaîté-Lyrique), Maurice Frigara (Opéra-Comique).
60 performances until May 1945.

22.

ROMA

Opéra tragique in five acts
Libretto by Henri Cain after Alexandre Parodi
Opéra de Monte Carlo, 17th February 1912
Opéra, Paris, 24th April, 1912

	Monte Carlo	Opéra
Fausta	Maria Kousnietzoff	Maria Kousnietzoff
Postumia	Lucy Arbell	Lucy Arbell
Junia	Julie Guiraudon	Jeanne Campredon
La Grande Vestale	Éliane Peltier	Le Senne
Galla	Doussot	Léonie Courbières
Lentulus	Lucien Muratore	Lucien Muratore
Fabius Maximus	J-F Delmas	J-F Delmas
Lucius Cornelius	Pierre Clauzure	Marcel Journet
Vestapor	Jean Noté	Jean Noté
Caius	Skano	Carrié
Un vieillard	Gasparini	Rey

Conductor: Léon Jéhin (Monte Carlo), Paul Vidal (Paris).
20 performances until 1918.

23.

PANURGE

Haulte farce musicale in three acts
Libretto by Georges Spitzmüller and Maurice Boukay
Théâtre lyrique de la Gaîté, 25th April 1913

Panurge	Vanni Marcoux
Frère Jean	Gilly
Pantagruel	Giovanni Martinelli
Angoulevent	Eric Audoin
Gringoire	Raveau
Alcofribas	Alberti
Brid'oye	Delgas
Trouillogan	Lacombe
Rondibilis	Godet
Raminagrobis	Royer
Malicorne	Garrus
Gymnaste	Marchand
Carpalin	Desrais
Épistémon	Lokner
Un héraut	Brefel
Un bourgeois	Guillot
Dindenault	Baillot
Colombe	Lucy Arbell
Ribaude	Maïna Doria
Baguenaude	L. Muratet

Conductor: Amalou.

24. CLÉOPÂTRE

Opéra in four acts
Libretto by Louis Payen
Opéra de Monte Carlo, 23rd February 1914
Théâtre lyrique du Vaudeville, Paris, 4th November 1919

	Monte Carlo	Paris
Cléopâtre	Maria Kousnietzoff	Mary Garden
Octavie	Lillian Grenville	Dyna Beumer
Charmion	Carton	Marie-Louise Dubost
Amados	Magliani	?
Spakos	Huchet-Rousselière	Charles Friant
Marc-Antoine	Maguenat	Maurice Renaud

Conductor: Léon Jéhin (Monte Carlo), Armand Ferté (Paris)

25. AMADIS

Opéra légendaire in four acts
Libretto by Jules Claretie
Opéra de Monte Carlo, 1st April 1922
Grand Théâtre de Bordeaux, 19th December 1922

	Monte Carlo	Bordeaux
Amadis	Vecla	Rougenet
Floriane	Nelly Martyl	Rizzini
Orlande	Lucette Korsoff	?
Beatrice	Florence	?
Simone	Dubuisson	?
Guillemette	Billion	?
Marguerite	Orsoni	?
Hélène	Rogeri	?
Une fée	Déliane	?
Galaor	Paul Lantéri	Cocheri
Le roi Rambert	Huberdeau	Avon
Moina	Curneval	?

Conductor: Léon Jéhin (Monte Carlo), Montagné (Bordeaux).

BALLETS

1. LE CARILLON

Légende mimée et dansée in one act
Scenario by Ernest van Dyck and Camille de Roddaz
Vienna Opera House, 21st February 1892

Bertha	Cerale
Karl	Frappart
Rombalt	Caron

Pit	van Hamme
Jef	Price
L'Échevin de Courtrai	Rumpel
Un héraut	Klasz
Philippe le Bon	Nunziante
Apparition de saint Martin	X

Conductor: Hellmesberger.

2. CIGALE

Divertissement-ballet in two acts
Scenario by Henri Cain
Opéra-Comique, 4th February 1904

La Cigale	Jeanne Chasles
La Pauvrette	Germaine Dugué
Le Petit Ami	Mary
Cigales	Mlles Richomme, Luparia
Madame Fourmi	Mesmacker
Le garçon de banque	Delahaye

Conductor: Eugène Picheran. Choreography: Mariquita.
10 performances until 1913.

3. ESPADA

Ballet in one act
Scenario by René Maugars (Baron Henri de Rothschild)
Opéra de Monte Carlo, 13th February 1908

Anitra	Natasha Trouhanova
Dolores	Valencia
Pacquita	Carrère
Anita	Bertrand
Elvira	Magliani
Morenita	Luparia
Consuela	Hanauer
Lolita	Fernando
Juanita.	Charbonnel
Florida.	Giussani
Alvéar	Fabert
Fernandez	Aragon
Bonita	Chalmin
Ruiz	Ananian

Conductor: Léon Jéhin.

INCIDENTAL MUSIC

Les Érinnyes. Leconte de Lisle. 6th January 1873, Odéon, Paris. Conductor: Édouard Colonne.

Un drame sous Philippe II. Georges de Porto-Riche. 14th April 1875, Odéon, Paris.

La vie de Bohème. Henri Murger, ad. Barrière. 1876. Odéon, Paris.

L'Hetman. Paul Déroulède. Performance suppressed, 1877.

Notre-Dame de Paris. Victor Hugo. 4th June 1879. Théâtre des Nations.

Michel Strogoff. Jules Verne, Ad. d'Ennery. 17th November 1880. Châtelet, Paris.

Nana-Sahib. Jean Richepin. Porte-Sainte-Martin, Paris. 20th December 1883.

Théodora. Victorien Sardou. 26th December 1884. Porte Sainte-Martin, Paris.

Le crocodile. Victorien Sardou. 12th December 1886. Porte Sainte-Martin, Paris.

Phèdre. Racine. 8th December 1900. Odéon, Paris.

Le grillon du foyer. Dickens, ad. Ludovic de Francmesnil. 1st October 1904, Odéon, Paris.

Le manteau du roi. Jean Aicard. 22nd October 1907. Porte Sainte-Martin, Paris.

Perce-Neige et les sept gnomes. Brothers Grimm, ad. Jeanne Dortzal. 2nd February, 1909, Fémina, Paris.

Jérusalem. Georges Rivollet. 17th January 1914. Monte Carlo.

ORATORIOS

1. MARIE-MAGDELEINE

Drame sacré in three acts and four tableaux
Words by Louis Gallet
Odéon, Paris, 11th April 1873
Stage production: Opéra de Nice, 9th February 1903
Stage production: Opéra-Comique, 12th April 1906

	Odéon	Nice	Opéra-Comique
Méryem	Pauline Viardot	L. Pacary	Aïno Akté
Marthe	Émilie Vidal	Hendrickx	Mathilde Cocyte
Jésus	Bosquin	Verdier	Thomas Salignac
Judas	Petit	Lequien	Hector Dufranne

Conductor: Édouard Colonne (Odéon), Dobbelaere (Nice), Alexandre Luigini (Opéra-Comique).

2. ÈVE

Mystère in three parts
Words by Louis Gallet
Cirque d'été, 18th March 1875

Ève	Brunet-Lafleur
Adam	Jean Lassalle
Le récitant	Prunet

Conductor: Charles Lamoureux

3. LA VIERGE

Légende sacrée in four scenes
Words by Charles Grandmougin
Opéra, 22 May 1880

La Vierge	Gabrielle Krauss
L'Archange Gabriel	Daram
Marie-Salomé	Élisabeth Janvier
Un Archange	Élisabeth Janvier
Une jeune Galiléenne	Andréa Barbot
Marie-Magdeleine	Andréa Barbot
Un Archange	Andréa Barbot
Jean	Laurent
L'Hôte.	Simon
Thomas	Caron

Conductor: Massenet.

4. LA TERRE PROMISE

Oratorio in three parts
Words taken from the Vulgate
Church of Saint-Eustache, 15th March 1900

Soprano	Lydia Nervil
Baritone	Jean Noté
Israel	Chorus
Tenor	12 tenors in unison

Conductor: Eugène d'Harcourt.

ORCHESTRAL WORKS

Op. 1. *Ouverture de concert.* 1863
Op. 13. *Première suite d'orchestre.* 1865
Scènes hongroises (2nd suite d'orchestre). 1871

Scènes dramatiques. (3rd suite d'orchestre). 1873
Ouverture de Phèdre. 1873
Scènes pittoresques. (4th suite d'orchestre). 1874
Sarabande du XVIe siècle. 1875
Scènes napolitaines (5th suite d'orchestre). 1864
Marche héroïque de Szabady. (Orchestration only). 1879
Scènes de féerie (6th suite d'orchestre). 1879
Scènes alsaciennes (7th suite d'orchestre). 1881
Parade militaire. 1887
Visions, poème symphonique. *c*. 1890
Devant la Madone. 1897
Fantaisie, for violoncello and orchestra. 1897
Marche solennelle. 1897
Brumaire, overture to the play by Ed. Noël. 1899
Les grand violons du Roy. *c*. 1900
Les Rosati. 1902
Concerto for piano and orchestra, 1903
Suite théâtrale
Suite parmassienne

INSTRUMENTAL WORKS

Piano, two hands:
Op. 10, *Dix pièces de genre*, 1866.
Improvisations, 1866.
Le roman d'Arlequin, 1870.
Toccata, 1892.
Deux impromptus, 1896.
Un momento musicale, 1897.
Valse folle, 1898.
Valse très lente, 1901.
Musique pour bercer les petits enfants, 1902.
Deux pièces, 1907.

Piano, four hands:
Op. 11, *Trois pièces*, before 1866.
Op. 17, *Scènes de bal*, 1865.
Année passée, 1897.

Dance music:
La noce du village, quadrille champêtre, piano, 2 hands, n.d.

Violoncello and piano:
Deux pièces, 1866.

CHORAL AND RELIGIOUS WORKS

Ave maris stella, motet for 2 voices. 1886.
Souvenez-vous, Vierge Marie, chorus, solo, organ and orch. 1887.
Narcisse, idylle antique, solo and chorus, 1877.
Biblis, solo and chorus, 1886.
Pie Jesu, with 'cello acc., 1893.
Ave Maria, based on the *Méditation* from *Thaïs*, 1894.
O Salutaris, 1894.
Panis Angelicus, 1910.

SONGS

Massenet wrote nearly two hundred and fifty songs for solo voice, duet, and various other combinations. Some of the most important are:

Poème d'avril (Armand Sylvestre), cycle of seven songs, 1866.
Poème du souvenir (Armand Sylvestre), cycle of six songs, 1868.
Poème pastoral (Florian, Sylvestre), cycle of six songs, 1874.
Poème d'octobre (Paul Collin), cycle of five songs, 1876.
Poème d'amour (Paul Robiquet), cycle of six songs, 1879.
Poème d'hiver (A. Sylvestre), cycle of five songs, 1882.
Poème d'un soir (Georges Vanor), cycle of three songs, 1895.
Quelques chansons mauves (A. Lebey), cycle of three songs, 1902.

WORKS DESTROYED OR INCORPORATED ELSEWHERE

Grande fantaisie de concert sur le Pardon de Ploërmel de G. Meyerbeer, for piano, publ. 1861, withdrawn by Massenet *c.* 1900.
Esmeralda, opera after V. Hugo, *c.* 1865.
Pompéia, suite symphonique, performed 24th February 1866, later utilized in *les Érinnyes*, etc.
La Coupe du Roi de Thulé, 3-act opera, libretto by Louis Gallet, 3rd prize in competition; 2nd act used for the 3rd act of *le Roi de Lahore*; also utilized for several other big works.
Méduse, 3-act opera, left unfinished, written *c.* 1868.
Manfred, opera, after Byron, left unfinished. *c.* 1869.
Introduction et variations, for string quartet, flute, oboe, clarinet, horn and bassoon; played but unpublished.
Rêvons, c'est l'heure, duet, (Paul Verlaine), publ. 1872.
L'adorable Bel'-Boul', operetta, privately performed, 1874, Cercle des Mirlitons; destroyed and suppressed by Massenet.

Lamento, for orch., on death of Bizet, 1875.
Bérengère et Anatole, curtain-raiser (Meilhac and Poirson), performed 1876, Cercle de l'Union Artistique; destroyed and suppressed by Massenet.
Robert de France, 'drame lyrique', *c.* 1880.
Les Girondins, opera, 1881.
Montalte, ? opera.
L'Écureil du deshonneur, burlesque operetta; work of his youth.
Les Deux Boursiers, one-act piece for the théâtre de la Tour d'Auvergne; destroyed.

WRITINGS AND SPEECHES

Notice sur François Bazin. Delivered at the Académie des Beaux-Arts, 19th July 1879.
Discours prononcé à l'inauguration de la statue de Méhul à Givet, le 2 octobre, 1892. F. Didot, 1892.
Discours prononcé aux funérailles d'Ernest Guiraud. F. Didot, 1892.
Comment je suis devenu compositeur, Scribner's Magazine, 1893.
Souvenirs d'une première, le Figaro, 29th August 1893.
Discours prononcé aux obsèques d'Ambroise Thomas. Le Ménestrel, 23rd February 1896.
Lettre-préface à: *Dictionnaire des connaissances musicales*, by Georges Bonnal. Bonnal, 1898.
Discours à l'occasion du centenaire de Berlioz. Revue Illustrée, 1st April 1903.
Reponse à: *Confidences d'hommes arrivés*. La Revue, 15th March 1904.
La musique d'aujourd'hui et de demain. Comoedia, 4th November 1909.
Mes souvenirs. Lafitte, 1912.

INDEX